THE CELTS

THE CELTS

The People who Came out of the Darkness

GERHARD HERM

Weidenfeld and Nicolson
London

Weidenfeld and Nicolson
11 St John's Hill London SW11

ISBN 0 297 77165 5

Printed and bound in Great Britain by
Morrison & Gibb Ltd, London and Edinburgh

CONTENTS

MAPS

Illustrations are reproduced by kind permission of: Bibliothèque
Nationale, Paris: 18; British Museum: 14, 15; Cosy-Verlag, Salzburg: 5;
Francoise Foliot: 13; Holle-Bildarchiv, Baden-Baden: 12; Christina
Herm: 1, 3, 6, 7, 8, 10, 11, 16, 17, 19, 22; Irische Fremdenverkehrs-
zentrale, Franfurt: 23, 24; Muséum Calvet, Avignon: 4, 9, 20; Jean
Roubier: 2.

ILLUSTRATIONS

ONE

The People who Came out of the Darkness

Along with terror, there sweeps over the warrior in a seething tide of blood-red waves, ecstasy.

Ernst Jünger, *Der Kampf als inneres Erlebnis*

To believe that we can penetrate the Celtic mind, and share the Celts' psychological condition and feelings, is a pure waste of time.

Stuart Piggott, *The Druids*

An explosive business, but its handling was almost comic. The two parties sat facing one another, both trying to avoid the real subject of their meeting. On one side, representatives of the Roman Senate, on the other Hasdrubal, the Carthaginian viceroy in Spain, with his advisers. The place: a town on the Iberian coast of the Mediterranean, probably called 'Kart Hadrash' by its founders, the Roman 'Nova Carthago' – today it is Cartagena. The date: 226 BC.

The Romans, whose forces had, a few years before, seized Sicily, Sardinia and Corsica from Carthage, thereby getting control of the western Mediterranean, alleged that they were worried by Carthaginian expansion in Spain. Their hosts pretended to take this concern seriously. Such a fear seemed logical in the circumstances. In a three-year campaign Hasdrubal had conquered a large part of south-eastern Spain, as recompense for the Mediterranean islands that Carthage had lost. Now he was in the happy position of being able to exploit the great silver mines of the Sierra Morena and build new fleets with the revenue. He had also evolved an ambitious stratégy for the further extension of Punic power in Spain.

It was these very plans that seemed to interest Rome's envoys in particular. They wanted to find out how much further north the Carthaginians intended to go. Would they not stop until they had reached the foothills of the Pyrenees? This was the heart of the matter, for on the northern slopes of this mountain mass that sealed off the Iberian peninsula there lived a people the Romans feared much more than they did Carthage – the Celts.

The North African mercantile city of Carthage had always aroused Rome's envy and jealousy; but the two had collaborated to mutual advantage for years, and even the First Punic War was more the outcome of misunderstanding and haphazard clashes than of political calculation. The Celts, however, were a constant threat to Rome's very existence, striking fear into its citizens. They seemed to be something out of a dark chaotic world, not a palpable military power. Now, in 226 BC, it seemed as if their hordes were again about to invade the central part of the Apennine peninsula. The Senate feared a possible alliance of three potential enemies divided by the Pyrenees – the Carthaginians in Spain, the Celts in France and the Celts in northern Italy. Rome could hardly have withstood the concerted might of such a coalition.

But none of the envoys who confronted Hasdrubal dared voice these fears; if they had, the impossible situation of the Roman delegation would have been obvious. Meanwhile Hasdrubal did not exploit his advantage unduly. He said that Carthage was prepared to halt her expansion at the Ebro, an undertaking which was confirmed by treaty. The Carthaginians were at the time nowhere near the river Ebro, and they thus obtained the right, with Rome's approval, to occupy yet another substantial piece of territory. On the other hand the Romans – in exchange for territory that was not theirs to give – got the assurance that in the struggle to come they would have to deal only with the pugnacious, but undisciplined hordes of a 'barbarian' people, and not with a Carthaginian-Celtic army led by experienced officers. Such a confrontation the Romans would have paid a high price to avoid. They could not have known at the time that Hasdrubal would be slain by one of the people they themselves so feared, and that his successor, Hannibal, would strive for just that Celtic-Carthaginian alliance they feared still more – though it came too late for Carthage. This was nevertheless the fruit of the treaty concluded at Cartagena. In 218 BC Hannibal crossed the Pyrenees to advance into Italy through France. Three years before his uncle Hasdrubal had been killed by a Celtiberian. There were Celts both to the north and south of the Pyrenees, and they inhabited a large part of Central Europe. It is not surprising that Rome was frightened of them.

This people, called *Galli* by the Romans and *Galatai* or *Keltoi* by the Greeks, did not fit in with any of the Ancients' notions of humanity. In the words of the Greek historian Diodorus (himself born in Sicily and hence known as 'Siculus'):

Their aspect is terrifying. . . . They are very tall in stature, with rippling muscles under clear white skin. Their hair is blond, but not naturally so: they bleach it, to this day, artificially, washing it in lime and combing it back from their foreheads. They look like wood-demons, their hair thick and shaggy like a horse's mane. Some of these are clean-shaven, but others – especially those of high rank, shave their cheeks but leave a moustache that covers the whole mouth and, when they eat and drink, acts like a sieve, trapping particles of food. . . . The way they dress is astonishing: they wear brightly coloured and embroidered shirts, with trousers called *bracae* [breeches?] and cloaks fastened at the shoulder with a brooch, heavy in winter, light in summer. These cloaks are striped or checkered in design, with the separate checks close together and in various colours.

This may sound like a description of some harmless, colourful, exotic people, addicted to embroidered peasant blouses and a sort of Scottish tartan about the neck; but Diodorus later shows that this love of colour was anything but primitive *joie de vivre*. Although Diodorus was only a compiler of contemporary eye-witness reports – he himself lived in the first century BC – we may none the less accept his account of what made the Celts not just surprising but also terrifying: their way of fighting.

Some of the Celts, he says, wore 'bronze helmets with figures picked out on them, even horns, which made them look even taller than they already are . . . while others cover themselves with breast-armour made out of chains. But most content themselves with the weapons nature gave them: they go naked into battle.' Before it began, however, they indulged in a performance that was

bound to confuse their enemies more than anything they had seen
before. It started with one or more of them leaving the ranks and
challenging the bravest of the enemy to a duel. As Diodorus
recounts: 'At the same time they swing their weapons about to
intimidate their foe; if anyone accepts the challenge, the Celtic
warriors break into a wild singing, praising the deeds of their
fathers and their own prowess, while insulting and belittling their
opponents, to take the edge off them before the battle begins.' It
was a ritualized psychological warfare, of a kind still employed in
pub-brawls in Alpine village-inns or Breton fishermen's taverns.
But there was more to it. After this prelude, the Celts would begin
their own moral preparation: 'Weird, discordant horns were
sounded', there was a chorus of shouting from their 'deep and
harsh voices', swords were beaten rhythmically against shields,
rage and war-lust were systematically whipped up. At last the
first warrior broke ranks and stormed forward. At the same time,
on the flanks, squadrons of four-wheeled war-chariots started
moving, usually manned by two warriors. One drove the horses,
while the other hurled javelins at the enemy cavalry. When he had
thrown them all, he would jump out and join the battle on foot,
while the chariot was turned around, to be kept ready in case a
retreat was necessary.

The horsemen fought in the same way. Each mount had two
riders: one threw javelins and then jumped off; the other turned
the horse about, tied it up and, like the javelin-thrower, took hold
of a sword or *lancia* (battle lance – the word is Celtic). Diodorus
says that the blade of such a lance might be up to eighteen inches
long and almost six inches across: 'Some of these lance blades are
straight, others are wavy over their whole length, so that a blow
not only slices into the flesh but can also lacerate it, and the wound
is enlarged when the lance is pulled out. . . . But their swords are
shorter than the javelins of other peoples.'

Yet it was not just the cruel weaponry that so terrified their
enemies, but the impression the Celtic warriors gave: the seething
rage, the fury of their attacks. However soberly they made preparations, in the midst of battle, for a possible retreat, when they were
actually fighting they were transformed, beside themselves,
entranced in a rage for blood. The Romans later described this
entrancement, for want of a better word, as *furor*, and they were
always in great fear of it.

If this incomprehensible battle-fury was not proof enough that
the Celts had come out of chaos itself, further evidence was provided by the most terrifying of their military customs. This was
their habit of cutting off their enemies' heads and nailing them over
the doors of their huts. As Diodorus put it: 'In exactly the same
way as hunters do with their skulls of the animals they have slain
. . . they preserved the heads of their most high-ranking victims in
cedar-oil, keeping them carefully in wooden boxes.'

Among the first inhabitants of the Apennine peninsula to lose
their heads and much of their property to the Celts were the
Etruscans. Around 400 BC this talented people had reached the

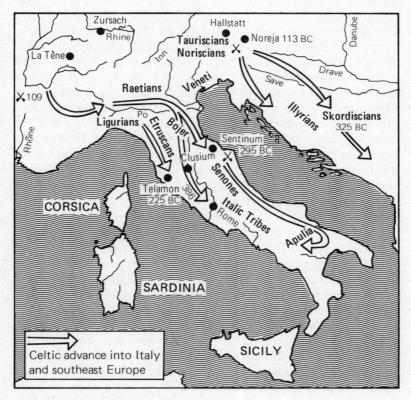

Map 1   Celtic immigration into Italy

peak of its five centuries of history. It held sway over the coast of
the Tyrrhenian Sea from the mouth of the Tiber to the northern
borders of Tuscany. It was organized in twelve mighty city-states,
had large ore-mines, for instance on Elba, maintained maritime
trade with Phoenicians, Carthaginians and Greeks, built perfect
roads, faultless drainage and irrigation systems, was famous for its
metal-working and, during its final flowering, had extended its
sphere of influence as far as modern Venice and the Alpine lakes
of Switzerland. The Etruscans' armed forces matched their
technology; nor are they likely to have been cowardly – witness
the high praise Homer had given their Trojan ancestors.

However when, around 400 BC, the as yet almost unknown
Celtic people came down over the Alps and, attracted by the
paradise of what is nowadays the South Tyrol and the lush
fertility of the Po valley, decided to settle there, neither courage,
excellent weaponry nor technology could save the Etruscans.
From their Danubian and Alpine villages the Celts had long been
doing brisk trade with Etruria. Now, as Polybius – an older
colleague of Diodorus's – laconically put it, 'without warning and
on a very thin pretext, they launched a large force against the
Etruscans, drove them from the lands around the Po and settled
the plains themselves'. Then they spread over the whole of
northern Italy. Polybius, an Arcadian Greek, wrote: 'In the area
where the Po rises, there settled the Laii and Libici; beyond them
the Insubres, the largest of the Celtic tribes. Their neighbours
along the river were the Cenomani. . . . The land south of the Po
by the Apennines was settled by the Anari, east of them the Boii,
towards the Adriatic the Lingones and, finally, on the coast, the
Senones.'

Unfortunately Polybius says nothing about the size of these
various tribes, though we can conclude from his list that the
Etruscans were confronted not with a group of wandering nomads
but with part of a vast migration. At all events, the Celtic invasion
marked the end of an era, and in the years after 400 BC the
Etruscans gradually fade out of Italian history – though there was
of course another people that contributed to this. South of the
Etruscan zone of influence, the community that would later
describe itself proudly as the 'Senate and People of Rome' was
taking the first, faltering steps towards statehood. The Romans
proposed to take over the Etruscan inheritance just as the Celts had

done. Indeed while the Celts drove the Etruscans back, the Romans subjugated them, incorporating Etruscan traditions into their own history books; it took them over a century to do so.

At first it seemed as if the blond invaders would be satisfied with their initial territorial gains. They settled, built huts and carried on a way of life that the historian Polybius, a friend of Roman nobles, must have found unspeakably primitive: 'Their villages were unfortified, their houses without furnishings. As they slept on straw, usually ate meat and did nothing other than fight and farm, their existence was very simple. . . . Individual possessions consisted of cattle and gold, because only such things could be carried about anywhere, in any circumstances.'

Yet it cannot have been that simple in the Celtic settlements. On the one hand in northern Italy Celts laid the foundations of some of the most important towns, among them Taurinum (Turin), Bergomum (Bergamo) and Mediolanum (Milan); on the other hand Polybius himself later says in his *History* that during his lifetime, at the beginning of the last century before Christ, more pigs were slaughtered in this part of Italy than elsewhere – 'partly to supply private consumption, partly to meet military demand' – that agriculture flourished and that guests were nowhere so cheaply and so amply provided for. He notes with astonishment that travellers did not make 'a separate contract with the landlord for each service he provided but pay an all-inclusive price for each person'. Full board and lodging was, it seems, invented in northern Italy. The prices were low: 'Even lavish conditions usually cost only half an *as*' (a penny or so). 'The large number of inhabitants' flourishing in these favourable circumstances, 'their stature and their beauty, and their prowess in war, may easily be discerned in the list of their achievements.'

We can thus conclude that the Celts, some of whose descendants must in Polybius's day still have been settled in these regions, by no means let the land fall into ruin, which in turn suggests that they had some knowledge of agricultural techniques. We may also infer that they were quite capable of recognizing spots favourable for a large settlement. Long before the Romans conquered it, Mediolanum was a rich and flourishing city, as was Taurinum. As Livy, who came from Padua, confirms, the Celtic invaders who settled in northern Italy had a lively sense of justice and protocol.

If we may accept what he says, the first conflict with the Romans was triggered off by the Romans' violation of international law, even though they were to become the arch-jurists of Europe. As a prelude to this, there occurred one of those bedroom farces much loved by Herodotus and other Ancient writers and included, with relish, in their accounts.

Aruns, the story goes, was a citizen of the Etruscan town of Clusium (Chiusi) in the province of Siena, which had not yet become Celtic. He obtained unmistakable evidence that his wife had been seduced by a young man, Lucumo (from *lauchme*, Etruscan for patriciate). Now Lucumo was not merely an accomplished Latin lover, but belonged to the influential and powerful ruling class of the Etruscan community. To avenge himself and, one suspects, take out his class resentment against this aristocrat, Aruns needed greater force than he could himself muster. He thought he had found the answer in the Celts, who had already advanced close to Chiusi. It is thought that he had already been of service to them, as Alpine guide, and no doubt he had some kind of business association with them. He seems in particular to have delivered wine to them, a beverage they loved immoderately and which was quite new to them for their own regions produced only beer. Aruns used wine as his weapon. He brought some to the Celts 'to entice them', in other words presumably to show them that the Clusium area had a particularly fine vintage, Montepulciano, which is still a very popular wine, though at the time it had a different name. The Celts came. Livy says that they were Senones, though it is possible that other tribes turned up in force as well.

The Clusians, who must have been well informed about the Celts by their fellow-countrymen further north, were nevertheless terrified 'at the appearance of so many enemies, and shapes and weapons they had not seen before. . . . They therefore sent envoys to Rome to beg for the Senate's help, though they were not allied, or even friendly, with the Romans.' But Rome was at this time bled white and completely impoverished by earlier wars, and there was no reason for it to mobilize an army to meet the request of a far-off city state, the more so as Clusium was a powerful and well-defended fortress. The Romans confined themselves to sending three envoys to Clusium, to find out what was happening and to mediate between the Etruscans and the Celts.

The Celtic aggressors were astonishingly reasonable in their first contact with Rome. Their leaders told the Roman deputation that

this was indeed the first time they had heard of them, but they assumed the Romans must be courageous people because it was to them that the Clusians had turned in their hour of need. And since the Romans had tried to help with an embassy and not with arms, they themselves would not reject the offer of peace, provided the Clusians ceded part of their superfluous agricultural land; that was what they, the Celts, wanted. . . . If it were not given, they would launch an attack before the Romans' eyes, so that the Romans could report back how superior the Gauls were in battle to all others. . . . The Romans then asked whether it was right to demand land from its owners on pain of war, indeed what were the Celts doing in Etruria in the first place? The latter defiantly retorted that their right lay in their arms: to the brave belong all things.

This section of Livy's tale obviously rings truer than the story of the cuckolded wine merchant Aruns, which Livy himself quotes only with some reservation. If things did really happen as described, we do not have to look very hard to find out what brought the Senones southward: their search for land. Either new tribes from the north must have threatened to expel them from the territories they had conquered, or malaria had begun to afflict them. The latter assumption is the more probable, because Diodorus Siculus, who must have been familiar with some traditional story to this effect, relates that the climate on the Adriatic had become 'too hot', which is why they decided 'to move once more away from this inhospitable settlement'. This seems probable enough. We do know that at this time in Europe a long sequence of cool summers was followed by a period of high temperatures, which dried up lagoons, turned their banks into marshes and thus gave the malarial mosquito (*anòpheles*) a favourable breeding-ground. In other words it was not wine that drew the Senonian Celts but necessity, and when the Clusians refused to part with their land the Celts 'took up arms and battle commenced'.

In all probability the fight that now began would merely have been one of a number barely noticed in early Italian history, had not something occurred which was to cause a subsequent quarrel. The Clusians were given help, 'counter to all international law', by the delegates of the Senate of Rome. The Celts could not permit this. After Quintus Fabius, one of the members of the delegation, had killed one of the Celts' leaders, 'they sounded the

retreat and threatened the Romans. Some even advised attacking
Rome itself. But the elders insisted that envoys should first be
sent to protest about the transgression and demand that the Fabians
(the family to which all three envoys belonged) . . . should be
handed over.' This was, at first glance, a bewildering train of events:
savages – in Roman and Etruscan eyes these warriors in their
multi-coloured apparel could scarcely have seemed anything else
– were appealing to current protocol. But it was not all that
bewildering: primitive peoples frequently have a livelier sense of
justice than those that have codified it. Once laws are passed,
people can begin to manipulate them. The Romans, with a law
'book' consisting of twelve bronze tablets already to their credit,
now felt driven to just such manipulation. The Fabians, whose
heads the Celts demanded, were no common-or-garden family of
citizens but among the oldest patricians. As Livy says:

The party structure would allow no resolution to be made against
such noblemen, as justice would have required. The Senate . . . therefore passed examination of the Celts' request to the popular assembly, in
which power and influence naturally counted for more. So it happened
that those who ought to have been punished were instead appointed for
the coming year military tribunes with consular powers (the highest that
could be granted).

The Gauls naturally saw this as an undisguised affront, a gesture
of arrogant defiance, and were understandably enraged by it:
'They loudly threatened war and returned to their own people.'
There the news that 'greater honours had been accorded to the
violators of international law and their embassy thereby held up
to ridicule' caused a storm that Livy finds quite pardonable,
though he seems to have been alienated by the way in which the
rage was expressed: 'This people have no self-control. They tear
their banners out of the ground and set off' – southward. Rome's
position was not just difficult, it was extremely dangerous, as its
citizens quickly perceived. To the end of their history, they would
neither forget nor overcome the shock of their first encounter with
these northern peoples. Blond giants, who 'filled the whole region
with their wild singing and horrible and diverse yelling' and who
when they arrived 'covered a vast area with their horses, men and
carts', were threatening a community that had already absorbed
the basics of Mediterranean civilization and evolved a quite
sophisticated form of government. An assiduously ordered world

seemed to be threatened by that very chaos against which all order
serves as a bulwark. As the savage host marched from Clusium on
Rome, peasants fled the surrounding villages to the nearest fortified
place. But the Celts had no intention of wasting their strength in
besieging mere towns. They had only one goal, the capital of those
who had insulted them, and they came daily closer to it.

Rome, in mortal terror, could see no way of halting that
approach. A defensive line was drawn up by the six military
tribunes at the spot where the little river the Ancient historians
call the Allia flowed into the Tiber, a mere eleven miles from
Rome. It must have been at the mouth of the modern Fosso della
Bettina. The Roman commanders had also thought up an im-
provised battle-plan. A slight rise was to serve both as battle zone
and place for reserves, and the remaining troops were drawn up to
the left of it. The plan was for a sudden flank attack at the climax
of the battle, and the Romans presumably counted on these
'savages' not seeing through this simple but well-tested strategem.
They were wrong. Brennus, the Celts' leader, had a good guess at
the possibilities and attacked the hill itself, ignoring the ranks of
soldiers to the side of it, and this in itself secured victory. The
reserves, caught completely unawares, were driven into the ranks
of the legion posted along the river-bank, which in turn became so
confused that, in Livy's words, 'it did not even put up a fight'.
Jostled by their own comrades, who struck at them in panic from
behind, these legionaries fled to the Tiber and tried to get away
by swimming to the opposite bank; many were drowned. The
soldiers on the outer flank, who had not had to fight at all, 'all
hastened to Rome and took refuge in the Capitol without closing
the city gates'. Others, equally panic-stricken, made off to the
neighbouring, formerly Etruscan, town of Veii.

'Thus the barbarians had not only luck but good leadership,'
says Livy. They were not, in other words, merely stout fighters,
but knew how to make the most of an opportunity. The panic they
had sown was caused by their savagery, the din they made and their
habit of attacking naked. But they did not exploit this victory.
Instead of pursuing the fleeing enemy at once into Rome itself, 'the
Celts spent the morrow of the battle cutting the heads off their slain
foes, in accordance with custom' – at least so Diodorus says. Meanwhile, he adds, they did not dare exploit the situation, as the
apparently open city seemed too obvious a trap. Evidently it did

not occur to them that the gates were left open because the enemy
had been so terrified by their attack. After their experience on the
Allia the Romans no longer trusted their own walls but fled at once
to the better-fortified Capitol, abandoning everything under this
castle-hill and temple to the enemy. However, before the sacred
geese of Juno, which were also kept in the Capitol, could raise the
proverbial cackling that prevented the complete fall of Rome, there
came a further scene that illustrated the clash of these two peoples
from different worlds with nightmarish vividness.

Three days after the battle, cautiously, sword in hand, the astonished Celts ventured into a Rome that lay wide open, in deathly
hush. They were both victors and vanquished. The extent of their
disquiet is depicted by Livy: 'Bands of them would enter nearby
houses to see if there were plunder. . . . But they always went back
to the market or its vicinity. The stillness frightened them.' Then,
in one of the abandoned yards, a bizarre sight awaited them: on
tall, ivory chairs, motionless, staff in hand, dressed in purple-
bordered togas, there sat bearded old men 'who, in their majestic
dignity, resembled Gods'. They were the city's senior patricians.
They had refused to go to the Capitol where they would merely
have meant extra mouths to be fed. Now they silently awaited
death in the abandoned city.

    The Celts were much too taken aback to act as they usually did,
and as the patricians feared. 'Instead, they gazed up at the old men
as if they were idols.' It must have been a scene that no surrealist
painter could have improved on: an empty court, in the radiance of
the midday sun, the solemn figures clad in flowing white robes and,
in front of them – as mundane and corporeal as peasants in a painting by Brueghel – the unkempt warriors in their gaudy plumage.
One of them finally plucked up courage to tweak the beard of the
old man sitting nearest him, as if to see whether he was awake. The
patrician, said to have been Marcus Papirius, indignantly raised his
staff and smote the Celt over the head. This quite natural reaction
broke the spell. The Celt drew his sword and the blood that flowed
from the old man's body extinguished the dream. Harsh reality
returned, and all the patricians were killed. The Celts rushed exul-
tantly into the exorcized houses. The city was theirs. Soon much of
it was in flames. Then they attacked the Capitol itself, and received
a painful surprise.

The defence of the steep slope of the Capitol hill was an easy task: 'The corpses lay in piles under their swords because, as the bodies fell, they dropped down back into the ranks of warriors below. The Gauls would not try this kind of fighting again, whether en masse or in groups . . . instead, they prepared for a siege.' But here too they had little luck. Since they had no organized supply units and since the surrounding territory they occupied was soon stripped bare, they were before long as much victims of hunger as the fugitives on the temple hill. Finally an epidemic broke out, caused by their neglecting to bury their own or the enemy dead. The commando operation with which they later tried, at night, to storm the Capitol was foiled, as is well known, by the sacred geese, who saw the Gauls creeping up and woke the sleeping sentries with their cackling. A former consul, Marcus Manlius, ran to the spot and 'smote the first Gaul to come up with the back of his shield' and threw him down just as he was climbing over into the Capitol. 'Soon the whole band of Gauls was rushing headlong back down.' Rome had acquired one of its most famous legends. The sequel was more bitter.

After seven months the two sides began to negotiate. The Celts promised to go away for a tribute of one thousand pounds of gold, a sum that, as Pliny remarks, the whole city must have found great difficulty in amassing. But when the gold was ready and about to be weighed, the Romans alleged the Celts were using faulty weights. This protest gave Brennus the opening for a dramatic gesture that has also passed into legend. He threw his sword into the laden balance and calmly uttered the words *vae victis*, 'woe to the Defeated'. It was the worst humiliation Rome suffered in her history. Even in later, more glorious periods this scene, and the Celts, remained a wound which was never completely to heal. The story also symbolized all the terrors that these blond barbarians from the north could, like no other people, inspire. The Celts had given rise to a Roman trauma. This is why in 226 BC, a good hundred and fifty years after Brennus, the Senate regarded an extension of Carthaginian power in Spain as a lesser evil than a new Celtic attack from northern Italy and France. On this latter occasion, moreover, the Celtic danger was no less than before. On the contrary, it was even greater.

TWO

A Roman Nightmare

Thus ended the war against the Celts, a war greater than any other known to history in the desperate bravery of the combatants, the number of battles, the list of the dead and the warriors who took part.

Polybius, *History*

The Celts were the most adventurous of all the barbarian peoples.

J. A. Mauduit, *L'épopée des Celtes*

It would no doubt be sensible, though mass psychology makes this scarcely feasible, simply to recognize defeats as such and accept their consequences; but defeated peoples usually try to compensate in another way. They tailor legends to add a retrospective gloss to the unpalatable facts and reduce the disaster to some minor historical mishap. Under cover of such moral opiates clever politicians can then begin to apply the sometimes painful remedies that are needed to restabilize the shaken community. It was in just this spirit that Rome reacted to the Celtic invasion of 387 BC.

A man named Marcus Furius Camillus served as the cornerstone of the legend. According to the historical record, he once captured the Etruscan city of Veii, but was then deprived of his offices and sent into exile. Legend now had it that he had set up a defence force for Rome while the Celts lay before the Capitol, and that he had deprived Brennus of the harshly exacted ransom before it could be removed to safety. However the judicious Polybius and even the somewhat more generous Diodorus would not accept this version – only Livy elaborated it and passed it on. In reality it cannot have been much more than a piece of Roman propaganda to quell the self-doubt and confusion the blond barbarians had caused; it was vital that the city's self-image remained intact.

Apparently the only reliable aspect of the tale is that someone like Camillus was indeed appointed dictator after the enemy army had gone, and that he did try to give effect to the only maxim that men getting on in years have always, for obvious reasons, felt to be valid: back to the good old ways, to time-honoured principles. What had happened was divine justice: a retribution for Rome's departure from tradition and custom. Now there must be a new consensus between deities and mortals. Thus, as Livy says, the legendary hero undertook 'to restore, delimit and cleanse all of the sacred places, for they had been in enemy hands'. This was no mere clearing-up operation; it was a sacral act, a re-consecration. Then, in an impassioned speech, he prevented the despairing citizens from leaving their ravaged town for nearby Veii. 'Here stands the Capitol,' he is said to have told them. 'Here a human head was discovered, and we understand the prophecy that this place will one day be the head of the world, the seat of its highest authority.'

It seems that the trough of depression was surmounted by this play on old myths and appeal to the dream of future power they enshrined. The psychological precondition for the necessary reforms had been met, and the Senate got to work. The aim was, first, the levelling of the grossest class-inequalities, to promote greater internal stability. Rome sought to use the shock it had sustained at the Celts' hands to the best possible advantage. At the same time it tried to strengthen its external position. This was, however, another matter.

The Republic, for all its strength, was still essentially a city-state which had gained a preponderant position in a federation of neighbouring peoples – Sabines, Latins, Hernicans. The members of this federation had received such a shock from the Celts that they now came more closely together. However by around 358 BC a new grouping to the south of Rome's sphere of influence had emerged, led by the Samnites, one of the most talented peoples among the Indo-European family of Italic tribes. Rome, bent on extending its power, fought them for five years; it might have been defeated had it not been for the sudden intervention of the Celts – this time with a happier outcome for Rome. The renewed Celtic attacks forced the Samnite leaders to join with the Roman Senate and send their troops together with Roman legions towards the Po valley.

This chain of events – war with Rome's southern neighbours, followed by an alliance with them; after this broke up, further conflict, with varying fortunes and various coalitions – went down in history as the First, Second and Third Samnite Wars, and the Latin War. But it was only a prelude to repeated and increasingly violent conflicts with the Celts. Even the Third Samnite War, which began in 298 BC, has to be classed as such. One of its high points, in retrospect, was the battle of Sentinum, which occurred in the fourth year of the war.

Near modern Sassoferrato, a tiny village on the eastern slopes of the Apennines, the legions of Rome took on a composite army made up – so rapidly did political constellations change – of Samnites, Etruscans, Umbrians, Lucanians and, in strength, Celts. The Romans had no doubt that the Celts formed the most dangerous ingredient in the mixture, though they also held the Samnites in great respect. Their commanders, Quintus Fabius, Maximus Rullianus and Publius Decimus Mus, therefore decided on tactics of containment and attrition. They hoped that, in Livy's words, 'as the war went on, the Samnites' morale would gradually decline, the Gauls' muscle would be weakened by the effort and the heat . . . so that if they began the battle with superhuman force, they would end it more helpless than women'.

However well-founded and rational these calculations may have been, it was not they that determined the course of the battle but two unforeseen occurrences that were anything but rational. The young Decius was responsible for the first. He suddenly ran out of patience at the half-hearted to-ing and fro-ing. He made for the Celts' horsemen but was beaten back – by fear, 'for, without warning, the enemy stormed forward on war-chariots and carts, with such a mighty rushing of horses and wheels that the Romans' horses took fright as they had never heard such a tremendous din. The cavalry, which had had victory in its grasp, ran off, stunned. Horses and riders fell victim to the senseless panic. . . . The Gauls' vanguard left them no time to regroup.' It looked as if the Celts had once more been helped by the dread that seemed their constant ally. But the victory was not complete, for Decius adopted a weapon that does not often figure in the arsenals of armies: anathema.

He ordered the high priest Marcus Livius to give him absolution, had all the formulae read to him and added, presumably in a very loud voice so as to be heard all over the field: 'Terror and ruin, murder and blood, the rage of the gods in heaven and below the earth I will carry with me, I will bring the curse of extermination to the standards, weapons and arms of the enemy. May ruin strike the Gauls and Samnites where I reach them.' Then he drove his horse into the Celts' lines and 'died, impaled on the weapons before him'.

His self-sacrifice had a remarkable effect: 'In their confusion, the Gauls' arrows missed; others stood stunned, unable either to fight or to flee.' When the Romans hurled their javelins, 'many fell unwounded, as if stunned, to the ground'. Seeing this, the Samnites took flight, whereupon the rest of the Celts were surrounded by Quintus Fabius's men and butchered. Rome had won the battle. Altogether this was a strange business, but not a completely imaginary one. If Decius's curse was impressive enough – and Livy says that priests did take part – it may well have managed, literally, to spellbind a horde of barbarians who were themselves deeply affected by belief in magical powers. Decius had deprived them of an ingredient of their strength: the trance, achieved by magic rites, in which they felt so much at one with their gods that death held no terror for them.

Despite Rome's success at Sentinum, it was still a long way from decisive victory over the coalition. Fabius and Decius had only prevented long-term unification of the Samnites from the southern Apennines and Campania with the Po valley Gauls. Only eight years later, when the Samnites submitted, did Rome's position improve, for then there were only some Etruscan towns and the Celts in the way of Rome's claims to central and southern Italy.

In 285 BC the Romans and the Celts were again at war. The course of this war is easily outlined. Polybius regards it as no more than a link in the chain of battles Rome had to fight with the Celts; and for most modern historians it was, at most, part of the aftermath of the bloody spectacle of the Third Samnite War. The Celts, had their people had historians, would no doubt have seen it in a different light, for it cost life and land to one of their proudest tribes, the Senones, even though they brought it on themselves.

As usual, their initial onslaught was made in irresistible strength. Before Arretium (Arrezzo, in Tuscany) they and their Etruscan allies annihilated a Roman legion. They then began their march southwards. Meanwhile the Senate had decided on a new strategy, believing that it was pointless to expose Roman troops again and again to the fury of the barbarians. To defeat them one would have to drive the axe into the roots of their strength: in less poetic terms, they had to be exterminated. The next Roman army was therefore sent, not directly against the advancing enemy, but into the Senones' own territory, the coastal region south of Rimini. There the legionaries staged one of the first planned genocides in European history.

With cold-blooded cruelty, unfortified villages were burnt down and women, old men, children – the whole defenceless population – mercilessly slaughtered or put to flight. Shattered refugees reached the settlements of nearby tribes and spread the terrible news. The terror, understandably, soon became rage and mobilized the whole Celtic people. The battle-hosts of the Boii joined with the Senones and Etruscans and once more marched on Rome. It seemed that there would be another battle on the Allia. However this time it turned out differently.

The Romans, who now had greater experience of Celtic tactics than in the terrible year of 387 BC, inflicted a crushing defeat on their enemies on the lower Tiber. The slaughter is said to have been so fearful that the river ran red as far as Rome itself; and if there was much Roman blood in the waters, there was even more Celtic. The Senones, who must have fought most frenziedly, were annihilated to such an extent that they ceased to exist as a people. The Etruscans' power was also finally broken. Only the Boii were able to withdraw in some order. In history books the conflict is called the battle of the Vadimonian Lake. Today the place is marked only by a little reedy pool, just off the autostrada between Orvieto and Rome, but locals say that its swampy banks still yield weapons and bones.

Despite this victory Rome did not spend much time on lengthy triumphs. Instead she exploited the new situation, occupied the areas settled by the decimated Senones, turned it into the *ager Gallicus* and secured it in 283 BC with a strong military colony, called Sena Gallica – known to modern sun-worshippers on the

Adriatic as Senigallia or Sinigaglia. The well-known resort of Rimini was originally founded for the same reason, two decades later, when it was called Ariminium. Both towns were the outcome of the Senate's new strategy, which had been tested in the war of annihilation. The Romans began to confine the fearsome warriors of the north with a string of strong border-forts in the Po valley, but they had by no means heard the last of them.

Generations born after the extermination of the Senones still lived with the Celtic menace, as a kind of ground-bass counterpointing all their political activities and accentuating their enemies' strength. Wherever the legions fought in the years to come – in Italy, Sicily, on the Balkan coasts – they were to encounter larger or smaller contingents of these dangerous blond-maned warriors in their gaudy dress. The Po valley became a kind of Red-Indian territory that only bold scouts, adventurous merchants and, of course, spies dared to penetrate. It was officially described as 'Gallia Cisalpina', that part of Gaul which lay this side of the Alps. On its borders, that is north of a line from Rimini to Pisa, the Senate's power stopped, even though it had taken over virtually the whole of the rest of Italy and only a few years later was to strike dread into the hearts of established Mediterranean powers.

It was partly thanks to the Celts that Roman legionaries had become such outstanding troops. As Polybius, without a hint of mockery, remarks: 'Once they had got used to being struck down by Gauls they were incapable of imagining anything worse; therefore they went into battle against Pyrrhus as highly-trained combatants.' The King of Epirus was indeed the next enemy they had to deal with. He was a sort of large-scale entrepreneur who used his forces much as a speculator uses his capital, and had crossed over from Greece with twenty-five thousand men and twenty war-elephants to win for himself an Italian kingdom. But although he was almost effortlessly successful whenever he encountered the Romans in the field, he was never able finally to overthrow a republic that was so well-versed in both tribal and guerrilla warfare. His 'Pyrrhic victories' remained just that. When he returned weakened, after a foray on the Greek-Carthaginian island of Sicily, the legions even managed to defeat him utterly in the field, although in this type of warfare he was supposed to be absolute master.

This final undertaking of Pyrrhus's was in fact the overture to the next great engagement: the war for Sicily, known to history as the First Punic War. Here too the Celts played a part, albeit as mercenaries. The mercantile city of Carthage, whose inhabitants were called 'Poeni' by the Romans, had always used mercenaries, mainly foreign, in pursuit of its interests. It bought up whatever it could get in the way of warlike tribes: Numidian cavalry from Algeria, Balearic sling-shooters, Iberian skirmishers and Celts from France and northern Spain. It was with these wild hordes that Carthaginian generals had, in campaigns that lasted for generations, wrested two-thirds of Sicily from the Greeks, conquered all Sardinia and overrun or held Corsica, Malta and Ibiza.

There had of course been problems with the mercenaries. These half-savages were considered to be fearless warriors, but they were also undisciplined and fractious, particularly the Celts. As garrison-troops at Agrigente they had once plundered the city out of hand when their pay arrived late. On another occasion their drunkenness cost them a victory that was already theirs. Immediately after the battle they had gone after the enemy wine-stocks; they were found 'stupefied, snoring on the straw' when the enemy returned that night and were 'butchered like animals'. Polybius does concede that these mercenaries cannot have been the elite of their people, 'for they had initially been expelled from their homelands for betraying friends and relatives' and had been accepted by the Carthaginians only 'as a wartime measure'. Like foreign mercenaries of later days, they seem to have been mainly the black sheep and the outlaws.

None the less, they caused the Romans a lot of trouble. The First Punic War cost the Roman Republic more lives than any conflict hitherto. As a result Roman respect not only for the Carthaginians, but also for their auxiliaries had grown. This partly explains why, twenty-five years after the conclusion of peace, the Romans allowed Hasdrubal to take over such a large area of Spanish territory: to deter him from alliance with the Celts. Polybius describes how essential this was.

When the ambassadors who had conducted the negotiations with Hasdrubal returned from Cartagena to Rome, they found a panic-stricken city. The citizens were so worried 'that they rapidly raised troops, laid in supplies of grain and other war-stocks, and soon sent off the army to the borders as if the enemy were already on the

march. . . . And this fear was not surprising, for the old terror of
the Gauls lay in their bones.' In fact the proliferating rumours and
reports that a further Celtic invasion was imminent seemed to have
become a certainty.

Polybius, who was born in 200 BC and could therefore have
known old people who had been involved in all of this, reckons he
can safely say that the Boii, Insubres and Taurisci of the Alpine
region had once again come together and formed a conspiracy
against Rome. He also says that their rulers had approached the
Celtic peoples who lived on the upper Rhône. Mercenaries were
raised there, whom he calls *'gaesatae'* and describes as professional
warriors; early ancestors, as it were, of the Swiss mercenary
Reisläufer of the Middle Ages, whose tradition lives on to this day
in the Vatican Swiss Guard.

The 'kings' of these mercenaries, he continues, were paid no fee
for their services by the Insubres and Boii, only a share of any
potential booty: 'They painted to them the great wealth of the
Romans and the plunder that victory would bring. . . . Nor was it
difficult to convince them, the more so as alliance was sworn at the
same time as the promises were made. . . . The leaders of the
Gaesatae were then seized by such a lust for battle that the whole
region never saw a more numerous, more imposing or effective
army.' If this is right, then Rome was well justified in preparing for
the worst and mobilizing its last reserves of strength. That is what
happened. Four legions, each of 2,500 foot-soldiers and 300 horsemen, were set up, and 30,000 other combatants were assembled
from among the neighbouring peoples. They were joined by alleged
'volunteers': 50,000 foot and 4,000 horse of Etruscan and Sabine
origin; 'the Umbrians and Sarsinatians of the Apennines provided
about 20,000 men, the Veneti and Cenomani another 20,000'. That
made in all a force of 134,000 soldiers, a no less motley horde than
that coming from northern Italy – the more so as, with the
Cenomani, it also contained Celts. This last point illustrates once
more that Rome had not only made military and political preparations for the battle to come, but had also engaged in intensive
diplomatic activity. It had apparently succeeded in dividing its
enemies. The Veneti, a people supposedly of Illyrian origin (in
France there was also a Celtic tribe of that name), had always been
on friendly terms with the Gauls. The fact that they, like the
Cenomani, stood on the opposite side from the Gauls 'obliged the

kings of the Insubres and the Boii to leave part of their forces to protect their land against the threat from there' (that is, modern Friuli and Venetia), which naturally reduced their chances of victory.

Even if they had succeeded in pushing south over the Apennines and defeating the huge army assembled against them, they would still have had to face, behind it, an equally multifarious reserve force, whose strength Polybius gives as '250,000 men on foot and 23,000 horsemen'. Even this was not the last force available to the federated peoples, for behind it stood a 'territorial army' of old men still able to bear arms, and boys who could do so in an emergency.

Why was this gigantic effort undertaken? Why was there such diplomatic activity in Venetia, even in far-off Carthaginian Spain? What was the reason for this mobilization of a whole people? It was in fact a force made up of a few barbarian tribes, hardly more than '50,000 foot-soldiers and 20,000 horsemen or charioteers'. The Celts must therefore have been even more terrible than the Ancient historians, with tales of their wild appearance and frenzy in battle, can convey. Since that summer when it had been saved only by cackling geese Rome had risen to become the leading power in Italy, and it must have known what it was doing in mounting an operation on such a scale. But the dread was now mutual.

The Celts in the Po valley also had every reason to feel threatened by the Romans. The people's tribune Caius Flaminius had used populist arguments to demonstrate that the *ager Gallicus* seized from the Senones should be divided up among Roman plebeians and settled by them. What this meant would be clear even to the least-politically-minded village elder: the Gauls were not only to be contained, they were deliberately to be driven out of their own settlements. For them there was no choice but to try and sever the noose around their necks: in 225 BC, as expected, they broke out. Their strategy was, as Polybius tells us, familiar: 'After the Celts had advanced into Etruria they ravaged the land unchecked, and as no one stood in their path they finally decided to make for Rome.'

The Romans, thoroughly as they seemed to have prepared for this war, were none the less surprised. For some reason they had expected the Boii and Insubres to attack not in the west, but towards the *ager Gallicus*. Accordingly fifty thousand legionaries had been assembled in and around Rimini, under Aemilius Papus; by far the largest contingent in the consuls' army. Now however the attackers stood a mere three days' march from Rome, at Chiusi, a region that, not least for its wine, was already known to them.

Messengers were of course hastily dispatched to all garrisons. On foaming horses they galloped to the Adriatic to warn Papus, or to Pisa where Caius Attilius Regulus stood with a further two legions. A third contingent holding the western borders was told only to shadow the Celts' approach, and on no account to attack. The senatorial military advisers seem to have elaborated a plan to manoeuvre the invaders into a situation where they could be simultaneously attacked from three different directions. It seemed that things were developing as desired.

But in the capital itself fear was greater than ever before. A soothsayer had found a prophecy, in an ancient book, that one day Gauls and Greeks would together take over Roman land. Who could be sure that this would not happen the next day? The confusion unleashed by the rumour must have been devastating. It must have reached such dangerous levels that the men responsible for public order felt they could counter it only with an action as barbaric as it was clever. A priest had recommended that the soothsayer's prophecy should be rendered harmless by appearing to carry it out literally. Greeks and Celts, a man and a woman of each people, would indeed enter the threatened land – by being buried alive. This advice was duly taken, and the gods seem to have been deceived. The Celtic army marched into the trap the Roman generals had set for it, though before this happened the Celts themselves managed a brilliant piece of deception.

When the leaders of the Boii, Insubres, Taurisci and Gaesatae saw that a strong observation corps was on their tail, they suddenly switched their line of advance. Instead of proceeding against Rome, they turned about and marched against the enemy in their rear, with the apparent intention of attacking. However that was only the first part of their plan. Once they had halted their pursuers south of Florence, they put into effect the second part. They put up their tents, as their enemies had done, ostensibly to prepare for the inevitable conflict of the next day. While the sentries in the Roman bivouacs merely kept in sight the Celts' camp-fires and listened to the savage singing that floated over, the Celtic army stole off soundlessly towards Fiesole. The noises heard by the Roman sentries came from only a few cavalry groups left behind who did not follow the bulk of the vanished force until dawn. The Romans naturally believed, when they had stormed the empty camp, that the Celts were trying to retreat. They set off hastily in pursuit without first doing what any semi-competent subaltern would have done in such circumstances – sent out spies. If they had done this, the lives of six thousand of their men would have been saved.

The Celts' only aim was to have the Romans in that formation in which an army is at its most vulnerable: on the march. This they achieved. They attacked down the slopes without warning, ripped apart the Roman column as it marched unheedingly forward and engaged in thousands of hand-to-hand combats. Those Romans who could not flee were killed, and it was only with difficulty that their officers managed to collect a few remnants of the broken corps on a hill that could with some success be defended against warriors whose qualities had never included perseverance. But this did not alter the fact that Rome had suffered a further bloody reverse at barbarian hands. What was even worse, the Roman trap had lost one of its teeth. The two remaining ones were to prove sufficient to complete the plan. Without knowing it, the victorious Celts had something to do with this.

One of their leaders, the king Aneroëstes, persuaded his allies to withdraw so as (in Polybius's words) 'to dispose of the plunder gained, not to risk everything at one go, and to return only when they were once more mobile to renew the fight with the Romans'. They therefore marched off towards the west, to reach their home along the Tyrrhenian Sea. They were pursued by Aemilius Papus's forces, which had reached the area from the Adriatic. Papus was likewise too cautious to launch an immediate attack, and waited for the arrival of the troops from Pisa. He was not to foresee that the Celts would run straight into these forces as they came south. On Cape Telamon the two armies met, to mutual surprise, while Aemilius Papus was already advancing. Aneroëstes and his vassals were in a trap. Enemy behind, enemy ahead: the situation appeared hopeless. Would the terror they always inspired save the Celts yet again? At first it almost looked as though it would.

When they saw that they were caught between two pincers, the Celts adopted all-round defence: one line turned to face the enemy force in the north, the other facing the enemy in the rear, with the camp and its vast booty between the two lines. The Gaesatae and

Insubres were to repel Aemilius Papus, the Taurisci and Boii the
soldiers of Attilius Regulus. Outside the lines were placed the two-
wheeled and four-wheeled war-chariots. Polybius asserts that this
formation was not only, as usual, 'terrible to see', but that it also
'suited tactical requirements'. He also wonders 'whether the Celtic
formation was the more vulnerable since it could simultaneously be
assaulted by the enemy on two sides, or on the contrary the more
advantageous since, as they were fighting on both sides, they were
also covering each other's rear'.

The Romans themselves seem not to have perceived this. They
reckoned to have all the tactical advantages on their own side, 'but
on the other hand they were again frightened by the imposing
appearance of the Celtic host in arms and the wild tumult. For the
Celts had innumerable horn-players and trumpeters, and since the
whole army took up a war-chant, a din arose so immense and
terrifying that not only the instruments and the warriors but the
very hills around seemed to be raising their voices in echo.' Once
more it was chaos itself that the Romans were confronting. The
Gaesatae must have been the most impressive, for while the
Insubres and Boii retained breeches and cloaks, such was the heat
that the Gaesatae threw off their clothes and attacked the enemy
in white-skinned nakedness, their blond, lime-hardened hair erect,
their golden bracelets and necklaces glinting in the sun.

But effective as terror might be as a weapon, it could work only
once: once the enemy had overcome it, the Celts inevitably became
for the Romans mere mortals, the more so as their nakedness was
covered by neither breast-armour nor thigh-plates. In the battle on
Cape Telamon, at the foot of the hill today called Talamonaccio,
the Romans seem to have learned this for the first time. A first
Celtic cavalry-charge failed, and when their infantry followed up
the legionaries realized that they were much better equipped
than the Celts. Tall men with shields too small to cover them offer
an excellent target for javelins and arrows, and the Romans cold-
bloodedly exploited this. While the Insubres, Boii and Taurisci
were effectively discouraged by the hail of missiles, the Gaesatae in
'senseless rage stormed against the enemy'. Hand-to-hand fighting
followed the skirmishing, and it emerged for the second time that
the Romans' ordnance experts had studied such fighting much
more thoroughly than their opponents.

'The shields of the Romans are better for protection and their

swords are better suited to battle, because the shield covers their
whole body while the Gauls' one is shorter; and the Roman sword
is good for thrusting, though it can also cut, while the Gauls' one
can only cut.' In other words the naked and lightly-clad Celts, prepared only for attack, were suddenly faced with a closed front of
soldiers who bore their tall shields like a moving wall and rapidly
struck out from the gaps in it. The Celts themselves could try to
break up this carapace of leather, wood and metal only by blows
from above, so that they had to expose their arms from above their
scant coverings. Moreover their swords, as Polybius rightly says,
had no point (rather, they were rounded) and were obviously of
poor material. 'They are effective only at the first blow, thereafter
they are blunt and bend such that if the warrior has no time to
wedge it against the ground and straighten it with his foot, the
second blow is quite ineffective.' Once more, as in the initial skirmishing, the legionaries exploited all these weak points. If a Celt's
sword were blunted against their shields or against the forward-
thrusting lances of the *triarii*, who usually stood in the last row,
they would press him so hard that he could not get in another blow.
It was a method that generals in subsequent Celtic campaigns were
to perfect. At Telamon, where it was developed, it was already
enough to annihilate the enemy. Of the Celts, who were now cut
down as they refused to flee – in any case no way was open – forty
thousand are said to have fallen. No less than ten thousand were
taken prisoner, among them one of their two kings. Aneroëstes, the
other one, killed himself, with his retinue.

It was a complete, so to speak a total, victory. However the
jubilation that greeted Aemilius Papus when he arrived in Rome
shortly afterwards – his colleague Attilius Regulus had been killed
– was aroused less by the captured arms he brought or the humili-
ated blond warriors who followed his train in chains, but rather by
relief that the nightmare was over, that a deep-seated fear had been
overcome, that Romans could now breathe freely once more in
their homeland. If there was still a lingering disquiet, it was
because the Celts were still in occupation of the Po valley and could
break out at any time. But that in itself did not seem to matter
much, for it was clear that an army with modern weapons and
methodical strategy could break even their *furor*. This lesson must
have been the most important outcome of the war of 225 BC.

All the later Celtic campaigns on Italian territory were a mere aftermath; not only the subsequent advance into the Po valley, in which Mediolanum was destroyed, but also – seen in this context – the Second Punic War: Hannibal's attempt to bring Rome to her knees with the assistance of the northern tribes. He could have succeeded, at the outside, only if the battle of Telamon had not struck at the roots of the power of the Gaesatae, Insubres, Boii and Taurisci, or if his uncle Hasdrubal had not concluded the treaty of the Ebro, which left the Romans time to deal with their enemies at home. But since he did, it was the Roman and not the Carthaginian scheme that succeeded. When Hasdrubal advanced to the Ebro, Rome ignored their agreement and used diplomatic means to upset his plans. This however set the fuse to the powder-barrel that Hasdrubal's nephew was later to ignite.

Roman treachery having supplied the *casus belli*, Hannibal seems to have prepared for alliance with the Celts very carefully. Delegates of the Boii, who at this time suffered particularly from Roman colonization of their lands, were by the winter of 219–18 BC discussing plans with him for a march through southern France towards northern Italy. An expeditionary force probably set up relay-stations over the whole route (two of these have been excavated near Carcassonne). When in September 218 BC the Carthaginian army reached the lower Rhône, there appeared Magalos, another prince of the Boii, who had presumably come to negotiate with the southern French Gallic tribes, who had already shown some signs of disrupting the army's manoeuvre. Without the help of such mediators from northern Italy, the Carthaginian army could probably not have advanced in such order across Celtic territory. On the other hand it was apparently only the Boii who sided with Hannibal from the start. Their fellow tribesmen, even the Celtiberians of Spain, were much less enthusiastic about Hannibal's far-reaching enterprises. Some ten thousand of them deserted even before the crossing of the Pyrenees, and others – local inhabitants for the most part – even served as spies for the Romans and reported via Massilia (the Greeks' 'Massalia' – the old Hellenic settlement now called Marseilles) to Rome that an army with giant grey animals they had never seen before, *elefantoi*, was moving towards the Alpine passes.

In these mountains it was initially the Celtic Allobroges who caused Hannibal further difficulties. They tried to block his path

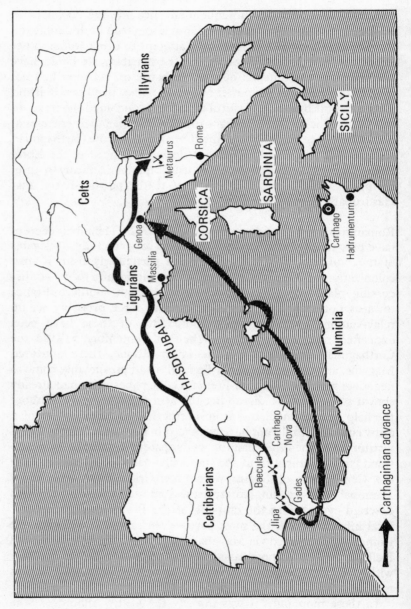

Map 2   Hannibal's advance from Spain to Italy

on the upper Isère and only a night raid on their lines, which they left in the evening, drove them back. Later the same was attempted by the Ceutrones, who lived in what is today Savoy. First they sent envoys to Hannibal with plentiful supplies; then, as Livy says, 'while the army was moving along a narrow path, flanked on one side by a menacing mountain-cliff, they broke out on all sides from concealed spots, attacked both front and rear, fought both at close quarters and at a distance, and dislodged great boulders on the column'. They probably only wanted the Carthaginian quarter-masters to pay them properly for the supplies they had given the vanguard. Hannibal's losses in this ambush were heavy, but 'fortunately more in beasts of burden than in men'.

All in all these events showed that the Celts were by no means all behind Hannibal, even though he was attacking their common enemy, the Romans. This may be perhaps understandable with tribes that had never faced Roman armies in battle, but it is some-what surprising with the northern Italian peoples whose territories Hannibal was now entering. Rome had bloodily defeated them and was threatening to invade their homelands. They stood literally with their backs against the great wall of the Alps, but evidently it was only the Boii who showed proper political judgment by allying themselves with Carthage. Was it insight into the situation facing them that they lacked, or was it a lack of solidarity? Or was it simply a resigned acceptance of their fate after the failure of the last march on Rome? Polybius may be absolutely right when he asserts that the Celts 'were governed not only in most, but effectively in all, cases more by disposition than by discretion'. They were a people who lived, attractively but precariously, from day to day. To outsiders they must have seemed volatile, unreliable and un-predictable. Of course Hannibal, whose people had for generations had dealings with the Celts, knew them well enough to have learnt how they should be handled.

When the Taurini, who lived in what is now Piedmont, in their turn showed little desire to co-operate, Hannibal stormed their capital. Then he tried another tactic. Before his assembled forces, he made the captured Celts a bloody offer: he told them through an interpreter that any of them could fight a duel with one of his countrymen, and if he won, could take a horse and weapons and would be free to go where he pleased. It is not difficult to guess what happened.

When the lots had been cast, all without exception demanded swords and action, each man anxious to be among those selected by chance for the fight. When his lot was drawn, the man who had been favoured would happily jump up and all would wish him luck. Without delay he would take his weapons as was the custom, with the leaps of a dancer. When they fought it was not just the other prisoners but also the spectators who rejoiced at the fate of both the victor and of the vanquished, who had met such a fine death.

It was, in other words, a spectacle after the Celts' hearts.

Livy also considers that it helped Hannibal to show his men the situation they were in. He is supposed to have shouted to the soldiery: 'Fate has given you bonds that are no heavier or harder to bear than those of the prisoners . . .; whenever you first encounter the enemy, you must win or die.' But this interpretation is rather contrived. It is much more likely that with this demonstration Hannibal was appealing to the Celts' sense of honour and their lust for battle, giving them tangible evidence that with him they could win freedom, life and rich booty. In a later speech that confirms this assumption, he even promised to give Carthaginian citizenship to all who joined his forces.

In addition, he knew that a swift victory over the Romans would be his best advertisement. He therefore sought battle as soon as possible. An opportunity came on the river Ticinus (Ticino), not far from Pavia. With one of his subtly devised attacks, he defeated the army of the consul, Publius Cornelius Scipio, and thus became master of a large piece of formerly Celtic territory. Scipio had in fact withdrawn after the battle towards Piacenza, one of the newest and strongest fortresses on the border with the Gauls, abandoning to Hannibal the whole of the eastern Po valley. For the Insubres this was the sign they must have been, in their vacillation, awaiting for so long. With fourteen thousand warriors they now joined up with Hannibal, while at the same time a whole series of Celtic units in the Roman army killed their officers and deserted to the Carthaginians – not forgetting, as custom ordained, to bring along the heads of their victims.

Hannibal's plans of alliance seemed to have worked after all. But they achieved little for him. In the next great battle, fought in a blizzard on the Trebia, a tributary of the right bank of the Po, it was in fact the Celts who deprived him of complete and crushing victory. He had placed them in the centre to hold the enemy attack long enough for him to take both Roman flanks. It was not a success. Before the intended pincers could close, they took to their heels and thus tossed away what the rest of the army was so close to achieving.

Had too much been asked of them? Or had they lost that frenzied bravery for which they were renowned? The truth probably lies in between. After so many defeats they no longer had their old self-confidence. Moreover their forces may have been made up mostly of inexperienced men. The majority of their seasoned warriors must have been slain in the various defensive campaigns that dragged on until 219 BC. Rome had managed to break the morale of the proud peoples of Gallia Cisalpina, something that Hannibal was often to appreciate in days to come. He did try his best to get the Gauls to co-operate and even is said to have learned their various dialects, but it brought him no worthwhile advantage. Soon after the battle of the Trebia entire Celtic units were returning to their villages, agitated by the rumour that Hannibal would give them the most dangerous missions so as to spare his own men. The temperamental barometer of this excitable people rapidly sank; they were indeed unreliable allies.

The few who accompanied Hannibal to southern Italy, his route paved with successes and ending in ultimate misfortune, came back years later disappointed and in despair, chiefly because the last attempt to halt Roman progress towards power over the whole of Italy had failed. Being the most politically adroit of the tribe, they also knew full well what this entailed. After the final overthrow of Carthage, the Senate would do its utmost mercilessly to extinguish the last trouble-spot south of the Alps. The inhabitants of the Po valley were faced with extermination.

As soon as peace with Carthage had been concluded, Rome again sent troops northwards. The senators had good reasons for doing so: Hannibal's crossing of the Alps had shown them how easily the unity of their state could be threatened from northern Italy. Even if the Celts had not been of much help to Hannibal, they still appeared to be the most stubborn of the many peoples that had settled in Italy and gradually been brought into the Roman structure. Since they would not bend, they had to be broken, above all the Boii and Insubres. However, as the Romans had meanwhile appreciated, armies alone were not enough for this. The last Celtic war on Italian territory was less a traditional campaign than a far-ranging operation in which one settlement after another was systematically attacked and destroyed. Those prisoners who were not put to the sword were transported south as slaves. The Celts met like with like, killing mercilessly, abandoned their colourful attacks and laid ambushes instead, waging guerrilla war for every yard of ground. In all, they held their enemies at bay for almost ten years. The peace treaty had to be concluded with old men, for scarcely any young ones remained. In some mountain valleys the fighting, in which the Ligurians were also involved, continued beyond 280 BC.

Even before this, colonies had followed the army. On this blood-soaked ground new Roman settlements grew up: Placentia, then Cremona, Aquileia, Modena, Parma. The province was still called Gallia Cisalpina, but the only Gauls in it were subjugated though capable farmers and, if Polybius is to be believed, inn-keepers with extremely low prices for full board and lodging. Nowadays a well-informed world tends to get worked up at stories of campaigns of annihilation in distant lands, only to forget them. At that time such news would be greeted by undisguised relief in those states of the Mediterranean who called themselves civilized. The Romans were not the only people who had to fight the Celts. Their *furor* had deeply offended ideas of order and civilization elsewhere too.

THREE

The Heirs of Alexander and the Celts

Majestix fears only one thing: that the heavens might fall on his head.
Asterix

You stupid Galatians! You must have been bewitched – you before whose eyes Jesus Christ was openly displayed upon his Cross!
St Paul, *Epistle to the Galatians*

On a late winter day in the year 335 BC thousands of armed men trudged painfully through the frozen snow towards that flat indentation in the chain of the Balkan Mountains that to the modern Bulgarians is the *Šipčenski prohod* or Shipka Pass. They would not have attracted much attention in that bald, barren mountain landscape. Over the centuries armies and wandering tribes had again and again made for this, the most important link of communication between the lower Danube and the fertile lands of the Maritsa valley, and all of them had looked more or less like this one. Wrapped in many-coloured cloaks, their heads hidden beneath flat iron helmets, armed with very long lances and round shields, these tall, long-haired and bearded men followed their commanders, who stood out from the rest with their superior weaponry, brighter breastplates and more elaborately wrought helmets. At their head rode a boy of twenty-one who would before long declare war, in the name of the Hellenes, on all Asia and who nowadays is regarded as the supreme incarnation of Grecian life and civilization, Alexander the Great of Macedonia.

The young king was however Hellenic more by education than by blood. The people he led and that had produced him struck their southern neighbours as a federation of half-savage mountain-tribes: men grouped round native princes in true fealty, their way of life reminiscent of Homer's heroes but regarded by the age as virtually barbarian. They liked wild drinking; no doubt to the Greeks' horror, wine was drunk neat, without added water. They liked boasting of their prowess, challenging friends to mortal duels, insulting enemies, listening to endless variations of heroic songs and on occasion – if the pebble mosaics found in Pella, one of their capitals, provide a true picture – throwing off their clothes in the heat of hunt or battle to stalk deer or to fight naked under flowing cloaks. Alexander himself is depicted thus.

If the Macedonians regarded themselves as Greeks, it was only because their rulers told them that it was to this people they belonged. In externals, but also in their way of life, they must have been much less different from the north Balkan tribes than from those they purported to defend. That was probably why they could so easily deal with barbarian peoples. When stone-filled carts rattled down on them from the slopes of the Shipka Pass, they were not nearly as frightened as the Romans on such occasions but coolly stepped out of the way or, crouching under their shields, let the carts roll over them. If ambushed they would withdraw until archers and javelin-throwers had driven the enemy from the undergrowth and their forces lay exposed in open country. When the Triballes, one of the tribes they had to fight, withdrew to an island in the Danube, a raiding party rowed after them at night and attacked them while they slept. Too shrewd to pursue horsemen as they escaped over the Romanian plains, they set up their own standards on the edge of the river and spread the news that a Macedonian prince had advanced to the extreme northern frontier of the Greek world and meant to keep it. This message must have counted as something of a sensation.

There came, from all corners, barbarian chiefs to visit the young man challenging them in their own sphere. One even came from the upper Danube, and his visit won him a place, albeit anonymous, in history. Alexander probably received him with especial curiosity. As a reader of Herodotus he was well aware that 'the Danube rises in the land of the Celts'. The man thus belonged to a people about whom he must at least have heard reports and with whom his western subjects, on the Albanian coast, must have had some contact for many years. Moreover, as his biographers rarely omit to mention, Alexander's father had been slain by a Celtic dagger. Now he too was to know one of the people who produced such weapons. The man stepped into his tent.

What Alexander discussed with him, and in what language, we do not know. Only Ptolemy, a friend of the young king, has recorded parts of the conversation for posterity. Alexander, he reports, asked the Celt what his people most feared, 'naturally in the hope that he would reply it was himself'. But the answer was unexpected. The Celt tersely replied that they feared nothing so much as the possibility 'that the heavens might fall on their heads'. His words must have impressed the officers present in the tent more than we can understand. What was so remarkable about a barbarian reacting impertinently to a chance observation and giving himself rhetorical airs, on the principle, one might say, that a silly question deserves a silly answer?

There must have been more to it. Ptolemy could still remember the Celt's answer when, thirty years later, and long since king of Egypt, he dictated a biography of his dead sovereign. Aristotle, Alexander's tutor, concluded that the Celts must be a people of remarkable rashness. Modern scholars have puzzled over this enigmatic reply until it became clear that what seemed a mere *aperçu* revealed an attitude to life that was shared by peoples of similar spirit, such as the Achaean Greeks, the heroes of Homer or the Turkic peoples from the regions of Lake Baikal. This in turn leads one to suppose that the Celt had uttered words that were, to him, tremendously important and therefore struck a common chord in the leader of the half-savage Macedonians.

We may assume that Alexander must have been moved. The young ruler, already in the process of conquering half of the world, was learning early in his career that there were men who respected no material barriers, recognizing only the limitations that fate imposed. In his situation this must have affected him almost like an omen. However the Celts were also impressed by him and his army. It was not until sixty years after this meeting on the Danube, when they were wandering freely and unchecked throughout half Europe and could take whatever they wanted, that they dared to cross the Balkan mountains into Greece.

Around the year 280 BC Tyche, the goddess of fate, 'unleashed a warlike rage which,' according to Polybius, 'overcame the Gauls like a pestilence'. The empire Alexander had created was beginning to fall asunder. On the Nile reigned Ptolemy, the chronicler of the scene with the Celt in the Danubian camp; the rest of the empire had, after all the other competitors among the Macedonian leaders had been eliminated, passed to Seleucus, also a former aide and friend of the late king. But of these Diadochs only the new pharaoh was to die peacefully. Seleucus was murdered by Ptolemy's son, called Ceraunos ('Thunderbolt'), just after he had won Macedonia. Expelled from Egypt by his stepmother, this prince became king in Alexander's homeland, a state stretching from the Danube to the Aegean. But he too was to rule for only a short time.

A few months after his successful usurpation, there appeared on the Danube, just where his father had fought the barbarian northerners, a wandering host of Celts that advanced, probably over the Shipka Pass, into Macedonia. Its leader was apparently Bolgios (or Belgios) and he brought, as his like had in Italy, terror. Ceraunos, an unscrupulous politician but a good general, gave battle to the barbarians – exactly where is not known – fought bravely and was killed. The Celts then overran and plundered the country for a time before disappearing with their booty.

However Bolgios had led merely a vanguard. The ruins of the houses burned by him had not been cleared before a new, and this time stronger, Celtic contingent appeared. It was led by a chieftain who had the same name as that mysterious hero of early Roman history, Brennus. Diodorus says that he had 150,000 foot-soldiers, 10,000 horsemen and 2,000 baggage-carts; but his army is not likely to have contained more than 30,000 men. This was however enough to give him free passage to the heart of Greece. An Attic force that tried to stop him, about a hundred miles north-east of Athens at the Pass of Thermopylae, was swept aside. A corps under his leadership made its way towards Delphi to plunder this town, the centre of the Hellenic world.

As always, wherever the Celts appeared, panic broke out. The guardians of the principal shrine of the Greeks turned to Pytheia to ask if they should remove their wives and children with the temple treasures to the nearest fortified town. As usual they received an enigmatic though comforting answer. In her 'raging voice' the priestess, writhing on the three-legged chair, replied that all oblations should be left where they were: there was no threat to the sacred precincts, for the god Apollo and the 'white virgins' would protect them. The trouble was that no one knew who or what these maidens were. There was hasty agreement on the virgin goddesses Athena and Artemis, both of whom were worshipped at Delphi.

It soon became clear that this was incorrect. No deities descended from Olympus. Instead it began to snow, though as it turned out this was very much like assistance from heaven. Brennus, who shortly before had laughed loudly in a temple at the Greeks' belief in gods in human form, was attacked in a snow-storm not far from the Oracle, at the foot of Parnassus, probably in the late autumn of 279 BC. He was decisively beaten. His victors chose to believe that 'white virgins' was merely a poetic name for the snowflakes driving into the faces of the Celtic warriors – which was plausible enough. Brennus himself probably no longer cared very much, for he had been so severely wounded in the battle of Parnassus that he had had to give his final orders from his deathbed. All the wounded, he told his senior lieutenant Acichorus, were to be killed and the baggage burned: only an army free of ballast would have a chance of escaping. Then, says Diodorus, 'he took a deep draught of un-mixed wine and killed himself'. After burying Brennus, Acichorus put to death the several thousand wounded or half-frozen men and with the remainder went back the way they had come. But they failed to reach the Danube, 'as not a single one ever returned home'.

This second Brennus was not given the chance of supplying Greek legend with its own *vae victis*. However, his attack was not without its consequences for Hellenic policy. It had suddenly become clear to the successors of Alexander that there lived, on the other side of the Macedonian border, peoples who could be just as menacing to the state as were their own ambitions. Antigonus Gonatas, successor of the usurper Ceraunos, therefore struck an agreement with Antiochus, son of the Seleucus murdered by 'Thunderbolt', by which a division of land and zones of influence were fixed. The former would retain and defend Macedonia. Beyond the Dardanelles and the Bosphorus, the latter wished to concern himself only with his possessions in Asia Minor, Persia and Syria. Both undertook to keep a wary eye on all the barbarian peoples. But this plan was not to take effect. The Seleucid was too

weak to hold together a state that ran from the Sea of Marmora to
the Indus. There were soon further internal power-struggles
which invited the Celts to invade the land a third time.

There has been much speculation about the three Gallic tribes
that appeared, a year after Brennus's defeat, on the western shores
of the Dardanelles. Their names are known, but this does not take
us very far. Even Strabo, the most famous geographer of Ancient
times, affirms more or less with a shrug that they were called
Tolistoagii, Trocmians and Tectosages, but he cannot say with
any certainty where they came from. However he believed that the
last, the Tectosages, came originally from the region around
modern Toulouse; moreover he cites a report that they participated in the advance on Delphi. But he knows nothing of the
two others, nor of the Prausians, the people to whom Brennus
apparently belonged.

The only thing about which this careful scholar was certain was
that after 280 BC there were power-struggles among the Volcae –
a tribe to which the Tectosages belonged – and that in the course
of these a great number of men and women were driven out of
their lands. They were joined by adventurers from other Celtic
peoples who accompanied the exiles towards Greece. But why the
fighting broke out in the Garonne valley, whether from factional
quarrels, dynastic disputes or simple overpopulation, no one
knows. Strabo seems to assume the last. We can say with some
accuracy only that the Tectosages, after their withdrawal from the
tribal homelands, disappeared in the mysterious darkness that
hung over the Celts' movements, to reappear in the light of
Mediterranean civilization with two other tribes attached or
absorbed. By then they were already in Macedonian territory.

The Macedonian generals had meanwhile learned how the
Celts fought, and could turn their knowledge into strategy. They
did this with the resolution native to them. Antigonus Gonatas
surprised the invaders at a time when their lust for battle was also
dormant: at night. He enticed them into a terrain that suited him,
and inflicted a defeat on them at Lysimacheia on the Gallipoli
peninsula which so enhanced his not very high reputation that the
Macedonians finally accepted him as king. The Celts who survived
the night action forced their way to the entrance of the Dardanelles
and crossed to Troy, where they became enmeshed in the net of
another ambitious petty prince.

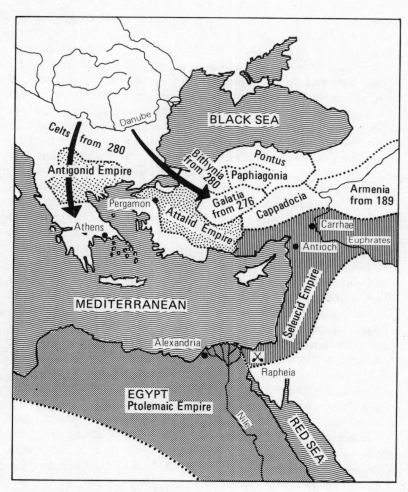

Map 3   The Galatians settle in Anatolia

Nicomedes, an aristocratic knight-errant from Bithynia on the Bosphorus, was among the many who were tearing, like a pack of hounds, at the giant carcass that was the Alexandrian empire. Lacking the strength to achieve his ends without the help of powerful allies, he suggested to the Celtic princes that they should fight for him against the Seleucid Antiochus, who still claimed sovereignty over all Asia and Asia Minor. The three tribes, who could have had no better passport to a world unknown to them, of course accepted. In the Bithynian's cause, they marched to and fro for two years across the western provinces of modern Turkey. They seem to have borne out all the terrifying reports that had preceded their advance since the march on Delphi. They burned, plundered, murdered and must have drunk whole wine-cellars dry. Not until 275 BC, when Pyrrhus had just conquered most of Sicily, did the powerful but heavily committed Antiochus feel able to deal with them. He had sixteen elephants specially brought from India and so terrified the Celts that they fled at the first encounter. But he too was unable to destroy them completely, which must have been as disagreeable to Nicomedes, who now had what he wanted, as to himself.

Nicomedes had hired the barbarians; they had given him the freedom of manoeuvre he needed to secure his own state, but he then faced the question as to what should now be done with them. To anticipate demands for pay or whatever he cleverly worked on the great longing that had impelled the three tribes to their wanderings; he offered them territory in that part of Anatolia east of his frontiers, the region around modern Ankara. This gambit offered a dual advantage: on the one hand, he would be rid of these guests; on the other he would create a buffer-state between himself and the wild Phrygians. Besides, the land was not even his.

He must have been visibly relieved when the Celts accepted the deal, moving forward and establishing a community henceforth known to the Ancient world as Galatia, land of the Galatians, i.e. Celts. This did not solve the Celtic problem in Asia Minor. Warriors with lime in their hair and multi-coloured clothing kept coming from the Danube valley into the areas east and west of the Bosphorus, disrupting sea-going traffic on the line of communication between the Black Sea and the Aegean, and being bought off only at considerable expense. These tributes were made not by Nicomedes but primarily by the wealthy city of Byzantium, modern Istanbul, whose vital artery was the Bosphorus. By this time a further Celtic state had been set up, extending over the Edirne (Adrianople) region: the so-called empire of Tylis. Finally a third Gallic tribe, the Scordisci, established itself in these years west of the Macedonian border and founded the town of Singidunum, which is today Belgrade.

If all these movements and settlements are viewed from the broad perspective that two thousand years' hindsight provides, a pattern emerges that Strabo could not have seen. To this geographer from Amaseia (Amasya in Anatolia), the Trocmians, Tolistoagii and Tectosages must have been an unaccountable phenomenon. He could say neither where they came from, nor what their motives were. We know rather more. Archaeologists have ascertained that Celts lived not only in Germany, France, Switzerland and northern Italy, but also in Hungary and Romania. This suggests that most of the tribes who invaded the Balkans came from beyond the Danube, and were all part of a single migration. Within a few years they made their presence felt and established their states and cities in rapid succession. It must have been a process similar to that which, one hundred and twenty years before, had brought the Insubres, Boii, Cenomani and their neighbours into Italy. This almost confirms Polybius's simplistic assertion that from time to time the Celts suffered from an epidemic of war-lust.

They must indeed at times have been seized by restlessness, which expressed itself in various ways. Whole contingents of moustachioed ruffians hired themselves out to any general who could pay. Pyrrhus used them, as did his rivals. Leaders such as Bolgios or Brennus would collect peasant youths with no patrimony and go off hunting for booty, followed by great hosts that not only fought and plundered but also intended to settle – though as we shall see there were also other reasons for this. So far as the three tribes are concerned, one's immediate assumptions are partly correct. Many bloody battles and two years' marauding, certainly not without losses, had left them still numerous enough to form their own state. The well-established theory that the Tectosages, Trocmians and Tolistoagii probably formed only the upper class in Galatia or *Gallo-Graecia*, as it was also called, does not particularly weaken the thesis. Rule over subject peoples also requires considerable strength, and they organized their community astonishingly well.

Each of the three tribes now settled in Anatolia took over its own province, as Strabo says. The Trocmians were in the eastern part of Galatia, the Tolistoagii in the western part, the Tectosages between them. For administrative purposes each of these provinces was divided into four, each division under a leader whom Strabo calls 'tetrarch' (literally, 'four-prince'), to whom a judge, military governor and two lesser commanders would be attached. These staffs were responsible to a 300-member senate, which represented the whole tribe and regularly met in a Drunemeton. The question of what these meeting-places were has occupied philologists and historians for some time. Now some agreement has been arrived at: the answer comes as the solution to a charade.

A *nemeton* was, in Celtic France and Britain as well, the peaceful, sacred place roughly corresponding to the *temenos* or original form of the Greek temple: here priests ruled and sacrifice was made to the gods. It was more difficult to establish the meaning of the prefix *dru-*. Pliny's final suggestion was it must come from *drus*, the Greek name for an oak. His modern colleagues have also taken this view; not for any lack of alternative solutions but because it is known that both Celtic and Greek were Indo-European languages with a common root. In Celtic Ireland the word for an oak was *daur*, and it must be obvious even to a layman that this word resembles the Greek equivalent as distant cousins sometimes do. The Drunemeton was thus a place of worship overlooked by oaks, both a sacred grove and a shaded stopping-place: hence the Galatian parliament must itself have been sacred in character. This is understandable because one of its functions was as supreme criminal court in the land, and because justice is almost always carried out in the name of a higher authority, whether god, king or people.

Both lower and higher civil justice, however, was a matter for the tetrarchs and the judges attached to them. In the Drunemeton only capital crimes were tried. All of this reveals a consciousness of justice and the state which would hardly have been expected of barbarians. But it did not preserve the Celtic federation from internal disturbances.

'In my day,' Strabo writes, 'the government lay in the hands of three kings, then of two, and finally only of one': in other words there were also power-struggles and dynastic disputes in Greek Gaul. But the three tribes gradually came to form a community under centralized government. Strabo does not say where its capital was. He mentions only a series of fortified garrison-towns in which the tetrarchs resided. The most powerful of these was thought to be Ankyra (Ankara), which seems probable. There is a citadel even today on the mighty rock dominating the Turkish capital, from which the Anatolian uplands parched by the summer heat can be surveyed. This rock is a commanding point and always has been – this was also true for the old Ankara, whose remains have been discovered by students not far from the modern city.

Strabo is somewhat more informative about the religious centre of the land than about the capital. He thinks it was in Pessinus, presumably not without evidence. The temple city was not a Celtic creation but an old centre of the cult of Cybele and her lover Attys. Even to the Romans this was one of the most sacred places of their empire. When the Celts ruled in the area, however, they must have forced their way into the place, not so much because the sacred black stone of the goddess mattered to them but because to be master of the Pessinus temple was to enjoy great prestige among the peoples of Asia Minor: this could be politically useful. The Galatians themselves did worship 'the great mother' under her Pessinian name, Agdistis, but they remained as faithful to their own gods as to their language. Even in the third century AD it was not quite extinct and a Gallic god was in that area worshipped as 'Zeus Bussurigios'.

Anyone with no more than a slight knowledge of their way of life is tempted to deduce from the New Testament that the Celts had hardly changed since leaving their homelands. In his Epistle to the Galatians St Paul warns them not only against idolatry, sorcery and jealousy, but just as strongly against hatred, murder, drunkenness, gluttony and the like. As to their inconstancy, he complained that, having started off so well, they were now stopping themselves from following the path to Truth. The Christian communities under the jurisdiction of the Drunemeton were among the oldest founded by this eloquent missionary on his travels through Asia Minor. We cannot tell whether it was merely chance that it was to them that his hymn to spiritual freedom was addressed, or whether he wished to combat an alternative, Celtic notion of what freedom was. He stresses that the fruits of the spirit are love, joy, peace, patience, mercy, goodness, loyalty, humility and meekness, that the Christian is not one who boasts or challenges others. He

added finally: 'God is not mocked, for whatever a man sows, that
he will also reap.' The Epistle of St Paul to the Galatians is
certainly the most humane of all documents on Celtic history: a
plea for humility directed at a people accustomed to putting their
trust in the sword.

Any assumption that the Galatians led a peaceful existence as
shepherds and farmers in their Anatolian refuge, with a wholly
bucolic year interrupted only by ceremonies amid the rustle of
oak-groves, misconceives not only them but the time and the place
in which they lived. All around them flourished states founded on
no more than armed force and strong will, or indeed on mere
money. Are we to suppose that these Celtic warriors turned their
curved lance-blades into ploughshares?

Pergamon, for instance, the principality on their southern
border, was the outcome of a transaction in the grand manner. Its
founder, the eunuch Philetairos, former treasurer of the Diadoch
Lysimachos, left him when his luck ran out and went over to his
rival Seleucus, without either returning the riches in his charge or
presenting them to his new master as dowry. Instead he used this
fortune to haggle his way into a new state of his own. He set about
it with cunning and method. At vast expense he first bought the
goodwill of his neighbours and then, through magnificent oblations to the great Greek temple, won himself the reputation of
a devout and generous patron; having thus consolidated his
position, he hired a mercenary army. Its generals were told to
extend the frontiers of Pergamon little by little, almost imper-
ceptibly: a task they fulfilled with growing success.

When, fifteen years before the three Celtic tribes appeared in
Asia Minor, Philetairos finally died, he was still not king: he had
never quite had the courage to secede from the Seleucid court. But
he left his nephew Eumenes a solid foundation for bolder, more
ambitious enterprises. Eumenes was not a man to pass up such
chances. He defeated Seleucus's successor, Antiochus, in battle at
Sardes, and became the most powerful man in Asia Minor. Then
he set about systematic extension of his possessions. He founded
new cities and reinforced his army, still using the contents of the
well-filled chest his uncle had left him. The embezzled money was
also his best weapon against the Celts. Now settled in Galatia, they
regarded Pergamon as a golden milch-cow, to be milked at will with

the assistance of sword and lance. Not even Eumenes could deal with them: to keep them away he had to pay, pay, and pay again.

The reputation the three tribes gained from this blackmail gradually became proverbial. They must to the peoples of Asia Minor have seemed a sort of divine scourge, a thorn in the flesh that smarted unbearably. Their presence provoked not only hatred and fear but also longing for some saviour who could free the civilized world from this curse. Any military leader who had managed to worst them would have been sure of enthusiastic welcome. Attalos I, Eumenes's nephew and successor, achieved this. In 230 BC he succeeded in intercepting and repulsing a Celtic horde that had advanced up to Pergamon. It was almost certainly not a crushing defeat, for it neither ended the Galatians' attacks nor shook their community to its roots. But it resulted in more jubilation and exaltation than virtually any other feat of Hellenic arms.

After his victory Attalos set up in the temple of Athena at Pergamon statues of Gauls dying and killing themselves. They have survived only in the form of Roman copies, but they have fascinated posterity considerably more than many an original and superior piece of sculpture of that time. Lord Byron was deeply moved at the recumbent Galatian warrior with the upper part of his body still raised but his head already bowed, in expectation of death. Art historians, however, generally regard this figure as second-rate, though they do concede that human tragedy is captured in uncommonly realistic and poignant terms by this warrior, as it is by his companion in suffering, who has killed his wife and is about to plunge his sword into his own breast. It is the 'human touch' that fascinates in the Gauls' statues of Pergamon. The sculptors certainly had no reason to love the Celts, or even to admire them. Yet they seem to have regarded them as a great, though barbaric people, not simply as bloodthirsty monsters. The British historian William Tarn felt that they had captured more of the Celtic spirit than writers ever did. This of course assumes an awareness of what this 'spirit' was – something extremely difficult for us to define today – and enables us to conclude that the Galatians inspired not only dread but also a certain admiration in their neighbours.

What was this admiration based on? Perhaps it was their imposing appearance that so struck the Greeks of Asia Minor, or

perhaps these over-sophisticated cities cast them in the role of the
'noble savage'. It is also feasible that in an age ruled by the most
cold-blooded political calculation, the Galatians were simply respected because they took such an active part in all the power-
struggles in the area of modern Turkey.

The Galatians continued to oppose the rulers of Pergamon in
varying coalitions; sometimes as allies of one of the Seleucids,
sometimes as allies of the Bithynians. But they could not prevent
the rise of Pergamon, the state built with an embezzled fortune, to
supreme power in Asia Minor. In 166 BC they received their first
crushing defeat, at the hands of Eumenes II; and it was only with
difficulty that they managed to resist their neighbours to the east,
the increasingly strong Iranian empire of Pontus. They had to
become accustomed to defeat and loss of sovereignty; they were
pushed into vassalage and subjected to forcible Hellenization. But
they were not finally conquered until the Romans incorporated the
states of Asia Minor into their empire after 88 BC. Pergamon was
bequeathed to them by its last king, Attalos III. Galatia was given
the status of semi-autonomous province.

Today its existence is recalled only by a quarter of Istanbul,
known as 'Galata' after the house of a no doubt influential Celt, and
by the famous statues in the National Museum and the Capitoline
Museum at Rome which give such a vivid image of his people.
When I myself, under the suspicious gaze of an attendant in the
latter museum, once tried to look the 'dying Gaul' straight in the
eye – to do this I had to lie almost on the floor – I was touched as I
have seldom been by a work of art. The face looking down on me
was not at all the 'noble countenance' one reads about but, on the
contrary, a face so ordinary that its wearer would not have stood
out if he had walked our own streets: unkempt hair, low forehead,
slightly snub nose and a Celtic moustache of the type that has for
some time been back in fashion. The mouth is half-open and the
features are frozen in an expression less of pain than of painful
bewilderment.

It seemed to me then that this might have been the face of a
young workman, perplexed by personal problems, someone with
whom I might already have drunk beer in some pub or other: a
likeable, not very complicated lad, whom one might happily have
helped, whom one could imagine as a friend, who could be relied
on. Not at all a warrior, capable of bloodthirsty rage and attacking

his enemy in wild *furor*, but a human being – I feel tempted to add – like you and me. It was my most direct and personal encounter with a Celt. It was in this frame of mind that I left and saw hundreds of young men like him sauntering through the streets: American hippies in worn T-shirts and faded jeans, young vagabonds from all corners of the earth with blond manes and moustaches, just like the statue inside, at once impatient and dreamy. As I said to myself, they are still among us.

Four Greeks Discover Gaul

Great thanks should be given to him who writes the universal history of mankind, for he has engaged his honour and his effort to serve the general good with his own labours and energy. In his history, he shows his readers the finest fruits of experience and thus teaches something really useful without the reader's having to face dangers to acquire the lesson.

Diodorus Siculus, *Biblioteca historica*

I shall also describe, in part what I myself have seen in my travels over land and sea, and in part what I found credible in those who wrote or talked about these matters.

Strabo, *Geography*

In an Arcadian country house some time between 146 and 133 BC, a vigorous elderly man with a distinctly authoritarian bearing was getting ready to dictate a book to his slave-scribe. It was to be a 'practical and descriptive' history, designed to 'demonstrate to all who hunger for knowledge how Tyche (the Goddess of Fate) has arranged the whole political course of the world towards one end' – namely, the Roman empire. The ambitious author was the same Polybius to whose work we must again return to reconstruct the early history of the Republic, if only because he witnessed its rise to world power from a ringside seat. At the time of his birth in around 200 BC in Megalopolis, a good sixty miles south of Corinth, this could not have been foretold. Everything seemed to indicate that he would follow family tradition and one day have a leading part in the government of his native city. From childhood he was brought up to be a politician, and achieved some success in this profession by the age of thirty. He became hipparch, or cavalry-leader, of the Achaean League, a federation linking Megalopolis and other cities of southern Greece against Sparta and her allies. This was an office that inevitably exposed a man to risk.

The Romans had long been playing the Hellenic communities off against each other, in order to conquer them. Finally they overthrew in its turn the federation to which Megalopolis belonged. Its representatives, Polybius among them, were taken to Rome as prisoners. Such a brutal interruption of his existence should have made the young statesman an enemy of Rome. But this is just what did not happen. With a mental leap that any modern intellectual schooled in the dialectic might envy, he overcame all imaginable resentment and joined his new masters, in a way as elegant as it was logical.

The pole assisting him in this mental vault was the highly abstract concept Tyche. He wrote everything that had happened to him down to her doing, and assumed that she intended to make Rome mistress of the world. In other words he strove to interpret his own fate as the outcome of a historically inevitable process and thus vindicate his captors. It was on a similar foundation that he constructed his *History*. It is possible that he was never quite satisfied by these arguments. Sometimes he interrupts his narrative with polemics against all who differed with him. He also rejects any supposition – and the reproach was ostensibly not unjustified – that he was writing for personal gain. As a charitable view his justification of Roman policy, though in places reading like propaganda, may also be taken as a sign of gratitude, for he did not do badly in Rome. As a tutor he had the entrée to the best houses in the city. He became friendly with the young Scipio Aemilianus, who in 146 was to capture Carthage, and accompanied him on many of his important campaigns.

But Polybius did not write his history from diary-entries alone. He tried to find out from travelling or in libraries what had occurred before his time. This was essential, for one of his ambitions was a continuation of the history of the Mediterranean world that his predecessor, the Sicilian Greek Timaeus of Tauromenion (Taormina), had broken off in 264 BC. This compelled him to turn first to the people that had caused the Romans as much trouble as the First Punic War that was just then breaking out: the Celts. It is here that Polybius impinges on our own interests.

Rigid as the system he imposes on history is, questionable as many of his arguments are, dubious as his own personal integrity seems, he never lacked thoroughness. He rejected out of hand the confused rumours circulating about the people in the Po valley. Instead he travelled there and, probably partly from eye-witness reports, composed his own colourful description of Celtic war customs, still fascinating reading after two thousand years. At the time it must have had a great impact precisely because of this chapter. There had been considerable puzzlement, amazement and vexation on the subject of the Gauls, but hardly anyone had any concrete knowledge of them. This was now decisively altered. Ancient scholars, starting with Polybius, marked out the first authentic description of the Celts that we have.

For most of the Mediterranean chroniclers of the last centuries before Christ the Galatai were merely an acknowledged phenomenon. Xenophon, Socrates's pupil, who recorded his Persian adventures in the *Anabasis*, notes in passing that they had been used as mercenaries ninety years before Brennus in the wars of Athens and Sparta against Thebes. Plato included them in his list of tribes inclined to drunkenness. The rest of his educated countrymen made do with a picture of the world in which there figured, alongside the civilized states of the Mediterranean and the orientals, three great barbarian peoples: the Scythians, somewhere to the north-east, the distant Iberians and the Celts in the near west. Beyond that region, that is, in the Back of Beyond, were thought to be the Hyperboreans, a race so little known that the frontiers of their homelands could only be shown as the north wind, the *Boreas*.

Even after Alexander's advance to the Indus, this confused picture did not acquire sharper contours. Men learnt of the Hindu Kush, Turkestan, the Arabian peninsula and the Persian Gulf; but modern Germany, central France, the British Isles and everything to the north remained, as before, a mystery. Only a few scholars took seriously the report of a journey made by Pytheas of Massilia, a contemporary of Alexander the Great, to central Norway, though this might have greatly extended their picture of the world. Thus it was left to a younger contemporary of Polybius to fill in some of the blank spaces on the Greek map of western Europe. He was a man of an altogether different stamp from Polybius of Megalopolis, who often seems crabbed and dry. Posidonius, who was born in 135 BC, came from Apameia in western Syria. In his day he was considered one of the outstanding philosophers of the school of the Stoic Panaitios of Rhodes. He was not so much a specialist as a polymath of quite remarkable range, interested as much by volcanic processes as by meteorology, forgotten myths as much as anthropological data.

In Rhodes, one of the most brilliant and powerful cities of the Hellenic world, he presided at the peak of his career over the academy he had himself founded. He was a member of the magistracy and intellectual sovereign in the sun-drenched halls, surrounded by a swarm of zealous admirers and students, listening with rapture. At this time he had not himself carried out much original or critical work. Instead he ordered, analysed, evaluated and commented on the knowledge that flowed towards him from all sides – and he did it brilliantly. But once he decided that it was time for him to go and examine for himself the subjects of his interest, he again turned out to be a master. In Gades (Cadiz), in the course of one of his many travels, he studied a phenomenon which much astonished the Greeks, the tides, and identified their connection with the phases of the moon. At Marseilles he assembled more evidence on the Celts than even Polybius had done, and related his findings to his. Unfortunately almost nothing he wrote has survived; but we can glean from the work of later authors what Posidonius discovered, for many later writers plagiarized him – Strabo and Diodorus Siculus above all, but also Caesar, who owed more to Posidonius than to his own observations. There are thus three men on whom we have to rely for first or second-hand knowledge of what the Greeks learnt and thought of their contemporaries, the Celts.

We cannot expect from the successors of Posidonius any systematic description of the Celts. In any case both Diodorus and Strabo relied too heavily on reports whose authenticity they could not always verify. They had therefore to make do with putting as many details as possible together to form a many-faceted picture, leaving the reader to draw his own conclusions.

This does not mean, however, that they uncritically bought up every rumour that came on to the market: on the contrary. Adopting criteria we do not know, they must have separated the wheat from the chaff with such care that modern scholars recognize the basis of their description as more or less correct. Posidonius especially must have been much less simple-minded than the anecdotal Herodotus, and even Strabo took great pains to be as dispassionate as possible (while producing a good narrative as well). But only Diodorus was bold enough to dig deeply in the superabundant treasure-trove of myth and legend, and to use images to explain what his reason could not understand. He was particularly partial to beginning his stories where human life itself generally starts: in bed.

He reckons that it is possible, for instance, to say that Celts are all descendants of Heracles. He says that this hero, in the course of one of his many journeyings, arrived in France, founded Alesia – later, the capital city of the Gallic Mandubii – and fell in love with a singularly shapely princess, who until then had coolly rejected all overtures for her favours. Heracles was the exception. This stranger, Diodorus says, so impressed the maiden

with his bravery and physical prowess that she passionately gave way to his embrace, though not without asking her parents' permission. The fruit of this union was a little Heraclid, called Galates, who outshone all the boys of his tribe in intelligence and strength. After he had succeeded to his grandfather's throne, he subjected a great part of the neighbouring country and carried out many heroic deeds. This made him so famous that he decided to call all of his people after himself, Galatai or Galli. From this derives the name Gallia, or Gaul.

This is an irresistible explanation for the name of a people. At the time it must have seemed reasonable enough, given that the Greeks believed their beloved demi-god and hydra-slayer had come to them from the far north. There he was said to have left a people that followed him and themselves settled in Hellas: the Heraclids, also called Dorians. The Dorian tribes that settled in Mycenaean Greece after 1200 BC were indeed a northern people and had much more in common with the Celts than with their remote descendants, one of whom was Diodorus himself. They equally resembled those they drove out or subjected, the kings and heroes of early Hellas celebrated by Homer. Modern research into the Celtic past has long been drawing conclusions, from the relationship of the three peoples, that are quite similar to those of

Diodorus, though of course without his mythical embellishments.

Strabo did not think much of the Heracles story. He soberly notes that a people living in the area of modern Narbonne were called *Keltai* by their neighbours, the Greek inhabitants of the city of Massilia, and that the name had become known to the world from the Massiliote trade-routes. Neither author provides us with anything scientifically tenable as to the origin of the name *Keltai/ Keltoi*, *Galatai* or *Galli*, and we have to be content with the supposition of modern philologists, who link the first of these four words with the Old-Norse *hildr*, 'war'. Celt thus meant 'warrior', though this cannot be proven.

However we probably can take Diodorus at his word when he describes the Gauls' country and inhabitants. It is with unconcealed horror that this native of Sicily depicts the rainy autumns and snowy winters. What astonishes him most is that on the rivers of the region can be found ice-floes strong enough to carry whole armies. The tribes living in such impossible conditions were up to 200,000 strong; most living west of the Rhine, but some east of it. The world, for him, ended effectively at this river; he had no notion about what might be happening on the other side of the Vosges.

Diodorus therefore turned with some relief to the favourite theme of all Ancient Celtographers, Celtic drunkenness. They were, he said, so greedy for grape-juice that Roman merchants in the wine-trade could name their price: 'for a jug of wine they could get a slave, for a single swallow, a servant'. Needless to say the people they swindled poured the wine down their throats 'unmixed'. They did the same with a brew 'made out of barley and water in which honey-combs have been washed out' – clearly mead was just as unfamiliar to this son of the wine-rich south as one of our own thin and over-fermented pilsners would have been. But one of their other customs is strangely familiar to him. In the middle of a flowing narrative he unexpectedly quotes a line from the seventh book of the *Iliad*: 'He honoured Ajax with a long piece of chine.' The descriptions of Celtic feasts that he was then studying evidently reminded him of the Homeric hero. In the camp before Troy these warriors often gathered round a slaughtered ox and cooked pieces on a spit: 'After, they rested from their labours and the meat was made ready, they feasted and their hearts were in this common eating.'

The Celts did the same. As Diodorus says: 'They squat, not on couches' – as did the Greeks and Romans of his day – 'but on the ground, with wolf or dog-skins as cushions. . . . Nearby are the fires, stoked up with charcoal and well-furnished with kettles and spits full of large pieces of meat. Brave warriors are rewarded with the choicest pieces' – for instance the chine which Agamemnon had served to Ajax after he returned from the duel with Hector.

It says much for this chronicler's acuteness that he at once saw the link between Achaean and Celtic table-manners. To expect a further commentary from him here would be to ask too much. He was not to know that in many Indo-European lands a communal meal among men had the status of a ritual, in which a sense of solidarity was expressed no less strong than that around the *Stammtisch* (regulars' table) in many German inns today. One of the customs was that the best warrior should be given the best piece of meat, a privilege that in ancient Ireland was defended if need be by the sword.

Otherwise, the feast was also a useful opportunity for the Celts to settle rivalries: 'During the meal they use the slightest pretext to start a quarrel and challenge each other to a duel. Their lives mean nothing to them for' – and now comes Diodorus's own most adventurous suggestion – 'they still hold Pythagoras's belief in the immortality of the soul and rebirth.' Thus, so it is reported to us, they even threw letters onto the pyre on which their dead were being burned, as if they, in the hereafter, could read them. This is a bizarre detail, but Diodorus is not likely to have made it up. The Greeks, who hardly ever wondered what happened after death, were obviously aware that the Celts did so. But since Pythagoras, with his strong influences from the East, was among the few great Hellenic philosophers who believed in the possibility of life after death, they could only conclude that his belief was related to that of the blond barbarians, or that they had taken theirs over from him. The Greeks explained this almost monstrous contempt for life by the fact that it seemed only logical that a man who knew that after death he would return sometime to earth or would enter some eternal after-life was hardly going to fear death. Diodorus found this neither sympathetic nor admirable, and not even Strabo can conceal a shudder when describing their blood-rituals.

The most hideous of Celtic customs, in Greek historians' eyes, was head-hunting. Diodorus tells us that Posidonius almost became ill when on a journey he once saw Celtic warriors with whole wreaths of victims' heads dangling on their bridles: 'though later, when he had become used to such sights, he could bear them easily enough'. A travelling scholar needs strong nerves, and the Stoic of Rhodes appears to have had them. Perhaps he was comforted by the knowledge that even generals of civilized peoples such as the Egyptians cut off their enemies' hands – for statistical purposes. For a general wanting to know, after a battle, how big his 'bag' was, this was simpler than counting corpses strewn all over the field.

This gruesome custom, together with the collecting of hunting trophies, must have originated in the demand for concrete proof of prowess as warriors or hunters. However, the Celts turned this practice into a cult, as we shall show in greater detail, much as the North American Indians did with another custom – once the white colonists had taught them scalping. But ancient Gaul knew no torturing, at least not at the stake: 'The inhabitants employ a very surprising and incredible custom when they want to know matters of great importance. They consecrate a human being to death, drive a dagger into his belly, above the abdomen, and draw conclusions about events to come from the squirming of the victim and the spurting of his blood. They have been practising this custom since time immemorial.'

Strabo confirms this, though he differs from Diodorus on one point: he says that the victim was slain with a blow in the back. Both writers seem here to depend once more on Posidonius, who may have observed similar rituals in the Celtic hinterland of Marseilles. He is also probably the source of a further detail about the special way in which the Celts used to kill a man which turns up in most of the authors who plagiarized him, including Caesar. Strabo describes it thus: 'They set up a colossus of wood and straw' – it must have been something like a gigantic basket-like plaited figure – 'shut cattle, wild animals and human beings in it, and set light to the whole thing.' Diodorus says the same, at less length; but both the Sicilian and the Anatolian agree that all of these human sacrifices expressed not so much cruelty as a – to them – incomprehensible religiosity. To emphasize this, they always stressed that even the bloodiest of rituals were superintended by the wise men, the so-called Druids.

No detail transmitted by Posidonius and his successors can have impressed readers more than the description of Celtic religion. Their contemporaries were just as satiated with accounts of the savage customs of barbarian peoples as we are today with reports of disasters from all over the world: human sacrifice was also practised in Carthage, and head-hunting was not the monopoly of Gaul. Anyone who liked reading horror stories by the fireside had no shortage of material.

But it was different when it came to the supernatural. This satisfied not only curiosity but the spirit as well: it offered food for speculation, could be adapted to one's own circumstances and might even supply an answer to the perennial question of the meaning of life. It seemed altogether possible that the truth, which virtually no one imagined was to be found in their own temples, lay elsewhere, that foreign peoples, however barbaric they were, had more direct access to the gods than the members of an over-civilized society.

The Mediterranean world had long become so complex that no one could say what inner laws it obeyed, and many people felt that it was out of joint. One of the results was that representatives and propagandists of oriental cults made a great deal of money. Since the west was at least as mysterious as the east, people seized on possible parallels, as hinted at by Diodorus, between Pythagorean mysticism and Celtic beliefs. It is even conceivable that this is why the great master himself worked such themes into his text. This is no doubt even more applicable to what he says of the Druids. Surprisingly he does not call them by their Celtic name, using instead the term 'philosophers', and ascribing to them astonishing powers: 'they are well-versed in the divine things' and can 'speak as it were, the language of the Gods'. In battle they sometimes stood between the two sides and kept them from fighting, 'as if they were placing a spell on wild animals'. He concludes: 'Thus does passion bow before wisdom even among the darkest barbarians, and Ares is overcome by the Muses.'

Strabo, with less romantic pathos and somewhat more detail, also covers this topic. He also cites the name 'Druid', though he gives no more precise definition of the role of the men who bore it. Instead he makes do with the assertion that they were particularly respected among the Celtic peoples, as were the bards and *vates* (soothsayers). If these last were some kind of natural philosopher – explaining what is and what will be – the Druids should be termed moral philosophers, explaining what ought to be: men who laid down and embodied moral criteria. The Anatolian writes that 'they are considered to be the most just of men, which is why they are called in to mediate in both private and public disputes. In former days they also decided on war or peace, and over cases of murder.' They were also among those who upheld the doctrine of 'the indestructibility of the human soul and the whole universe', though they admitted that sooner or later the world would be destroyed by fire and water.

All this, though announced in tones of sober reportage, must greatly have stimulated the imagination of Strabo's readers. It read half as a fairy-tale and half as a story about some Utopia. A community run and led by philosophers had already been conceived by Plato. That a barbarian tribe had realized it was an altogether refreshing thought, the more so as the Celtic social order had evidently been erected on the basis of an uncommonly comforting doctrine. Posidonius and his epigones thus not only provided information, they also launched virtually a new myth – one moreover that has to this day lost little of its fascination. Exaggerated ideas of the wisdom of the Druids were current in Germany, France and England alike, in countless myths and sects. In the whole history of Celtic studies, as will be shown, they had effectively the key role.

So far as the name of the office is concerned, it is nowadays believed that, like Drunemeton, it can be deduced from the Greek word *drus* (oak) and the Indo-European *wid* (wisdom), which produces the apparent absurdity of 'oak-knower'. None the less we can conclude that in the assemblies held in sacred groves from France to Galatia the Druids had the last word in matters of justice. In all the later literature, they are always depicted walking through rustling oak-glades. But there were in ancient Gaul, other, less edifying characters.

The Celtic women [Diodorus writes] are not only as tall as the men, but as courageous. . . . But despite their charm, the men will have nothing to do with them. They long instead for the embrace of one of their own sex, lying on animal skins and tumbling around with a lover on either side. It is particularly surprising that they attach no value to either dignity or decency, offering their bodies to each other without further ado. This was not regarded as at all harmful; on the contrary, if they were rejected in their approaches, they felt insulted.

Strabo confirms these homosexual practices with the brief mention that the young men of Gaul are 'shamelessly generous with their boyish charms'; while Athenaeus, another of the writers who dug deep in the treasure-trove of Posidonius, also says that the Celts generally slept with two companions in a bed – and not because the winter was very cold.

We can therefore suppose that this was a warrior-society strongly characterized by man-to-man bonds. As soon as they were old enough to bear arms, young people lived almost wholly with others of their own sex. They learnt riding, swordsmanship, hunting, drinking; they had to prove themselves in the field, were (or were not) honoured at the feast, and saw their like as the only suitable company. It is not hard to see that this placed enough emphasis on the latent homo-erotic component of many male friendships to turn them into true homosexuality. His comrade became the object of admiration and desire for a man, his driver for the passenger, his spear-carrier for the warrior. Thus Achilles loved Patroclus as did Alexander the Great Hephaestion. Wherever there was no taboo, such relationships understandably gave rise to a cult of the male body.

'The Celts,' says Strabo, 'tried to avoid becoming fat or pot-bellied, and they punished any boy whose waist was larger than the standard they set.' Moreover, Diodorus goes on, 'they put on arm-bands of all sorts and wear about their necks heavy rings of solid gold'. These were the famous Celtic torcs, and any self-respecting museum of pre-history has a few on display. Even the Gauls' statues at Pergamon have them: massive rings, richly decorated and with a finger-sized opening at the front. I have often wondered how they were put on: they are too narrow to have been pushed on over the wearer's head, and yet cannot be bent open. Perhaps they were welded round the young men's necks. Strabo and Diodorus did not investigate this problem. They were content to give a fleeting picture of well-grown lads and men who, for all their arrogance and their finery, seemed to neglect the primary duties of a good cockerel.

In view of such less than innocent practices, one naturally wonders what part was played by women in the male-dominated Celtic society of the day. Unfortunately none of the Greek writers gives a complete answer, which is in itself significant. The Hellenic scholars do not seem to have been let into those areas where the female part of the population lived, because they were sacrosanct or because they were private. We may suppose that women were limited to the three classic K's of Germany: *Küche, Kemenate und Kinder* ('kitchen, boudoir and children'). By virtue of the prevailing moral code, the bed was less a place for pleasure than for marital duty. The women conceived and bore children, which won them respect and a high social status.

This can also be deduced from Diodorus's observation that they were reckoned to be just as courageous (and perhaps just as haughty) as their menfolk. We can see this also in the love-story of Heracles and the mother of Galates, which, even if pure invention, still reflects Celtic ways. Its heroine had preserved her chastity until this powerful stranger appeared. She then discussed what should be done with her parents and, no doubt, with him as well, and this must have been the prelude to a wedding. Only after it had been performed did she enjoy in his arms what other young men withheld from those such as her. The mythical Galates was thus certainly legitimate.

Yet not all women can have been mere prisoners of household and nursery. Just as the men used their masculine opportunities, so some of the women must have used their feminine ones somewhat uninhibitedly. Unhappily the section where Strabo indicates this is less clear than anything else he wrote about Celtic women.

On an island in 'Okeanos' (presumably the Atlantic), he says, lived Celtic women who paid homage to Dionysus. They formed a sort of order, given to mystical practices and arcane initiation-rites. No man ever sets foot on the island. The women themselves occasionally go away, have sexual relations with men, and return at once. It is one of their customs, as Posidonius has shown, each year to uncover and re-cover the roof of their temple in a single day. Each carries her share of the material needed, but if one of them drops anything she is then and there torn to pieces by the rest. Crying 'Ev-ah' they carry the parts of her body round the temple again and again, and do not stop until the fury is over. And, Posidonius says, it always happens that one of them causes that woman to stumble who has been predetermined for this fate.

The Anatolian presents this story without commentary or evaluation, and without evident reaction. No doubt this is because he found nothing astonishing in such rituals; indeed even in Greece there were ecstatic bacchanalia in which people were torn to pieces.

The cry 'Ev-ah' was the hallelujah of these Maenads, of these sisters of Dionysus. But how do we explain that this Hellenic god of intoxication was worshipped on an Atlantic island far from the Mediterranean? Strabo does not say, probably because it was believed that Dionysus had been in the north or even that he had come from there to Greece.

We are left with the question whether the Celts really did have cults similar to the bacchanalia. To suppose that Strabo merely picked up wild rumours would be too hasty. As we have seen, he generally described the Gallic people quite accurately and without prejudice; we must thus return to this subject in another context.

The Celtic women also have a claim to fuller treatment than they got from Posidonius's successors. They were not simply chaste maidens and dutiful housewives but quite capable of assuming starring roles in the *comédie humaine* of their people, with their own Juliets, Medeas, Kriemhilds, Xanthippes. It scarcely matters that the stage was suitable at best for rustic comedy.

The impression of life in the Gauls' villages to be had from the French comic-books depicting the adventures of the mighty Celtic atom, Asterix, and his friends, is not entirely misleading. The authors seem to have read at least Strabo quite thoroughly and describe as he does – though with a pinch of salt – a colourful rustic idyll. Between large houses, some of which have dome-shaped roofs and which are made of 'board, wickerwork and a great deal of straw', run half-wild pigs, 'bristly creatures that are so extraordinarily large, audacious and swift that not only can they be troublesome to men not used to them but can even chase away a wolf'. Pork cutlets and leg of mutton appear to have been the favourite meat of the originals of Asterix. They had sufficient of both animals to 'guarantee a surplus of woollen coats (*saga*) and salt meat'. The inhabitants of Gaul even exported great quantities of the pickled meat to Italy, thus revealing healthy capitalist instincts.

They loved gold, washed it from the rivers of their country and hoarded it in temples, which seem to have served as the forerunners of banks because they were protected – less by law than by superstition – against attempts to break in. But men who wanted both liquid cash and credit carried their wealth on their persons in the form of rings and chains 'and even corsets of solid precious metal'. The torcs were thus not just an expression of male vanity but what economic historians call 'decorative money'; they may even be regarded as an early form of that modern method of payment, the credit-card. Posidonius's epigones concluded from the items they saw glinting on the Celts' rippling muscles that these people must be fairly wealthy, and we can see from their descriptions that the Celts' circumstances were quite comfortable. But whether this wealth was equitably distributed is another matter. Celtic society, as the Greeks show, was hierarchical. A small upper class must have had by far the greatest share of the people's wealth, including land. Everyone else was, in varying degrees, dependent on them. Free and semi-free peasants had, according to rank and class, the duties of loyalty and tribute, in return for which their property was protected or their livelihood guaranteed. What this amounted to was that a man living in such a society was obliged to seek recognition as vassal by a nobleman, just as a nobleman's power stemmed from his ability to collect and retain as many adherents as possible, by force as well as by munificence and justice. Real sovereignty ultimately rested with the sword and the traditions founded on it. At the base of this pyramid were the slaves, though of course not many, for, as Diodorus says, they were either sold or sacrificed in blood-rituals; at the top, chieftains who on occasion would have to demonstrate that they deserved their privileges. The great middle stratum of retainers seems also to have had some democratic rights.

Before his time, according to Strabo, tribal leaders were elected at annual assemblies. But later there were meetings at which debate and counsel were guided by strict rules of procedure: 'If anyone interrupted a speaker, he would be called to order by the advisor in charge; if he did not obey, then the councillor would cut a piece off his coat and repeat the act if need be until the *sagum* could no longer be used.' Strabo does add that this was a custom identical or similar to that of other barbarian peoples. He no doubt means that the Celtic social order followed a basic pattern that was widespread. He would certainly have been right, had it not been for the existence of Druids, *vates* and bards – a class of wise men who, though not priests in the traditional sense, led an existence that is difficult to determine alongside the warrior society of the Celts. They served the tribes and clans as judges, prophets, soothsayers, wise men and as keepers of the collective memory, but they were not bound by the ordinary rules of behaviour. In the midst of quarrelling, rivalry and feuding they seem to have stood for what was common to all, the essence perhaps of some 'Celthood', whatever that may be.

It was in the twenty-third of the fifty-two volumes of his lost *History* that the founder of the academy of Rhodes discussed this people which, from a political viewpoint, was such a thorn in the flesh of Apollo. But despite the wealth of information which we owe to Posidonius, he is scarcely the authority to help us judge how far such a thing as 'Celthood' existed. (We shall thus have to return to this question and also discuss the Druids more fully later.) For all their oddity they were part of his own world and much closer to him than to us, which is why he describes many of their customs without explaining them. On the other hand the Gallic people were to him simply an object-lesson for a thesis. Posidonius was primarily the adherent, defender and interpreter of a particular philosophy, the Stoic, and he tried, as Athenaeus says, 'to bring his researches into line with his convictions'. Through his study of barbarian or semi-civilized peoples he wished to find out what mankind had been like in the primitive state he considered to be the ideal. The Celts were thus one of the stages through which *homo sapiens* had passed since the Golden Age, the Greek paradise, into that world which he, like any critical spirit at almost any time, regarded as in dire need of change.

But he did not idealize the Gauls, as did many later scholars of the school of Alexandria, as noble savages. With all his tendency to romanticize, like Strabo he remained a man to respect facts, even when they did not square with his preconception. Stuart Piggott, a noted expert in European prehistory, therefore calls him a soft-centred primitivist; unlike Rousseau's later precursors, who were merely soft and for whom the Celts were no more than a kind of nobler and more unspoiled Redskin – so noble, indeed, that even their head-hunting was forgiven.

In other words what Posidonius and his successors provide is not a sharply focused photograph of the Celts as they really were but an image of how their age saw them. These scholars assembled not all the available facts but those that they could command. Their portrait lifts one of the veils that shroud this people and affords us a glimpse of what happened at that time in the central regions of western Europe. Needless to say in those days the knowledge stored up in the archives of Rhodes was of real political, not to say strategic, value.

In the year 113 BC when Posidonius was just twenty-two, Rome was once more in terror at the prospect of a new barbarian horde approaching from the north-eastern border of Italy. The first reports must have come from the territories of the Scordisci, who lived in modern Serbia and Croatia. The next came from the Carinthian region and from Salzburg, in which the Illyrian Noricians and Tauriscian Celts lived. Both of these peoples were on good terms with the Romans and even seem to have requested their help to fight off invaders.

The great power of Rome, which still trembled at the mention of blond, blue-eyed giants from somewhere in the north, treated all these reports with deadly seriousness and immediately sent an army against the unknown invaders. The forces met at Noreia, the Norician capital south of modern Klagenfurt, and it was a fiasco. The foreign hosts were put by Plutarch at 300,000 men. Like the warriors of the first Brennus, they possessed 'invincible strength and courage: in battle they attack with the force and speed of five and no one can withstand them.' The Roman army under Papirius Carbo was annihilated and panic reigned once more. There was talk of a 'second Celtic invasion' and apprehension about what would happen next, for all these barbarian peoples were known to have only one aim: to conquer Rome. But the intruders did nothing of the kind. Instead of pressing on south they marched along the northern slopes of the Alps towards the west and disappeared almost completely for four years. They did not reappear until 109 BC, this time in Provence, which Rome had just annexed. There was a repetition of Noreia: two small senatorial forces were crushed and a third, larger one did no better. At Arausio, modern Orange, the tall berserkers triumphed a fourth time.

Posidonius was at this time a rising star in the Greek academic firmament and he was perhaps, like other scholars, busy collecting what he could about the new wandering people. Their name seems to have been known. Artemidorus of Ephesus, one of the leading ethnographers and geographers of the day, reckoned that he could say what they were. It was not difficult; as the Cimbri, as they were called, had come towards the Alps from a north-westerly direction, they must therefore be Celts. Another scholar unknown to us but

quoted by Plutarch is more specific in traditional fashion. He seems
to have thought that their march was as much from the north-east
as the north-west, from which he concluded that they should be
called 'Celto-Scythians', for the north-east was the Scythians'
region.

   From these meagre details was developed the theory that the
intruders must have belonged to the same Cimbri who had lived on
the Black and Azov Seas, were driven out by the Scythians and
moved to Asia Minor, though not of course all of them. A small
section of them must have gone north, settled on Chersoneus
Cimbrica, modern Jutland, and then marched south again. This
was the accepted view when after the defeat of Arausio Rome again
conferred consular rank on her best soldier, the bravo Gaius
Marius. This twenty-five-year-old general, a military man to his
fingertips, completely reformed the Roman armed forces. He
turned a militia into a professional army, recruited in the main
from landless proletarians. These .poor souls he drilled as no
sergeant-major before him. With a full load of trenching equipment and stores he made them undergo, as Plutarch says, 'long
route-marches and forced them to prepare their own food'. He also
insisted that every man should be able at all inspections to present
himself and his kit scrubbed and polished and his weapons
sharpened. Luckily he did not have to fight the Cimbri while carrying out these parade-ground orgies. After their latest victory they
again did not turn towards Italy but wandered, apparently aim-
lessly, through half of Gaul and north-western Spain. Only in
102 BC did they again emerge on the Roman borders, in southern
Provence. Marius went after them at once with his reorganized
legions. On the lower Rhône he set up a strongly fortified camp
with its own communications canal, making the silted-up river
delta navigable for supply-ships.

   However not only the soldiers but also the scholars and spies had
been uncommonly busy since the battle of Arausio. They knew
now that Rome was dealing not with one but with three peoples,
Cimbri, Teutones and Ambrones, all equally to be feared. Marius,
who in southern France encountered only the two latter, strictly
forbade his men to leave their camp. Instead, Plutarch says, he had
them go 'in turn to the wall and ordered them to look round and
thus get used to the appearance of their enemies and their hideous
savage yelling'. Only when the Teutones and Ambrones, wearied

with these delaying tactics, withdrew towards the Alps did Marius follow them, in carefully protected marches. Only at Aquae Sextiae, modern Aix-en-Provence, did he fight the famous battle to which the place gave its name.

When it was over so many slain barbarians littered the field that the earth 'yielded up the following spring an incredible amount of fruits'. But it was none the less with some unease that the Roman

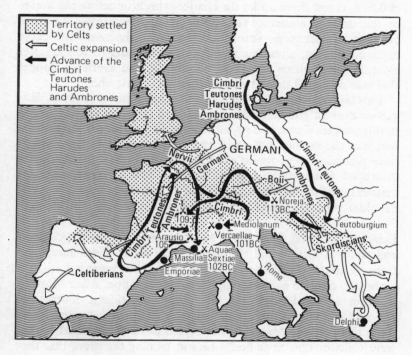

Map 4   The movement of the Cimbri

victory was celebrated in the capital. The Cimbri, the third tribe of the wandering people, had meanwhile advanced into northern Italy and there awaited the Roman army that Marius was to bring. In spring 101 BC at Vercellae, modern Vercelli in Piedmont, the leader of the tribe, who bore the clearly Celtic name of Boiorix (literally 'king of the Boii'), challenged him in the usual way to a duel and, when Marius declined, to battle. It was arranged according to rules, like a sporting event. Nowadays it figures in the

history books as one of the great Roman victories in this war. The
Cimbri literally let themselves be slaughtered. When their worst
enemy, the heat, had so weakened them that they could barely
stand, they bound themselves together with chains and awaited
death. Anyone seeking refuge among the carts was killed by the
women who had remained there, 'even if they were their husbands,
fathers or brothers, with their own hands they throttled their little
children, threw them under the chariot-wheels or before the horses
or the draught animals. Then they killed themselves.' Plutarch
called it 'a most tragic scene' and went on: 'the common people
declared Marius, after this victory, third founder of Rome (after
Romulus and Furius Camillus) because he had averted a danger
that was reckoned in no way less than the Celtic one'.

   This last comparison is striking. Were the Cimbri really as dangerous as the Celts? Plutarch himself had said that they belonged
to this people. Was this now, all of a sudden, no longer the case? If
not, was the famous *furor* that the poet Lucian was later to call
furor teutonicus to be found elsewhere than in tribes that had once
destroyed Rome and, if so, in which? This contradiction was
neither noted nor examined by Plutarch, but it was investigated by
his older colleague, the Stoic Posidonius.

Look up 'Cimbri', 'Teutones' or 'Ambrones' in an encyclopedia
and you will merely find the laconic indication: 'Germanic tribes
from Jutland'. Posidonius, who was then regarded as the
authority, came to a more complicated explanation. After Marius's
triumph he undertook his frequently mentioned journey to
Massilia and Spain, hoping in effect to gain some knowledge of
these three tribes. Above all he wanted to discover whether they
were Celts or not. Specifically he was looking for proof that they
fitted into the traditional scheme: a Scythian north-east, a Gallic
north-west. Inevitably he found that the Cimbri, who had come
from the north, had appeared first among the Scordisci and then
among the Tauriscians. Thereafter they had gone through the
territory of the Helvetii, who were likewise Celtic, and so strongly
impressed this 'people rich in gold but peaceable' that three of their
tribes joined up with them, the Teutones included.

   We could therefore conclude that the latter were Celts. But
Posidonius's faithful interpreter Strabo describes them, like the
Cimbri, as Germans, using a term probably unknown in Greek

scholarship before the Massilia journey, for Strabo himself explains it. The Germans, he said, were a people living east of the Rhine. They differed from the Celts of the left bank, being 'even taller, more savage and blond'. Otherwise there was close resemblance in all respects: 'Thus I imagine that the Romans who lived in Gaul called them "Germani" because they wanted to indicate that they were the "authentic", the real Celts. *Germani* means in their language "genuine" in the sense of original.'

Thus the Teutones and Cimbri were Germans; these in turn were not just one of the great Celtic family of peoples, as opposed to the Scythian one, but the very heart of that family. They were the most Celtic of the Celts. This is a surprising enough line to take, and there has since been considerable dispute about it. What can have caused Strabo to adopt it? Perhaps it was misinformation, or misunderstood replies made by Gauls whom he asked. But that is too simple, for the whole complex of problems is a great deal more confused than modern scholars were prepared to admit for many years.

How do we explain that a Cimbrian, i.e. Germanic, king was called 'Boiorix'? Similarly, what conclusions may we deduce from an incident related by Plutarch in his account of the battle of Aquae Sextiae? He says that the Ambrones, attacking Marius's army, used their own tribal names as war-cries. When the Ligurians, auxiliaries on the Roman side, 'heard and understood the cries, they too shouted out their old names, for the Ligurians are known after their origins as Ambrones'. It is at least clear that the topic is complicated, but what is the key to it? Who was what? Were Ligurians Ambrones, Ambrones Germans, and Germans Celts?

The ancient authors can be of no further help in our attempts to settle this. They have provided us with a picture of the peoples contained within the Celtic, Scythian and Celto-Scythian orbit and have done all they could. We will now show how far contemporary scholars can augment and correct this rough sketch. Armies of experts and amateurs have set themselves to the task. Many of the theories they have come up with are hardly less wild than those of Posidonius and his successors.

FIVE

It Began on the Volga

Celts (Gr. *Keltoi*, also *Galatai*; Lat. *Celtoi* and *Galli*; Fr. *Celtes*):
Indo-European people.

(Grosser Brockhaus, 1955)

The Indo-European wanderers were terrible, unruly, plundering.
Mariya Gimbutas, *The Indo-Europeans: Archaeological Problems*

It is hardly likely that a people that swept through the whole of
Europe as restlessly as did the Celts could be a home-bound one.
Peasants leave their land unwillingly and drive their well-fed herds
along dusty tracks to unknown and meagre pastures only when
forced to. They are attached to what they know, the regular pattern
of sowing and reaping; they are accustomed to long-term planning,
to thinking in terms of generations. All of this requires computable
qualities, familiar circumstances, a stable world within known
horizons. Adventurers are cast in a different mould. To react in a
crisis by pursuing some promise of paradise just over the hill, or
even, if need be, to base one's existence on vague hopes alone, is to
have vagabond blood and a nomadic character. Such a person
regards property as something tangible that can be easily mobilized. This makes him a speculator who places his capital where it
can produce the highest return.

The Celts sometimes seem to have thought in such terms. The
first Brennus sought in Rome the riches that his native fields could
not yield. It was, if Strabo is right, an internal quarrel that forced

the Tectosages to move; and nor can we suppose of the second Brennus's people that they would have preferred to stay at home sunning themselves outside their huts. But wanderlust is one thing; the capacity to satisfy it quite another. To set thousands of men on the march requires a capacity for organization and some technology. At the very least, there have to be solid carts, draught animals, tents, portable furniture, shepherds who can keep great herds together and waggon-drivers or riders who can make sure of the day's route by going on ahead. The whole people has to be able to withstand this gypsy life.

Since this was obviously the case with the Celts, one is tempted to assume that, at least at an early stage of their history, they were nomads, and adapted only later to some degree of settlement in regions they liked. Even in such places it seems they were not very good at settling. Like Posidonius and his successors, Polybius reports that their huts were little more than shelters constructed out of necessity and that they always tried to keep their property as movable chattels rather than as land or buildings.

A further illustration of this is that they were excellent horsemen and charioteers. Their cavalry always frightened the Romans more than their infantry. An important component of their tactics was the attack by yelling and mounted spear-throwers and the inbuilt preparations for withdrawal. A preference for the greatest mobility corresponded to their fiery temperament: rapid attack, rapid victory, a fixed aim and an easy plunder. Equestrian peoples have generally been of this character. If, with this in mind, we now look for the point at which Celtic history can have begun, we have to go back to the days when the horse first began to play an important role in man's existence. To be exact, we must look to the first hunter who captured a fleet-footed tarpan – the ancestor of our various species of horses – and, instead of killing it, tamed it. When this had been achieved life began to change considerably for the majority of mankind.

Some men soon discovered that they could travel with more speed and comfort in a cart drawn by a horse than in clumsy ox-carts. Others recognized that their life had become more perilous: they could be attacked and plundered by hordes who vanished as they appeared, leaving behind them smoking ruins and empty paddocks. Horse-owners began to feel themselves masters of space, seeing distances dwindling, acquiring a taste for speed and regarding the far-off as a challenge. Their mentality changed accordingly. Settlements became springboards for endless plundering which, in a few days, could bring in much more than several years' painful toil. When at last it became clear that this effortless profit could be secured in the long term if the people attacked were also permanently enslaved, the history of great armies and great military leaders began. Warrior-castes evolved and laid claim to noble status; modes of conduct were developed that, in their period of greatest refinement, we term chivalric.

The first profit ever made must have come from an attack of this sort. Even the Mycenaean Greeks knew business – so long as it was peaceful – only in the form of exchanging goods of equal value. Profit they would try to obtain only through war. The later Gauls knew nothing of such things, for they were already good businessmen in the conventional sense. But they continued to cultivate a certain horse-bound mentality; fighting, boasting, drinking, living for the day and to the full. What was lost today could still be won tomorrow. Meanwhile the tankard was passed round and meat dripped from the moustaches. The world was vast, and somewhere in it a man could either make his fortune or find his grave. Huns, Pandurs, Hussars, cowboys – and of course the Celts – were all alike in this: the horse had made them what they were. As early as 3000 BC the horse progressed from hunted to domesticated animal. To look for the forefathers of Brennus as far back as this would be to demand too much of research; we must make do with a later period. Can archaeology supply an answer?

Research into prehistory can now achieve remarkable results. It can, as the French scholar Jean-Jacques Hatt has observed, 're-construct, hundreds or thousands of years on, the gesture of an artisan at his labours or a worshipper before his God'. From pieces of pottery, remnants of cloth, traces of colour or even smell we can reconstitute the milieu in which mid-Stone Age hunters lived. Archaeologists can as it were smell with the noses and feel through the skins of human beings long turned to dust. But one thing they cannot do: they cannot loosen the tongues of the dead.

This is a severe handicap. A people is essentially a linguistic community. The man who first wished his wife good day in Celtic must count as the first Celt. But since an excavated piece of ankle-bone does not tell us what dialect its owner spoke, the results of archaeological enquiry often seem very abstract. The diggers themselves seldom speak of peoples but only of 'cultures': globular-urn people, Funnel-Beaker people, Battle-Axe people, Urnfield people. They leave open the question whether those who produced these objects had in common only their attachment to certain types of utensil, weapon, burial-rite, or whether they spoke a common dialect. There are good reasons for this. An archaeologist of the distant future would be grossly in error if he took the world-wide occurrence of huge quantities of Coca-Cola bottles as an indication of a unified world language.

Thus the analyses of potsherds by pre-historians resemble finger prints which are unaccompanied by any real information about the culprit – his origin, nationality, distinguishing marks. Not even the Celts' place of birth can be determined. It is to the philologists that we must turn to learn more, but there is no guarantee of quick results. It is true that they have produced a complete reconstruction of Celtic, a long-dead tongue. But this test-tube language, bred from a few personal and place-names, a few Celtic words that passed into Latin and from dialects such as Breton, Irish, Welsh, Cornish and Manx, adds little to what we can already tell. The question where it originated remains. For an answer we should have to know out of which language that of the later Gauls developed, as Spanish or Italian did from Latin. We should have to know how the Celts' ancestors communicated with one another. On this point we have some information which is supported by evidence. From old river-names we may conclude that around the middle of the second millennium BC in the whole region between the Baltic and the Alps, the British Isles and Hungary a single idiom predominated. The Indo-Europeanist Hans Krahe calls it the 'Old-European language' and surmises that around 1000 BC it began to disintegrate into individual languages such as Italic (the early form of Latin), Germanic, Slavic, Baltic and of course Celtic. His reflections give us ground for supposing that the history of which Polybius wrote a late chapter began some time around the beginning of the first pre-Christian millennium.

This may be taken to mean that the speakers of 'Old-European' were those same warriors who tamed the horse and set up a new hierarchical social system on this basis. But they can hardly have discovered the horse in western and central Europe; probably they brought it from where it originated, the steppe. Krahe adds that these early Europeans were Indo-Europeans. To trace the growth of a people in whose life horses played such an important part and who had nomadic inclinations, changing their abode from time to time and preferring portable possessions, we need more information. We must once again have recourse to the philologists, for the name 'Indo-Europeans' is exclusively their invention. For almost two centuries men have been trying to make this abstraction concrete. Their difficulties started towards the end of the eighteenth century in India.

Sir William Jones (1746–94), from 1783 a judge of the supreme court in Calcutta, was one of those fortunate civil servants who manage to use their spare time creatively. His hobby was comparative philology, and it led him to an astonishing discovery. He established that Sanskrit, the ancient Indian classical language, is more closely related to early European languages than had hitherto been thought possible. To take one or two simple instances, the word for 'king' was *raj* in Sanskrit, *rex* in Latin and *rix* in Celtic; 'fire' was *agni* in Sanskrit and *ignis* in Latin. Even a layman can see that these words obviously had some common root.

Sir William was not to know that his work was helping a new discipline to come into being or that he was inaugurating a scholarly debate that has continued to our own day. The new discipline, Indo-European studies, took its name from the peoples that interested its practitioners. The debate, fought out in countless books and international congresses, always centres on the question whether there was ever a single language from which all these related idioms developed, whether a people that spoke it ever existed and where that people lived. In the philologists' terminology these are referred to as the *Ur*-language, the *Ur*-people and the *Ur*-homeland (*Ur* = 'proto' – 'original').

We have of course made progress since Sir William Jones's day. Scholars now know that no less than eleven basic idioms are related in the same way as Latin and Sanskrit. Among them are Tocharic (spoken by an extinct Russian steppe-people), Indo-Iranian, Hittite, Armenian, Slavic, Baltic, Greek, Illyrian, Italic, Germanic and Celtic. From these, almost fifty modern languages have developed, from Russian to Serbo-Croat and Norwegian. Their root, the *Ur*-language, has been similarly reconstructed by scholars, though they cannot tell if it was ever actually spoken. The results they have arrived at are none the less interesting.

They suggest that the German *Pferd* (horse) was called in proto-Indo-European *ekuos* and horned animals *peku*. From this they draw the obvious conclusion that this hypothetical people knew and raised both of these animals and were probably pastoral. They can be more exact than this, however, for the first *peku* that grazed on Indo-European meadows was, they believe, a sheep. This much emerges from an equation in which the known quantities are the Latin word *pecus*, the Sanskrit *pasu* and the Greek *pekos*. *Pecus*, like *pasu*, means 'cattle'; while *pekos* means 'pelt': but all three are obviously related. If we now take into account that in Latin *pectere* means 'to comb' while in Greek *pektein* means 'to shear', it emerges that the proto-Indo-European *Ur*-livestock provided not only meat and milk but also skins that had to be combed and sheared, and therefore must have been sheep. We can then presume that the name of this animal was later transferred to others.

Once one has followed the scholars this far it is not easy to swallow the alternative arguments that write off such reconstruction attempts as nonsense. However both views are contested with equal vigour. The battle is by no means over. That it has gone on for so long seems in part due to the misuse that has been made of the concept 'Indo-Europeans'.

When, around the middle of the last century, the possibility of an *Ur*-people was discussed, countless publicists took it up and tried to make it into an ersatz myth. This was understandable, for it looked as though this early linguistic community was the basis for a re-ordering of the world.

What enormous power these tribes must have had, whose descendants lived in both India and Iceland and populated the whole area in between. The way in which this new idol was fashioned was, however, highly dubious. Scholars seized by nationalist ambition threw into the pot what seemed to them the most noble of the Greeks, the Indians, the Persians and the Germans, added Cyrus and Achilles, Vercingetorix and Arminius, Caesar and Leif Erikson, in order to cook up a superman with the wisdom of the Brahmin, the courage of Alexander the Great and, needless to say, the best qualities of their own people.

Each naturally sought to locate the *Ur*-people's home as close as possible to his own land. Poles insisted that the Indo-Europeans came, if not from their own country, at least from the neighbouring

Ukraine; Bulgarians took endless pains to demonstrate that the
Balkans had been their cradle; while Germans postulated that the
originals must have been much like the Germans as described by
Tacitus – simple, heroic, uncommonly gifted. Many of them also
began to confound the terms 'Aryan' and 'Indo-European', until
the former was used exclusively for the Persian-Indian branch of
the linguistic community.

Since Germany was one of the most important centres of Indo-
European research, the so-called 'Nordic thesis' that was formulated here carried greater weight than all others. It held that the
Ur-people had come from the Baltic region, including southern
Russia, and despatched its members to furthest Asia. This theory
was still upheld with such vigour that wealthy Indians felt obliged
to travel to Pomerania and southern Sweden to familiarize themselves with the Ur-home of their ancestors. One of them set down
the results of his investigations in a work significantly entitled
Confession of Indo-Germanic Faith.

Such 'confessions' were of course presented with suitable
'scholarly' underpinning. To demonstrate what the writer wanted
to believe, a comprehensive mechanism had to be set up, embrac-
ing both anthropology and what was called 'linguistic paleontology'
– the history of the animal and vegetable kingdom as an auxiliary to
philology. The most famous instance is the 'beech-tree argument',
according to which the tree called in botany *fagus* must, since it has
a name in many of the languages (in Celtic, *bagos*), have been known
to a great many Indo-European peoples. Hence the proto-Indo-
Europeans had their homes in a region in which there were beech-
trees. That could be found only west of the line Königsberg–
Odessa, for east of it hard woods do not flourish because the
ground is not humid enough. Ergo: the proto-Indo-Europeans
must have been Central Europeans.

Virtually no one takes this seriously nowadays. The Indo-
Europeanist Heinz Kronasser mockingly says that by the same
methods we could conclude that the Slavs came from an area where
there were elephants, for no less than eleven – i.e. almost all –
Slavic languages have the word *slon* to denote this animal. It was
not just methodological errors that discredited the Nordic thesis,
these being an unavoidable risk in an area as dependent on
hypothesis. It was, rather, the ideological fog with which it was
enveloped. Critics were especially irritated by the unqualified way

in which the Indo-European and the Nordic super-race were equated, and the whole question of *Ur*-people became anathema to them. This was not of course true of all. Indeed contemporary scholars have reached, virtually along parallel lines of thought, the conclusion that there must have been a people speaking Indo-European, whose members must therefore count as ancestors of the Celts, as of the Indians, Armenians and Romans. But this people did not live on the Baltic.

To discover the *Ur*-homeland we have to follow the hoof-tracks. Alfons Nehring, a prominent German Indo-Europeanist, suggests that the cradle of this people could only be in an area which offered the many peoples who spoke Indo-European languages easy access to all corners of the globe – the Balkans, the Baltic, the Hindu Kush. This reflection, simplistic as it may appear, he complements with the demonstration that proto-Indo-European has affinities with other linguistic groupings – with Uralic and with Caucasian-Mediterranean, spoken in pre-Greek Hellas and in Anatolia. This leads to his next deduction: the place we are looking for cannot have been too remote from the Urals and western Siberia, but must also have had links with the Caucasus: all in all, a clear enough pointer.

If we now consult a map it is clear what Professor Nehring is getting at: we will see that the region that meets these conditions is on the lower Volga. There is flat land both to the east and the west; it is not too far from the Persian uplands where the Aryans settled; nor is it too far from modern Turkey, which was occupied by the oldest of the Indo-European peoples, the Hittites. Even the route to western and southern Europe does not encounter insuperable obstacles in the Balkan mountains or the Carpathians. For men living at the mouth of the Volga, the world was open on all sides – so much so that, given a modicum of adventurousness, they must have been near enough sucked out of the area.

If we accept this argument, the hitherto highly abstract notion of an *Ur*-people suddenly comes to life. Since it seems established that its members knew *ekuos* and *peku* (sheep) we may legitimately assume that there already lived on the steppe nomadic or semi-nomadic shepherds with some inclination towards farming. Some of them may later have gone west, crossing the endless Ukrainian plains, leaving the gentle hills of White Russia behind them and reaching the Baltic or the Mediterranean. They would arrive at the mouth of the Danube, whose valley forms a broad highway leading to the Iron Gates and, beyond them, into the heart of Europe. These wanderings were made possible by their mobility. What they owned they could carry with them on horseback, proving to everyone they encountered that portable capital is best. The only questions now remaining are when and why these tribes and their herds left their native settlement.

As to date, Alfons Nehring suggests that in proto-Indo-European there was only one named metal: copper. This means that the Indo-European speakers must still have been living together when man first discovered ore that could be utilized, and that by the time men learnt to produce bronze a few centuries later the community had split up into individual peoples. Professor Nehring's arguments thus point to the New Stone Age. Artisans who could make simple copper utensils existed in Europe after 2200 BC.

Introducing the horse into the argument, Nehring's colleague Wilhelm Brandenstein comes to similar conclusions. The *Ur*-people must still have been together when *ekuos* was domesticated, but towards 2000 BC they must have begun to disintegrate for at this time the first Hittites appeared in Anatolia. To sum up: at the end of the third millennium BC bands of a steppe-people of the lower Volga bridled their horses, collected their herds and families and set off to find a new home. Why they did this is rather easier to guess: a few simple reflections and a second glance at the map suffice.

The most westerly salient of Eurasia is, in comparison with the regions east of the Carpathians, a true paradise. Low mountain-chains or hills divide the area into small, easily surveyable districts and prevent cyclones or other climatic disasters. A multitude of rivers irrigates a multitude of valleys. The seas that surround the European peninsula on three sides make for an equable climate. There are by and large neither Siberian winters nor torrid steppe-summers. The earth is mainly fertile. The woods are rich in timber and game.

It is no wonder that, with the glaciers of the Ice Age barely withdrawn, men from the east filtered into this land. But two thousand years later, at the time of the Indo-European migration, western Europe was still an attractive objective, the more so as the climate was considerably milder than today. It therefore seems virtually superfluous to assume that abrupt climatic changes drove the *Ur*-people from the *Ur*-home, though for the period 2300–2000 BC a series of extremely hot summers is attested. Instead, growing population pressure would probably have sufficed, whether on its own or as an added factor, to set the first nomadic tribes on the move. When those that stayed behind learnt what riches awaited them in the west, the brakes were off.

However what these Indo-European scholars have put forward is only a hypothesis, for which there is no concrete evidence. Only the archaeologists can provide this, and it has been their task to dig at the mouth of the Volga in order to find out if the philologists are correct.

In Moscow I asked Vadim Mikhailovitch Masson, a Soviet archaeologist of international renown, what he thought of the German philologists' 'Volga thesis'. His answer was as concise and clear as could be imagined. For him and his colleagues there had been no doubt that 'Indo-Europe' must have been sited on the lower reaches of the Volga, and he added that, in the Soviet Union, both philologists and pre-historians had reached this conclusion: 'The former sketched out the route that the latter followed, spade in hand.' Despite such apparently well co-ordinated collaboration between disciplines, the most comprehensive answer as to the original homeland of the *Ur*-people comes not from the Soviet Union but from the United States. As early as 1963 the archaeologist Marija Gimbutas, by origin a Balt, went ahead with a short survey of Indo-European history and published it, to her Soviet colleagues' chagrin, before they could present their own results. What Mrs Gimbutas says bears out almost to the last detail the suppositions of Nehring, Brandenstein and others. At the same time she supplements her outline with details that they could not have known.

For instance she reports that there was a 'culture' flourishing in the third millennium BC, north of the 'Pontus Euxeinos', the Black Sea, and which she therefore calls the 'North Pontic'. Its people must have been farmers. They lived in villages on the banks of the Dnieper, the Don and the Donets, raised cattle, pigs and also dogs, though they seem not to have had horses. Men and women wore ornaments of boar's teeth, shells and carneoles, and on occasion copper-bands and bracelets. When they died they were buried in mass-graves, where they lay stretched out on a bed of luminous

red-ochre flanked by painted flat-bottomed jugs. To the south-
east on both sides of the Caucasus there was a further, somewhat
different culture. These people lived in villages high in the
mountains and were possibly cattle-raisers who also cultivated the
land. In contrast to the North Pontians, they could already make
carts. Furthermore, battle-axes and globular mace-heads of
polished stone have been found in their villages.

Soviet scholars classify these mountain-dwellers as a 'New
Stone Age Trans-Caucasian culture'. Mrs Gimbutas opts for the
more striking 'Trans-Caucasian Copper Age culture', for this
metal was already known to them. But there is a third group of
greater interest than the North Pontians or Trans-Caucasians.
They lived, at the same period, in the very area where philologists
believe they can locate the home of the Indo-Europeans: the area
between the lower Volga, the Caspian, Lake Aral and the upper
Yenisei – in other words, the steppe. These people were more
gracefully built than the squat Ukrainian farmers, with narrower
and longer skulls. Originally they must have been hunters; later
they took in cattle and finally domesticated the horse, which
increased their mobility and dangerousness.

Marija Gimbutas has none the less given them a very peaceful
sounding name, the 'Eurasian Kurgan Culture' (from the Russian
kurgan, 'mound'), after the single graves in mounds where their
dead were placed with stretched-out legs and covered with ochre.
The Soviet scholars who had preferred the clumsier term
Drevnyaya yama ('old grave') were once more trumped. 'Kurgan'
gained currency because the burial-mound was the characteristic
feature of Indo-European culture in Europe. Does this mean that
these nomadic hunters from Kazakhstan were the long-sought
Ur-people? Their discoverers believe so, though with some
reservations.

The Kurgan people do not seem to have left their homes
specifically to conquer the far west and far east. There were more
immediate goals. Between 2400 and 2300 BC they invaded the
territory of the North Pontians and, somewhat later, that of the
Trans-Caucasians. Both actions, particularly the latter, greatly
changed them. The mountain-people they encountered had long
ceased to be barbaric. They had had contact with the great
civilizations of the Euphrates valley, knew Sumer and Akkad and
must have profited from this. Their achievements in civilization,

slight as they may have been, could only be of advantage to the
Kurgan people. From inherited and acquired elements a new,
superior way of life developed, and possibly along with it the
Ur-language.

Near Maikop and Tsarskaya in the Kuban basin, archaeologists
have discovered royal graves with fabulous ornaments of gold,
silver, pottery, hammerhead axes of semi-precious stones, statues
of bulls and lions, turquoise, pearls, dagger and lance-points of
copper – i.e. ornamental weapons. The battle-axe was used to
denote this mixed culture, together with 'corded' pottery (decorated by impressing lengths of cord before baking), and it was
established that the influence of this culture had been felt as far as
northern central Anatolia. This brings us within reach of the first
Indo-European people whose existence is attested in written
documents: the Hittites. They advanced around 2000 BC into
what is today Turkey, where they founded, a good four hundred

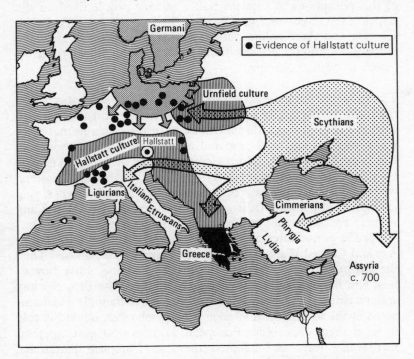

Map 5 The Scythian advance into Western Europe in the Hallstatt era

years later, one of the most powerful empires of the ancient world, which at its apogee reached into Syria.

These steppe-warriors could not have acquired the capacity to set up and govern a state in their homeland. This they presumably learnt in the Trans-Caucasian region, where they had to test their own hierarchical order against a more highly developed people. Their military prowess will also have benefited, for the mountain-people seem, like themselves, to have been of a warlike disposition. While the Hittites' forefathers were setting off, the Churri, who probably lived in Armenia, left their homelands and set up several states in Mesopotamia that were dominated by chariot-borne armies. Half a millennium later they were followed by the Cassites, who conquered Babylon and held it for almost four hundred years. Some scholars reckon that, though not Indo-European, both peoples were at least led by Indo-European chieftains. They were at all events characterized by a rigidly hierarchical social order. All of this permits us to suppose that a warrior people lived on the slopes of the Caucasus, in the modern Soviet republics of Armenia, Georgia and Azerbaidjan, which at one time had not only the military but also the organizational capacity to undertake the great march to western Europe.

The Indo-Europeans – as we can now call them – did not arrive in their new territories as a disorderly and savage host, nor even in scattered little groups. Marija Gimbutas instead reckons that there was a planned and well-prepared occupation. Otherwise we can hardly explain why the cultures already settled there ceased to exist overnight and almost completely went over to their new masters' way of life. This must have been imposed on them by rulers strong enough to implement their aims by political means. Marauding robbers are not usually successful at this sort of thing.

For the period after 2000 BC elements of the Tumulus, Battle-Axe and Corded Ware cultures can be found in the Balkans. Then the steppe peoples emerge in the middle Danube, move further west and finally reach even Denmark, southern Sweden, Norway and the British Isles. Only France was barred to them. It was domi-nated by the so-called Bell-Beaker peoples who were obviously able to repel them. The older European cultures now gave up their matriarchal ways and adopted the Indo-European patriarchal system, renouncing their earth-oriented fertility cults, turning instead to sun-gods – those to whom horses and bulls were sacrificed in the steppe. Moreover they acquired the habit of interring their dead in burial-mounds.

They in turn also influenced the invaders from the east. Each group of invaders took on some of the characteristics of the regions they had selected. With this the old community gradually broke down. Single peoples began to develop. In the middle Baltic emerged the proto-Germans, east of them the Balts, then the Slavs in the north Carpathian region. The Cimmerians and the Scythians grew up in the now empty Pontic and Caucasian area; the latter people was decisively to influence the Celtic culture, although the Celts themselves cannot as yet be discerned.

This is perhaps because the tribes from which the Celts emerged selected an area of settlement so central that continual new arrivals and different influences from all sides prevented the emegrence of specific groups for many years. They settled in Bohemia and Lusatia, an old cockpit of European history. It must have been dominated at that time by a constant coming and going and an unrest that can be explained not only by its central position but also by the rich ore deposits of the Bohemian and central German mountains. There was gold and silver and, what was more important, copper, even tin: in other words the basic constituents of bronze, the material that gave its name to the era which now dawned. It was greatly sought after, not just by peaceful merchants and artisans but by warlords who wished to secure their supplies of raw materials.

The occupants of the lands in which the Celts emerged would therefore be capable of defending what they possessed, and would also have the chance to amass a considerable treasure, which these former inhabitants of the steppe seem to have done with particular success. In Bohemia they founded one of the richest cultures of European prehistory. Named after a site near Prague, the Únětice culture extended over central Germany, the greater part of modern Czechoslovakia and southern Austria, and was in contact with the Bell-Beaker culture, which extended from the middle Rhineland to nearby Lower Bavaria. Other finds reveal that the products of the Únětice culture were taken to the Mediterranean and Baltic areas. In Jutland they were bartered for the most highly prized ornamental material of the day, amber (the Samland finds are of later date).

The distinguishing feature of the Bohemian–central German culture was still, until the mid-Bronze Age (which in Europe began around 1500 BC), the burial-mound. Not until 1300 BC did this archaeological indicator give way under pressure of catastrophe to one less obvious. The Lusatians and Únětice people then began burning their dead, placing the ashes in urns and putting these in cemeteries. We now therefore talk of an 'Urnfield culture'. Cremation remained a custom for a whole series of later peoples – for instance the Italic, Venetian and Illyrian. This in turn permits the conjecture that the area in which this Urnfield culture spread was the cradle of the three linguistic communities – perhaps also of a fourth and fifth, the Phrygians and Armenians – who around 1200 BC settled in Anatolia. So long as they were together they must all, with their neighbours, have spoken the idiom that later developed out of Indo-European and which Hans Krahe, in his attempt at definition, calls the Old European language. He believes that it has been preserved in river-names such as Albina (Elbe), Regana (Regen), Visara (Weser), Aventia (Switzerland), Arante (France) and Arga (Lithuania). Latin in particular retained its richness in vowels.

An interim report would give the following picture: five hundred years after the Indo-Europeans had left Russia a series of new cultures arose in Europe and Asia, ranging from the Aryan Indians via the Hittite Empire and the Mycenaean principalities of Greece, celebrated by Homer, to the Únětice culture. All had certain features in common. Their farmers preferred solitary farms to enclosed villages and laid great emphasis on raising animals rather than cultivating the land. Their masters led a courtly life, with war, hunting and elaborate festivities. Their priests sacrificed to sun-gods. Their warriors knew the battle-axe and the two or four-wheeled chariot. They were therefore not yet horsemen, but may have shared this mentality through their nomadic inheritance and the hierarchical principle cultivated by the aristocracy. But although all of this is also characteristic of the Celts' ancestors, it would be premature to claim that this people existed before 1500 BC or to look for proto-Celts. The later Celts lived in an Indo-European community whose individual groups had not yet taken on separate physiognomies and would not do so for centuries to come.

But it can be said that European history began with the invasion of these eastern tribes. A people, more restless, more active and more ruthless than most others that we know of, had secured the base from which it was to go on to conquer the greater part of the world. Success rs of the Indo-European people set up the empire of Alexander the Great, the Roman empire, the British empire, the Spanish colonial empire; they occupied northern and southern America, colonized Africa, penetrated Siberia and created most of the few states that today control the earth's riches. Moses, Christ and Mohammed came, however, from a different world. Only Prince Siddharta, known as Buddha, could perhaps have traced his ancestry back to some Kurgan chief.

I asked Vadim Masson how he viewed his own work, though the spartan office in the Soviet Academy of Sciences in Moscow hardly seemed the right place for speculative remarks, nor did he seem the man to entertain them. Soberly, he answered: 'You know, we hardly dare draw any far-reaching conclusions from our finds, or to re-structure world history on the basis of the one or three cultures we have discovered. The romantic era of archaeology is over. I am not even happy when I have to talk of "cultures". I prefer to talk only of men who lived in this or that way.' This raised a smile on my part, for Masson's assistant had told me shortly before that his chief was just about to discover a new 'culture' that might possibly explain the origins of the Parthians. But instead of pursuing this I asked: 'But you do agree with the philologists that the people from the Caspian were actually ancestors of the Greeks, Romans, Germans and Celts?' 'Yes,' he replied, 'that point has already been cleared up.' 'Then we, your descendants, are all of us Russians?' It was his turn to smile: 'You might put it that way.' But as if by way of apology, he at once added: 'Though of course you are not obliged to.' Masson was not just being polite, he was right. Kurgan people may have been the proto-Indo-Europeans, but they themselves were only a people that had emerged from a long prehistory of fusion with other peoples. Where did they come from?

Mythologists have for long been aware that sagas and fairy-tales from areas as far apart as Polynesia and North Germany show extraordinary similarities. They conclude that men and cultures of all times have always influenced each other and that, very early on, there were extensive migrations from Pacific to Atlantic and vice versa. There is little likelihood that we shall ever be able to feel our way back to those times.

Thus the steppe-people of the lower Volga marks only a random fixed point in the flux of history that can be taken as the beginning of a particular phase. If we wished to go back to the beginning of this beginning, we should have to find out when and from where man first spread over the globe. That would be the place and date of birth of all peoples and all languages – including the Celts – something like a Garden of Eden.

But where do we locate Paradise? Even the fertile, green, well-watered region of western Europe that had seemed so enticing to the nomads from the steppe did not have everything it had promised. After a millennium their descendants learnt that man is as exposed to natural catastrophe amid mountain-ranges and high forests as at the mouth of the Volga.

SIX

When Atlantis Sank

Very many types of mass-destruction of human beings have taken and will take place, the greatest through fire and water, other, lesser ones through a thousand other mischances.

Plato, *Timaeus*

All the great events of history were not caused by peoples; rather, it is they that caused peoples to come into existence.

Oswald Spengler, *The Decline of the West*

In the second half of the fifteenth century BC the whole world experienced a series of disasters such as has never since been recorded. It began with a fall in the water-table to seven metres, with the result that springs dried up, rivers became trickles, bogs stopped growing. This drought was preceded by a climatic optimum that went on for thousands of years with long summers and mild winters. This had also produced long periods of drought, as for instance just before the Kurgan people's withdrawal from the Caspian area. But in general it must have been warmer in Europe after about 5000 BC than at any time before or since in the past twelve thousand years. Vines grew in southern Norway, the whole of Scandinavia lived in the shadow of mixed and deciduous forest, there were glaciers only in the extreme north. These times are probably recalled in the Greek saga of Phaeton. He, mortal son of Helios, asked his father's permission to drive the sun-chariot across the firmament. He could not control the unwieldy vehicle and was hurled by the four winged horses across the entire universe, up to the stars and down to the earth. There he let loose an inferno, for the glowing chariot set alight woods and cities, made seeds turn into coal and is said to have scorched the Moors black. Even the sea shrank, and large lakes bubbled away. Phaeton himself was killed.

In his *Metamorphoses*, a history of the world from its beginnings until his own day, the Roman poet Ovid describes the same event in a less allegorical fashion. He maintains that not only the Rhine, Danube and Rhône were dried up, but also the Nile, Euphrates, Don and Ganges: in other words it was a worldwide disaster. His remarks seem to be borne out by the fact that Libya, until then covered by savannah, became a desert. Herodotus relates that at that time there was a famine in Anatolia that forced the Lydian king Attys to send half of his people to the land of the 'Umbricians' (Umbrians), i.e. to Italy.

That too can be verified. Ancient historians such as the Viennese Fritz Schachermacher have shown that between 1300 and 1200 BC peoples from Asia Minor settled in Umbria. But their migration was only one of many started by the abrupt climax of the climatic optimum, and the drought was only the prelude to a worldwide tragedy. A far more dramatic note was set by earthquakes of unprecedented violence, registered throughout the Mediterranean area and again enshrined in Ovid's verse. 'Everywhere the ground bursts,' he says at the end of his two hundred and fifty stories of transformation, 'the light of day breaks through the cracks into Tartarus and frightens the king of the deep and his wife.' More soberly, an Egyptian eye-witness reports: 'All settlements are destroyed. . . . Great and small alike say they wish they were dead. . . . The palace has collapsed in minutes.' Thebes valley records the battles with the invading Sea Peoples around 1200 BC. In the old Hittite empire, a similar catastrophic register was revealed.

A second climax followed. On a spring day about 1470 BC a submarine volcano erupted on Thera (Santorin), an island of the Cyclades, and destroyed villages, livestock and people within a radius that certainly included the northern areas of nearby Crete and the Peloponnese, and probably also the coast of Asia Minor, some hundred and fifty miles away. A few years earlier, both Etna and the volcanoes of Sinai and Iceland are thought to have become active. It appears the world was undergoing one of its sporadic contractions, the direct consequences of which were disastrous.

Seismic tidal waves such as always accompany great earthquakes and eruptions caused the sea to recede from the land and even sucked out the rivers. There was a deathly silence. Then the towering tide rushed back – a roaring wall of green glass as tall as a house – and mercilessly shattered whatever stood in its path on the shores. All these facts were assembled by Jürgen Spanuth, a student of Atlantis, who also used them to explain the destruction of the Egyptians who pursued Moses's fleeing hosts into the Red Sea. The straits had been so shallow that the Children of Israel were able to cross it almost without getting wet. Then there came a raging tidal-wave which covered the chariots and horsemen of the whole Egyptian horde. (But this occurred around 1250 BC, and cannot be connected with the earlier catastrophe.)

At the height of the climatic optimum there occurred an almost equally catastrophic period of rainy summers and cold winters. Everywhere on the edge of the Mediterranean cloudbursts flooded the parched earth, streams and rivers then washed the mud into the sea. What remained, according to Plato's *Kritias*, was 'only the bones of the sick body . . . the emaciated body of the land'.

Any visitor to Greece would find this to be accurate enough, but it also applies to Anatolia or Syria, not to mention the North African coast. Climatic experts and geologists both confirm the words of Plato's fictitious interlocutor. Before this great drought the southern reaches of the Balkan peninsula were 'covered with rich soil, its hills crowned with thick forest'. Afterwards it consisted of bare rock, thin topsoil unable to retain water, scrub-grass and dry valleys. In central and northern Europe it was even worse after the great heat. Glaciers expanded, the sea-level sank, vines stopped growing in Scandinavia and what the Swedish prehistorian Count Eric Oxenstierna has called the 'brilliant Bronze Age' came to an end. North of the Alps it has never since been so warm as before 1500 BC. Men who had got used to this agreeable climate must have thought that the gates of Paradise had been slammed in their faces. Along with this Garden of Eden there vanished highly developed cultures which may have been the equal of Mycenaean Greece or Minoan Crete, though scholars are hesitant to go further.

The experts are rightly suspicious of attempts to show what really happened in the second half of the fifteenth century BC. The fragments of information out of which such accounts are assembled are too variegated, too much speculation is required to hold them together and, in any case, the picture presented is not always coherent. In-academic circles no one would keep his job for long if he described the period of climatic change as I have done – something that ·Spanuth, on whom I have primarily based my account, discovered to his cost.

Around Jürgen Spanuth and his theories there has been for some years a bitter debate, which has so far produced nothing but bruises on both sides. Some of the experts who have sought to refute him have had to admit that they were themselves guilty of bias. The pastor – Spanuth is an 'amateur' – could be accused of a tendency to tailor pieces of prehistory to fit his own 'Atlantis theory', which will be discussed below. This practice is not, however, uncommon, even among reputable scholars. Indeed, used in moderation, it is quite legitimate. It is rather like trying to do a jigsaw that refuses to come out by starting at a different corner. If it works, so much the better. If it fails, the attempt should not be condemned out of hand but should be classed among the many models that have, over the years, been set up only to be knocked down again. Indeed many useless hypotheses belong among those sorts of wrong answer that must be given so that we can know why they are wrong. In our attempt to account for what may have happened at the end of the Bronze Age, it is thus appropriate at this stage to set up what may be called test-questions. The existing facts have grown into such a mountain that a survey would take a whole lifetime, without guarantee of result. Hypothesis has to be our core-sampler: with it we can probe the mountain, in the hope of being rewarded with unexpected insight. I have in what follows had occasion to use such methods, and studies whose arguments, though plausibly founded, cannot be conclusively proven. At best the result will be a picture that ought to be looked at with caution: this is how it might have been. If it was not, no doubt we shall one day find out.

One of the classic theses of historical enquiry rests on the Latin idiom 'ex oriente lux', a poetic way of saying that the sun of civilization rose first in the Near East and Egypt and then gradually began to illumine the dark regions of the north-west. This notion was based on the fact that almost all the oldest surviving cultural artifacts were dug up from the sands of the Nile or Euphrates valleys. Today this, along with a great many other respectable theories, seems to be losing ground.

It was for instance long believed that the megalith-builders'
route, the 'dolmen route' along the Mediterranean, the Spanish
and French Atlantic coasts to England, with a branch from the
Rhône delta to Brittany, was the road along which myths and ideas
moved from the Mediterranean region to northern Europe. Seafarers, merchants and missionaries of Egyptian, Helladic, Cretan
or even Phoenician origin were thought to have set up these sometimes huge monuments along this road, rock structures that were
to give later generations material both for fantastic speculations
and fairy-tales and heroic sagas.

There is in fact support for this assumption. The oldest of these
megaliths are never more than a hundred miles from the sea and,
though of many different types, they indicate sacred or meeting
places in Libya, Corsica, Malta and Sardinia, and also in Micro-
nesia and Easter Island. Did not, asks the French ethnologist J. A.
Mauduit, old Jacob at Bethel set up a stone to worship his God?
And does it not follow that the custom of ramming rocks into the
ground, or putting them together to form a gigantic monument,
spread from Palestine, eastwards and westwards over the globe?

It is certainly a seductive thesis. However, we may object that
erecting stones may always have been the simplest way for people
to express their beliefs. Moreover the megalith styles are so dis-
similar and fulfil so many different purposes that they can hardly
be traced back to a common source. The *nuraghi* in Sardinia are
rough defensive towers and places of refuge; the standing-stones
called menhirs are perhaps the primitive equivalent of statues; the
dolmens are burial-places; and the prehistoric stone structures on
the Pacific Marquesas are something similar to temples. Finally,
and this effectively destroys the argument that all at least of the
megalithic grave-stones simply spread out to the west over Europe,
is is not easy to see why Mediterranean peoples took the dangerous
route round Cape Finisterre and the Bay of Biscay if they wanted
to go north-west. It seems more probable that they would have
taken the easier land route from the Rhône delta. Though they are
said, of course, to have sailed as well.

Since these contradictions are so obvious, it is necessary to
change our perspective and look at things from the north. Here
we can observe that Atlantic coast-dwellers, used to the rough seas,
would have been much more likely to develop a ship suitable for
such perilous voyages. Indeed there exist, if only from the early

Bronze Age (1800–1500 BC), rock-paintings found in Bohuslän, southern Sweden, of a craft with high poop and stern, low, long and streamlined, which looks like a primitive version of the highly seaworthy Viking dragon-ship. The Phoenicians had similar ships, though not of course until about 1100 BC.

The stone structures of the Mediterranean region and the Atlantic coast are much older than the first high-seas ships of the Phoenicians. It is thought that the 1,169 menhirs which stand in seemingly endless rows at Ménec near the Breton resort of Carnac – looking as if the children of giants had been trying to set up a number of complex slalom routes – were erected between 3510 and 2500 BC. The jewel of megalithic monuments, Stonehenge in Wiltshire, undoubtedly dates from long before 1400. If it was the Mediterranean peoples that erected these monuments or inspired the natives to do so, they would have had to travel through the Straits of Gibraltar at a time when the most sophisticated vessel in the Mediterranean was a kind of raft or flat-bottomed canoe, which kept within sight of the shore. If the impulse came from elsewhere, we have to assume that even in the Stone Age there arose an archaic high culture on the Atlantic whose people could reach the Mediterranean.

Scholars have for many years been concerned with this possibility, but not until 1971 did anyone clearly affirm that it was a likely explanation. Colin Renfrew, the British archaeologist, wrote that pre-historians had considerably underestimated the originality and creative drive of prehistoric Europeans. His statement, which caused something of a sensation, was based mainly on the work of two American scholars, who had shown for their part that the most important chronometer of pre-historians, the so-called 'radio-carbon clock', was giving false results.

This chronometer was developed in 1949 by a chemist, another American, Charles F. Libby, who had noted that during their lifetime plants and animals – and human beings as well – store up in their cells not only ordinary carbon ($C12$) but also radioactive carbon ($C14$) as it comes from the cosmic rays of the atmosphere. On death the $C14$ begins to drop – to about half of the quantity in 5,600 years – while the $C12$ remains. We can thus use the ratio of ordinary to radioactive carbon to determine fairly accurately the age of excavated bones, wood, seed-corn and the earth in which they were found.

Libby's method, the object of worldwide admiration, has in the past quarter century come to be regarded as the archaeologists' absolute measuring-scale. It has been used by them all the more willingly as it seemed more or less to confirm what they had arrived at by more circumstantial methods. The whole process has, however, a weak spot. Its inventor started out from the assumption that the atmosphere had at all times had a constant measure of C14. This was not the case. The chemist Charles Weyley Ferguson of the University of Arizona deduced from his study of tree-rings in four-thousand-year-old American giant trees that before 1500 BC the radiocarbon content of the atmosphere was considerably less than later.

This implied that all remains of that era must be older than Libby's atomic clock could show, for his count allowed for a greater amount of C14 than can actually have been present. Hans P. Suess, a colleague of Ferguson's, reckoned that the Libby clock was in error by up to seven hundred years. Thus a find dated at 1800 BC must in fact be from 2500 BC.

If this improved system of measurement is now applied to the Atlantic megaliths, we can see that the oldest of them were not erected at a time when the notion of the state was emerging in Egypt but much earlier. The pillars of Stonehenge were already standing in the meadows of Wiltshire before the Mycenaean Greeks had even laid the foundations of their rich civilization. The Achaeans could not, as was long supposed, have influenced the style of this structure. Colin Renfrew was right to call the two Americans' discovery 'revolutionary', in that it put an end to notions of an east-west diffusion of civilization. It changes a whole view of the world.

Instead of western Europe as a dark, primitive and barbarian area in the shadow of the brilliant eastern centres of civilization, we can imagine an age that had at least two poles of civilization, one in the eastern Mediterranean and one in the Atlantic north. Both flourished under the blue skies that covered the whole of the Ancient world after 5000 BC. On the Atlantic, peoples of various origins had set up their megalithic civilizations, built dolmens, erected menhirs and perhaps even – as the German ethnologist Kurt von Boeckmann assumed as early as 1924 – found a way into the Mediterranean via Palestine and Mesopotamia and thereby made contact with the civilizations of the Persian Gulf, which in turn had links with those of the Pacific. Each of these communities took their predecessors' achievements and extended them by their own methods. The Indo-Europeans did this too: their inheritance has been clarified by the Harvard astronomer Gerald S. Hawkins. He demonstrated, and had his results tested by computer, that Stonehenge was none other than a 'Stone Age calculating machine', with the help of which eclipses of the sun and the moon could be precisely foretold, over a period of three hundred years.

Such knowledge of celestial processes, handed down from generation to generation, must also have helped navigators as their narrow keel-boats probed the waters around the coasts from England, Brittany, Jutland. They may well have reached Gibraltar, even the Canary Islands, where ship-drawings similar to those of Bohuslän have been found. If so, the Egyptians must have known about them.

In fact Plato quotes in the *Kritias* a report allegedly from the archives of Egypt that mentions men who live on a sea 'called the Atlantic'. Their kings are said to rule 'many islands situated there' and later apparently extended their rule over 'those who live within the Pillars of Hercules up to Egypt and Tyrrhenia'. Their capital was supposed to be Atlantis. Hardly a single expert now believes that Plato was merely telling a fable; but where was the legendary city? There are many opinions. It is sought at Crete, Cadiz, the Canaries, even in the Atlantic. Jürgen Spanuth says, however, that it lay near Heligoland in the Bight, and of all the many Atlantic theories his, the product of long research, is by far the best founded. If Spanuth is correct, Plato's description of the vanished empire is the most comprehensive that we have of the Bronze Age successors of the megalith-builders in the area between western France, southern England and northern Germany. Presumably these people were, as Spanuth says, identical with the men of Atlantis. The description Plato gives is very thorough.

The Atlantians had artificial harbours, a royal palace the walls of which were covered in 'brilliant oreichalcos' (possibly molten amber), as well as highly disciplined armed forces, 'ten thousand battle-chariots', including 'double-harness ones without a seat, which could carry a lightly armed warrior and next to him the driver of the two horses'. There was also a gigantic fleet. The sacrifice of bulls and fire-ceremonies played a part in their cults. The ceremonial dress of their kings was 'a fine dark-blue garment' and their land was so fertile that it had two harvests a year, one moistened by the winter rains and one by artificial irrigation. They could also ride, and on their largest island there was a race-track 'the breadth of which is a stadion' (215 yards). Above all, their public buildings were virtually stuffed with gold, silver and 'oreichalcos'; the statues of their gods were of gold, as were their ancestral figures and sacrificial bowls, while the walls of their temples shone with silver.

If all this comes from eye-witness reports, Atlantis must – even given a sailor's taste for tall yarns – have been a highly civilized, rich and powerful community. This is by no means impossible. Pre-historic research has long demonstrated that roughly in the area of southern England, Schleswig-Holstein and Jutland there were in the Bronze Age princes who enjoyed considerable riches. They acquired gold from Ireland, silver from Spain, found amber off their own coasts, got ornamental pins from central Germany, urns from Greece, faience beads from Egypt and must have paid for these imports largely with the tin that could be mined in greater quantities in their regions – particularly Cornwall – than anywhere else. They were not yet thinking in terms of maximizing profits but simply of 'presents'; these however could only be acquired if something of equivalent value was offered in exchange.

Given the climate of the time, it is not all that unlikely that their land was exceptionally fertile, as Plato's informant says. Horse-drawn vehicles had already brought the ancestors of the 'Atlantians' from the steppe. Finally, the allusion that these vehicles carried, like the later Celtic ones, at most two men makes the unknown informant still more credible, for in Ancient Greece they were usually meant for only one man. Similarly the race-course mentioned is not necessarily an invention. Near Stonehenge there is the so-called 'Cursus', an arrangement of earth banks that immediately calls to mind a race-course, even if the excavators themselves (in the seventeenth century) – inclined as always to label everything they cannot explain a place of worship – believe it to be a processional route. The Cursus is about a mile and a half in length, one hundred yards wide, and narrowly elliptical in shape.

It is quite possible that the horse-lovers of this community not only raced around the track in chariots but also rode. Mounts strong enough to carry a man over long stretches came, experts believe, from a cross between the descendants of the light steppe

tarpan and the heavier cold-blooded types of animal native to areas
west of the Vistula. Thus it is as likely that the first cavalryman got
into the saddle on some north German heath as anywhere else.

The horse was as sacred as the bull to descendants of nomads.
Poseidon, whom *Kritias* says was worshipped by the Atlantians in
their temples, was originally depicted in the shape of a horse – as
witness the Trojan Horse itself, in reality a statue of the King of
the Deep (something that Homer no longer appreciated). Fire, too,
was for most Indo-European peoples a divine phenomenon, as was
the sun, from which it seemed to originate.

It is more difficult to say how these people approached their
gods. Their priests may well have worn 'very fine dark blue garments'. The art of weaving was astonishingly well developed in
the Bronze Age, and textile producers had also mastered dye-
techniques. In Danish bog-graves there have been found remains
of flowing cloaks and shirt-like garments, even a 'miniskirt', made
out of hanging threads.

Putting these few details together we get a picture of a community that must have greatly impressed a foreigner, whether by
its wealth or by the luxury in which at any rate its upper class
lived, by its colour or by its way of life. Of the archaeologists who
have dug in the area they are said to have inhabited, at least one,
the late J. F. S. Stone, has dared suggest that they were at least 'a
barbarian copy of what is described in Homer's poems'. But we
could add – if we take Plato's account seriously – that this was no
copy and that they were no barbarians: on the contrary, that it was
they who influenced the Achaeans.

The 'agonal' attitude (from the Greek *agon*, 'competition') that
scholars so admire in the Achaean Greeks may have developed just
as easily further north, on the Atlantian race-tracks, as on the
Peloponnese. Love of games, sport and the human body does not
seem to have been a characteristic limited to southern peoples –
particularly if we recall that in the warm era before the great
climatic change it was possible, even in regions fog-bound today, to
tumble around in the open air naked or lightly clothed for the
greater part of the year. This must also have been true of Bohemia
and central Germany. There is evidence that they had considerable
links with the self-contained northern civilization of the Bronze
Age. When it collapsed in the face of earthquakes and seismic tidal
waves, they too were naturally involved in the catastrophe. It was

for all of them a time of bloody unrest and profound change, brought about by the collapse of the land which may have been Atlantis.

Earthquakes had destroyed the northern empire, if we are to believe Plato's fictitious interlocutor, Kritias. The sea had flooded it and created, on the site of the disaster, an 'impenetrable sea of mud'. We think we know what this meant. In the earthquake period of the fifteenth century BC, towards the end of the middle Bronze Age, a broad and fertile stretch of fenland along the western coast of Schleswig-Holstein was completely destroyed. The Kiel geologist von Maack has estimated that, perhaps provoked by Icelandic and other quakes, sixty-foot-high waves must have unleashed a flood 'whose height and destructive force far surpassed any other known to history'. His colleague Wildvang established in his borings, early in this century, that 'throughout [the sunken land] the tops of fallen trees point to the east, which may bear out the assumption that the catastrophe was caused by a storm from the west'.

It was, according to Spanuth, on the fens joining Heligoland with the coast that Atlantis was situated. The *Edda*, he continues, contains a reminiscence of the cataclysm that destroyed the city, exemplified in the three verses which read, literally: 'In storm, the sea rises to the skies, and then falls on to the land; the air becomes foul; there is a blizzard and a great wind; and then it is the end for the *Ase*' – these latter perhaps being the rich Bronze Age princes. A large part of the fertile land that had given two annual harvests was now covered by the sea. The sky was filled with clouds and the temperature sank. There would remain nothing for those who had survived this 'twilight of the Gods' but to search, numbed with cold, for new regions where there was still the warmth to which they were accustomed. They donned their horned helmets, took up their lances – many of which had those flame-shaped blades that Diodorus found among the Celts – girded the 'Germanic hilted-sword', one of the finest weapons ever to be forged, and went south with their forces. The peoples whose regions they marched through prepared themselves for the worst.

The inhabitants of Hungary, influenced by the Únětice culture, put strong palisades round their villages. In Greece existing fortress walls were hastily extended or strengthened. Even the rulers of Crete set up chariot squadrons though they had hitherto felt able to

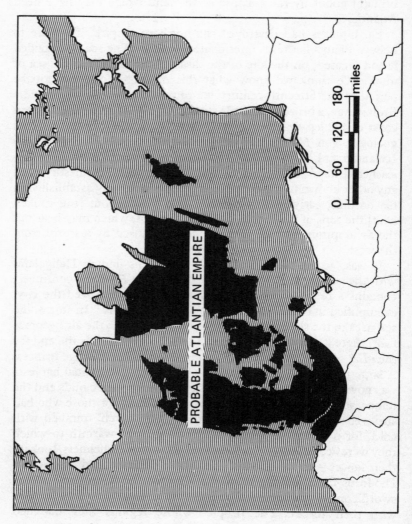

Map 6   The Nordic culture: Atlantis?

entrust the defence of their island to a strong war fleet alone. But that was not much use. The bands of emigrants went up to the Elbe or the Oder, then with one part of their forces to the Alps and Italy, and with another into the Hungarian plain. Had there been a political map of Europe, it would have needed radical alteration.

Those tribes that reached the Apennine peninsula settled and became the Umbrian people, using the Indo-European language and at first calling themselves Ambrones. This perhaps explains the incident at the battle of Aquae Sextiae related by Plutarch, who confuses the Umbrians with the Ligurians. But there were also Teutons or 'Teutani' at that time in Catania, which comes as no surprise when we learn that the word *teuta* occurred in many of the old European languages. The Celts had a god named 'Teutates'; the early Irish had the concept of *túath*. Both – *teuta* and *túath* – merely meant 'people', and from this root emerged the word *deutsch*.

This great movement, which brought the early Teutons and Umbrians to central Italy, may also have driven the Veneti to northern Italy, the forefathers of the Illyrians (related to the Veneti) to Yugoslavia and their cousins the Phrygians and proto-Armenians to Anatolia. It may further be assumed that the whole Únětice culture to which they belonged was caught up in this upheaval of peoples. As the Illyrians had personal names such as Teuticus, Teutomus or simply Teuta, we may assume that this was the matrix of Indo-European and Old European alike. The refugees even got over the Balkan mountains to Greece from Hungary.

All this must have happened after 1220 BC when the Thera volcano erupted. The invaders from the north had scant opportunity to test their siege strategies against the Mycenaean castles, as these had already been levelled or burned, possibly through that same natural catastrophe. As the land was too exhausted by the continuing drought to sustain large bodies of men, the wanderers simply continued to Anatolia to menace the empires there, above all that of the Hittites. At the same time they probably built sea-going ships and made for more distant shores. A king of Ugarit in Syria wrote to his colleague in Cyprus: 'Enemy ships have been sighted on the sea; be prepared!' The clay tablet on which this message was scratched was not in fact sent: the enemy had gone through Anatolia and destroyed Ugarit. They approached the borders of Egypt. With this they left the darkness of pre-history,

the province of archaeology and its sister sciences, and for the first
time entered the light of recorded history. Egyptian chroniclers
described them as 'the Sea-Peoples'.

Who the hordes were who, in the reign of Ramesses III (1198–66
BC), attacked Egypt, has for many years been the subject of debate.
If we collate what we know of this event, we come to the inescap-
able conclusion that it was connected with what prehistorians
describe as 'the great central European migration' of the late
thirteenth century BC, i.e. the movements launched by climatic
change. People in all populated areas between the North Sea and
the Aegean were stirred up, thrown together and dragged along by
the peoples of the north in the movement towards the south.
Among them may have been ancestors of the Celts as well as
Mycenaean and Mycenaeanized Cretan noblemen with their
retainers; and alongside these, Umbrians and Teutons who had
found no rest even in Italy.

If this motley host appeared to the Egyptians as a single people,
it was because they came from regions that overwhelmingly bore
the imprint of a culture that was, in essentials, unified. Relying on
Krahe's albeit not uncontested findings, we could even assume that
most of the wandering 'Sea-People' had a single language, Old
European, and that they had similar customs. The Egyptians have
depicted them on the walls of the mortuary temple of Ramesses III
at Medinet Habu (at Thebes) as warriors who, without exception,
wear their hair in a very stiff style. These might be plumes on
extremely flat helmets; equally, and more probably, it could be hair
combed up and then held by nets or hardened by a lime-wash.

Pharaoh was not alarmed by this strange custom, however, and
told posterity: 'I secured my borders. . . . I have prepared the river-
mouths with a strong wall of warships . . . fully manned with brave
warriors from bow to stern.' Then he defeated the attackers in two
land battles and one naval one in 1195 BC. The causes of the
invasion appear to have been known to him. Texts on the walls of
Medinet Habu assert that the invaders' homelands had been 'torn
up and blown away by the storm'. Now they had failed to find a
substitute in the warm Nile valley. The survivors of the Sea-
Peoples lived a precarious existence on the coasts of Palestine, Syria
and Cyprus. Large contingents managed to set up the Philistine
federation of towns in that same land to which Moses's refugees

had also been drawn, while still others co-operated with the Canaan people in the Lebanon and assisted in the creation of their commercial empire, the Phoenician. They were certainly more capable than the original inhabitants of the Mediterranean region of building the ships needed for such an undertaking. In the lands through which they had wandered, a new life gradually developed.

The lords of Mycenae seem to have rebuilt some of their shattered cities. The culture to which they belonged survived the Sea-People's invasion for a good hundred years. Only then did new hordes of invaders appear, the Dorians, who brought up the rear of the great central European migration, to complete what the others had not attempted. They overran the Peloponnese.

The myths, the collective memory and subconscious of the Greeks, evaluated this positively. Drawing on this, Thucydides says it was the Heraclids that invaded the land, descendants of the great and beloved national hero of the Hellenes, who according to rumour had, like Apollo and Dionysus, sometimes travelled north and had there produced the first Celt. The Greeks also thought Heracles had had something to do with the Phoenicians. Did he then return with the Lebanese descendants of the Sea-People? Or was he one of the Indo-European gods? The same is supposed of his father Zeus and of Poseidon.

However mysterious the myths, they must be regarded as faded memories of a past that Achaeans, Dorians, Sea-Peoples and many others shared. In any event they are the last remnant of that Old European culture whose beginnings go back to the Stone Age and of the soil in which the roots of new civilizations grew. In Greece, Hellenistic classicism emerged from it, the product of an 'agonal' man who loved to pit his strength in the arena and his intelligence in the debate. On the edges of this cradle of the West, in the ravines of the Balkans and in the Macedonian forests, were tribes that followed this evolution so slowly that even in Alexander the Great's time they lived like the Achaean heroes described by Homer. They drank unmixed wine, loved bardic songs and were organized in retinues.

This was also true of those that remained on the Sea-People's route further north, the remaining inhabitants of Bohemia. These people, adopting to a climate that had degenerated, exchanged the skirts of their ancestors of the middle Bronze Age for trousers and jackets, though they still coloured their garments brightly.

They also kept the horned helmets and the stiff hair-style which the Dorians, under the influence of Mediterranean civilization, gradually began to abandon – though if it became very hot, they still threw off everything that hindered their freedom of movement and ran naked to the games or into battle.

In the lee, as it were, of the great central European wanderings, in the western European heaths devastated by the climatic catastrophe, began developments that produced later civilizations. Their founders had once more to start at the beginning, to fit their inheritance to fundamentally altered circumstances.

SEVEN

The Birth of Celtic Europe

We still know little about how the Celts arose. It is certain only that they were not immigrants, but came from a process of biological and cultural fusion that cannot as yet be analysed.

Rudolf Pörtner, *Before the Romans Came*

It is a sombre picture: a black lake with a few thin white wisps of fog, the Dachstein mountain grey-blue in the reflected light. In silhouette is a boat, with a straight hull and a raised prow; in it stands a man. Through the shifting mists, a flat craft glides across the lake, propelled and steered by a single oar, a cross between a dug-out canoe and a Venetian gondola.

A little later the mist lifts and the canoe, known locally as a *Fuhr*, has vanished. What the picture now gains in colour, it loses in atmosphere. Houses appear – yellow, white, timbered, packed as tightly as if knitted together – and a church tower with a baroque dome. After the earlier lyrical scene, this one is almost earthy. Hallstatt, in the Upper Austrian Salzkammergut, lies hemmed in between the steep slope of the mountain and the lake. Above the roofs you can see the brilliant spray of a waterfall. There is a great deal of history crammed into the tiny space the village occupies.

Its cemetery gives the first indication. Next to the Eyss von Eysselberg family, who gave the Austrian monarchy in the First World War a naval staff doctor, lie a baker, Leopold de Pretis, and farmers, fishermen and innkeepers with names such as Schoisswohl,

Gamsjäger, Mistlberger, Schopfhauser, Höll and the 'salt-mine cashier's widow', Josefine Reisenbichler. But not all of them will lie there until the Last Trump. People who do not have family graves are dug up after fifteen years. Their skulls, carefully marked with names and dates of birth and death, perhaps also painted with crosses or flowers, are placed in the ossuary. The bones also end up there, unmarked. The most recent admission to this final resting-place that I could see was Josefa Kugler, who died in 1952. I was informed that relatives of many of the dead still come by so they can say, 'that's granny'. But, famous as the cemetery is, beloved as it is by the tourists, the village has much more impressive burial-grounds, even if they are less photogenic.

On a steep slope high above the place, in 1846, a mining-inspector named Johann Georg Ramsauer discovered the burial-ground thanks to which Hallstatt has lent its name to a whole era of early European culture. Having set out to find deposits of pyrites that would be worth exploiting, he discovered two skeletons, a bronze ornamental band and an axe. Later he came across the remains of seven more dead with their grave gifts. Luckily Ramsauer was neither superstitious nor easily frightened; still less was he ignorant, but an enlightened and conscientious official. He reported what he had found to Vienna and received, by a second stroke of luck, funds from the curator of the imperial collection of coins and antiquities that enabled him to continue his digging.

In a single summer he found fifty-eight more graves. Nineteen years later, the number had already reached 193 and, in all, over three thousand objects: enough, the pre-historian Rudolf Pörtner believes, 'to fill a whole museum with pins, brooches, belts, torcs, earrings, daggers, spear-heads, axes, bronze pots or earthenware vases, bowls and dishes'. Influential amateurs in particular were attracted. In 1907 Grand Duchess Maria of Mecklenburg had the graves surrounding Ramsauer's discoveries combed, found what she wanted and took it away. The booty was later auctioned off in New York. Other enthusiasts followed, but even so there are still some four hundred graves that still await opening.

Not even such mishaps could diminish the significance that Hallstatt acquired almost overnight. The finds represent a great, self-contained culture, virtually unknown until the mid-nineteenth century. As a result a rich era of early European history has been given the name the 'Hallstatt period'. It began around 700 BC and ended around 450 BC. That so many finds were made in such a remote corner of the Alps and that a place like Hallstatt was apparently the centre of a whole culture is neither accident nor the product of bias: both are to be explained, in part, by the fact that the mountain is one of the richest salt-deposits in Europe.

It was not for its natural beauty that the Austrian Salzkammergut was settled as far back as 4,500 years ago, in the Late Stone Age. While the first inhabitants were still taking the salt from salt-wells, there must have been, in the late Bronze Age, proper salt-mines near the present ones. Some miners clearing caved-in galleries in April 1734 had this confirmed in a hideous way: according to their own account, in among the fallen rock they found 'the natural body of a dead man . . . this was wholly embedded in the rubble, but some pieces of his garments were to be seen and shoes on his feet'. Unhappily this corpse, mummified in the salt, did not survive. But later finds confirmed that men armed with bronze picks were, as early as 800 BC, climbing down into the depths on gnarled trees to mine the Haselgebirge, a layer of rock made up of clay, lime and rock-salt. They thus not only supplied their own needs but sold what they dug out to others.

Salt was, and is, essential to life. With it a man may become as rich as if he possessed a gold mine. It is one of the oldest known commodities, the basis of early trading empires and even today – as in the Salzkammergut – the source of considerable wealth. A trader must of course have good lines of communication. A mountainous region, we might suppose, would hardly seem ideal. But there is an old road out of Hallstatt, leading over the Tauer into Carinthia, and another one along the Traun into the valley of the Danube. Even in prehistoric times there were two great trade-routes crossing the Alps, linking the amber-fields of north Germany and the copper and tin mines of central Germany with the Adriatic. The salt-miners probably had access to these routes, and in exchange for their salt they certainly acquired goods with which they sometimes endowed their graves.

Thus they not only owned inestimable mineral wealth, they also lived in a relatively accessible area. Better conditions for economic prosperity would be hard to find. We must next ask ourselves what kind of people these were, so obviously capable of exploiting economic possibilities to the full. The answer is not easy, for although we know a great deal about the Hallstatt culture we know almost nothing of the men who created it.

In Gmunden on the Traunsee, not far from Hallstatt, a hill-cemetery was investigated in 1948 which must have been laid down between 1500 and 1400 BC. Each corpse was buried under large, carefully layered heaps of stone, covered by only a thin layer of grass. Their legs stretched out, faces turned towards the east and lying on their left sides, they were provided with everything a man might need on a long journey – daggers, arrows, clothing-pins and knives. On the slope of the Hallberg, where Ramsauer had first dug, there is no trace of such prodigality. The skeletons were still well provided for, but were in some cases in multiple graves – where the dead were not simply burned.

We may then assume that the earliest Bronze Age settlers in the Salzkammergut belonged to a tribe that had come west with the Indo-Europeans and had introduced the kurgan. But because of 'rationalization' it was replaced by cremation. The reason for this was that new peoples uprooted in the great central European migrations had arrived in the Alpine regions and there could profit from a culture that had developed much as the Únětice. They brought their burial customs, but not much else besides. In their place of refuge they had to recover their strength and subject themselves to further influences before they could shape their surroundings as they liked and thereby acquire a specific character of their own.

One could say that they arrived as nobodies, mere refugees, and had to become somebody. But pre-historians with a very different viewpoint call these Urnfield people the very first Celts. French scholars in particular claim that the Gauls' ancestors lived over as broad a time-span as Germanomanes had claimed for the Germans' ancestors. However, scholars with no reason to assert that the ancestors of Brennus were already living in a separate clan even in prehistoric times set at the most 600 BC as the date of their emergence.

We might simply take the average between these two dates and make do with the statement that they emerged in Hallstatt for the first time between 1300 and 600 BC, but this would mean abandoning any possibility of getting a few centuries closer to the date in question. We should never be able to reach the point when, in the laconic phrase of Friedrich Morton, who has given us the most thorough archaeological account of Hallstatt, 'suddenly the Celts arrived'. No people enters into history fully equipped with language, national customs and culture, as Athena emerged from the head of Zeus. There are other factors to be considered: in this case, events outside the Alpine region.

That Celts were involved in the Hallstatt culture is beyond question. That the Urnfield people are their ancestors is likewise uncontested. But they themselves required a great deal of foreign influence before anything could emerge which bore their distinctive stamp. What came to them from the other side of the Alps – i.e. from Italy, which since 900 BC had been Etruscan – certainly belongs in this category, as does their inheritance from the Bronze Age. There was, however, more to it. We have to consider a whole set of characteristics, elements of style and also technical innovations that they could have acquired only from the east, from the regions in which there once lived the *Ur*-people.

On the Caspian Sea there grew up, possibly as early as 1800 BC, the third of the three great barbarian peoples among whom the Greeks also included the Iberians and the Celts: the Scythians (though the earliest archaeological evidence dates from around 700 BC). Herodotus tells a story about them that rings true enough:

Each of them cuts off an enemy's head and takes it back home. He then skewers it on a long wooden stave and sets this up so that the head sticks up far above the house, often above the chimney. They maintain that the head is put there as guardian of the whole house. . . . With the heads of their worst enemies they proceed as follows: once they have sawn off everything below the eyebrows, they carefully clean out the head. If the owner is poor he will merely stretch calf-leather round it and use it thus. But if he is rich, he will also line the inside with gold and use it as a drinking vessel. . . . When . . . guests arrive he will bring out these heads and say how they . . . attacked him, and how he defeated them.

Of yet others Herodotus says that they regularly scalped their victims and made towels or garments from the skins. What is more, members of the nearby tribe were said to be magicians, every year changing themselves for a few days into wolves; and the tribe itself was said to be composed of cannibals.

What we have since learnt of the Scythians is sufficient to absolve Herodotus of the charge of telling horror-stories: there was an element of truth in at least two of his reports. The steppe nomads really did believe that their ancestors had been animals. They therefore carried images of them as totems or coats of arms and crowned their rulers with head-pieces shaped like bears, bulls or other animal heads. A man who thought he was descended from wolves may well have worn the open jaws of the proto-dog on his head and imagined himself to be a kind of werewolf. Besides, as regards Herodotus's other story, the Scythians and their neighbours were indeed led by shamans (*shamana*, the Sanskrit word for such priests, means 'magician'). The third detail he mentions, head-hunting, can be written off as a curiosity only if we ignore that the Scythians are among the progenitors of Celtic culture.

What is certain is that towards 1100 BC the steppe people must have come from the Caspian basin – some even say from Iran – towards the Dnieper. Between 800 and 700 BC they drove the neighbouring Cimmerians along the east bank of the Black Sea into Asia Minor. Then the Scythians took the old road into western Europe. Their vanguards reached Silesia, Lower Lusatia, Hungary and perhaps even Bavaria. In all these regions they must have encountered the Urnfield people, whether peaceably or not we do not know. They seem to have influenced and impressed the indigenous peoples, possibly forcing some of their own chiefs on to them as sovereigns. At least the contact did have positive consequences.

The Scythians were by no means savages. Archaeologists have shown that they produced highly developed arts and crafts, a firm political structure, accomplished horsemanship and the capacity to build vast kurgans. One of these 'ancient' or 'thick graves', as Soviet archaeologists call them, was opened at Ordzhonikidze on the lower Dnieper in 1971. It was neither the first found in the Ukraine nor the largest, but it was sufficient to impress its finders.

An enormous quantity of earth had to be removed to get at the principal grave and an adjacent lesser one. Six horses and three grooms were buried around the former. In the stone chamber itself lay a chief or prince. His subjects had provided him with a golden necklace consisting of two dozen tiny cast animal figures, each one perfectly shaped. In the lesser chamber lay the skeletons of a woman and a boy. The boy held a large bracelet, his clothing covered all over with plaques of gold, the largest of them again in animal shapes. The woman had, among other items, a little lacquered box, a bronze mirror with a silver handle and – which impressed the archaeologists most – a glass receptacle dyed a delicate pink. Of course only splinters remained, but the question as to its origin obviously arose – Iran, Mesopotamia, Phoenicia? Even in classical Greece, glassware was a luxury.

The Ordzhonikidze find confirmed what had already been known for some time: that the Scythians were inclined to making exquisite ornaments in animal form, decorating weaponry and clothing with golden or bronze deer, ibexes, lions, bulls, that they were horse-lovers and cattle-raisers and that they wore sleeved smocks and trousers. A carpet that has survived, intact, two millennia in the ice of the Altai mountains shows, moreover, that they threw multi-coloured plaids over their shoulders, grew moustaches and combed their hair up straight.

There are three main conclusions to be drawn: first, that this steppe people had customs similar to those of the original Indo-Europeans, and were thus perhaps related to them; second, that much that seems Celtic in the old Europeans was in reality taken over from the Scythians – as for instance head-hunting and moustaches; finally, that the invaders from the east brought back customs that the descendants of the earlier nomads had gradually forgotten – thus reviving the old inheritance.

This is however only speculation. There is evidence only that later Celtic ornamentation was greatly influenced by Scythian modes. It is also certain that the eastern people gave the westerners a completely new feel for horses, for they provided their mounts with snaffles with two-part bits and movable side-reins, which must have enormously simplified riding. They also stopped the practice of cremation and instead went over to individual burial. The most important feature was the cultivation of an aristocracy, whose members saw it as their privilege to go about on horseback. This too had existed, with chariots, among the Old Europeans since the Indo-European invasion; but with the incursion of the Scythians such features re-emerged correspondingly altered and connected to political practice.

In France the regional cultures of the Urnfield people declined by 700 BC. Shortly after there appeared a new, younger and more variegated culture that spread so rapidly from the east over northern and western Europe that it is assumed to have been carried by the Scythian aristocracy or, as we have mentioned, by the Scythian chiefs themselves or their descendants.

The invasion from the Danube, Silesia and Lower Lusatia occurred in two great phases. Between 900 and 700 BC the first wandering tribes emerged in France and encountered a people of whom we know next to nothing, the Ligurians. They seem to have been farmers, short, muscular and so dangerous in battle that even the tall blond warriors hesitated before taking them on. At the peak of their history they must have spread out west to the Atlantic and south into Italy, where a narrow coastal strip on the Gulf of Genoa bears their name. After the great central European migration those who had settled in the Romagna were expelled by the Indo-European Sabines; others in Provence were still enjoying a certain prosperity eight hundred years later.

Their settlements, which they generally established on high ground, contained stone houses put together without mortar and coated on the inside with a mixture of mud and broken straw. Such a hill-village has been dug up near La Pègue on the lower course of the Rhône. It illustrates a whole segment of Ligurian history and also makes clear what the invaders from the east in the main owed to this people: contact with Greek merchants and their civilization.

In the remains of these square stone dwellings were Attic pots and also native pottery which imitated or transformed the Greek style. This shows that Greek seafarers who sought a route to the Spanish copper-mines in the seventh century BC, mainly from the town of Phocaea in Asia Minor, had developed vigorous trading links with the Ligurians of southern France. Around 600 BC they founded what is now Marseilles east of the mouth of the Rhône. Some decades earlier, at Istre on the edge of the Rhône delta, had arisen the settlement of Mastramele. Both points served the same purpose: control of the end of the ancient trade-route by which tin was transported from Brittany to the Mediterranean.

The Ligurians, too, profited from dealings in this important commodity. Now newcomers tried to get a share in what must have been, at least to start with, a peaceful enough attempt. At the foot of La Pègue arose a non-Ligurian settlement, a trading-post or agency, a feeler extended by the stronger power that was already being established further north. It was not the only such outpost. After the mid-sixth century BC links between the Greek towns on the Mediterranean coast of France and the area of the upper Rhône and the Danube grew closer and closer. There developed an economic activity that was to be astonishingly fruitful. Market-places

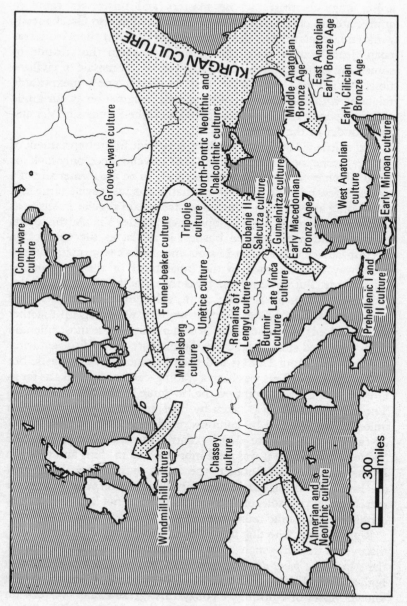

Map 7   The spread of the Kurgan culture in Europe

arose, huge fortresses whose masters and mistresses came to appreciate not only Etruscan bucchero vases but also Greek metal-work and, in particular, the sweet, heady wines of the Mediterra-nean. Jean-Jacques Hatt even imputes to them the creation of something approaching a 'European market', a mosaic of civiliza-tions 'which had very close and, at first glance, inexplicable relations with one another'. With a little imagination as our guide let us now look at two of these potentates, the Princess of Vix and the founder of the Heuneburg.

Vix, a little village near Châtillon-sur-Seine in the department of Haute-Marne, needs no landmark: the traveller need only look for a hill which even from a distance appears to be the former site of a castle. A few miles north-west of Châtillon is just such a large hill, protruding above the meadows and streams, as regular in shape as if it were man-made. On its slopes there nestles Vix. At the top its surface, hidden by stunted bushes, is as flat as the deck of an aircraft-carrier. That Mont Lassois once had a castle on its summit has always been known to the inhabitants of the surrounding countryside. But not until 1929 was the rumour, which archaeolo-gists had written off as mere myth, substantiated. In a ten-year campaign over a million pieces of pottery were dug up together with hundreds of weapons and ornaments and – the most splendid items – worked amber and coral. An interpretation of the evidence revealed that Mont Lassois had been crowned not by a castle but by a whole town. This was both a trading-centre with links as far as Greece, and a check-point on the tin-route to the Mediterranean. The valuable metal was taken by boat up the Seine to Vix, then unloaded and carried by columns of pack-animals or caravans of ox-carts over the Côte d'Or's central mountain-range into the Saône valley, where it was once more stowed in ships and taken to Lyons and along the Rhône to the Greek coastal cities. What part the lords of Vix played in this forwarding enterprise – whether merely by levying tolls or as co-organizers – is not known, but they certainly made some money out of it.

René Joffroy, who dug into one of their graves in January 1953, discovered treasures such as have seldom been found on this side of the Alps. The *pièce de résistance* was a bronze receptacle five feet high and weighing four hundred and fifty pounds; it was the largest known vessel of Antiquity. Today this 'great Crater' (Greek for 'mixing-jug') is in the museum of Châtillon-sur-Seine. It is debatable whether we should call it beautiful or merely imposing. It resembles a toy for giants or for an ostentatious millionaire. Its handles bear grinning masks with their tongues sticking out; its rim is decorated with a column of Greek warriors on foot and in two-wheeled chariots. It probably came from Laconia and is faultlessly worked. But I cannot avoid the impression that the whole piece was constructed for export only, to underdeveloped lands – much as we manufacture automobiles with gold-plated radiator grilles to gladden the hearts of Arab potentates.

But the Crater, at least in death, did not belong to a man. The grave where Joffroy found it was that of a young woman, whose personal ornamentation shows undoubted taste. Her half-moon-shaped diadem of twenty-four-carat solid gold is of such timeless elegance that it would have brought credit to a modern designer. She was given everything a well-run household needs: Attic black-figured wine cups, Greek wine-jugs, Etruscan copper beakers and even a four-wheeled cart – at least its wheels. As to who this lady might have been, there has been a great deal of understandable puzzlement among pre-historians.

The Crater cannot, despite the attached wine-sieve, have been used exclusively for mixing wine, a practice that in any case few peoples went in for in northern Europe. It could just as well have been used as a receptacle for the blood shed at ritual sacrifices. Does not Strabo tell us that the Cimbri cut their prisoners' throats over sacred vessels? Do not the Berne *Scholien* (a medieval commentary on the writings of the Greek poet Lucian) talk of Celtic tribes which, to honour Teutates, 'put men's heads into a pot so that they would be stifled'? This is admittedly speculation, but sacral vessels were indeed an important element in barbarian cults in western Europe.

The other question – whether women were capable of performing or supervising such brutal practices – only makes ethnologists and experts in the field of Antiquity frown. What about the priestesses of Dionysus who tore their victims apart? Is it therefore not possible that the tender lady of the grave of Vix owed her high social rank not only to noble origins but also to the dark cult amid which she lived? Standing on Mont Lassois, surrounded by peaceful farming country, it is hard to imagine that this remote spot was an important trading centre, a focus of power and wealth, and the site of dark ceremonies to protect men from the envious Fates.

And yet gold and blood have always gone together, though we ourselves are now less conscious of it for today it is only in seemingly
distant parts of the globe that men die for our prosperity.

Once you have seen Mont Lassois you can quite easily track
down its German counterpart, the Heuneburg on the upper
Danube. Both have a similar situation by a river, and both equally
dominate the surrounding countryside. But the hill of Vix stands
isolated, a purely geological phenomenon, whereas the Heuneburg
rises up out of low mountains and was man-made.

What the archaeologists discovered here was not so spectacular
as the gigantic Crater, but it was sensational enough. Around the
Heuneburg were built, in the sixth and fifth centuries BC, when the
men of Lassois were carrying on their tin trade, two other great
forts and four so-called 'square earthworks', meant for religious
purposes, and a series of the inevitable burial mounds. Of these
buildings the Heuneburg, overlooking the little village of Hundersingen, is by far the most imposing and interesting. Earth ramparts
thirty feet high protected an inner area trapezoid in shape and three
thousand square yards in area. Outer works of ramparts and
trenches leading to the Danube gave additional security. Several
generations participated in the construction, the first of them as
early as the period of the central European migration. At the time
it may have served as a fortified refuge. It was completed by an
architect who either came from or had visited the Mediterranean
area.

He did not use the usual local building materials but tried
instead to erect a wall of air-dried mud bricks interrupted, at regular intervals, by forward bastions. Similar fortifications can be
found on some hills in Provence. There they were made out of
natural rock and have survived. The brick walls could not long
have withstood the humid German climate, and the builder may
have foreseen this. He set them up only on one side of the central
trapezium, the one that seemed least vulnerable.

So long as this wall stood it must have dominated the Danube
valley even more impressively than the earth-walls of today, less a
place of refuge than a centre of power that also controlled traderoutes and established 'world-wide' connections. The Heuneburg
could have been another centre of that 'European market' that men
with clear political and commercial instincts were beginning to set
up in the middle Hallstatt era. To visualize them, we have to

imagine a prince anxious to secure his own possessions by the most up-to-date means possible, who put out feelers simultaneously to Ligurian trading posts, Etruscan manufactures, Greek ports and perhaps also staked his own forces in a game whose prizes were the products of advanced industries, as well as gold, metals and wine.

Life in the castle seems however to have been provincial rather than brilliant. The inside resembled a small peasant village, with houses for men of the retinue and servants, rustic banquet-halls and taverns, stables and coach-houses. It was the starting-point for warlike or commercial expeditions (much as would be the Hohenzollerns' nearby family seat, on the edge of the Schwäbischer Alp). Men came back defeated to lick their wounds, unless they had found some more impressive residence far away, where they could forget the thick mud around the native hearth and the path-ways between the stables and the living-quarters which in rainy weather turned to marsh.

The lord of the Heuneburg was, like the Princess of Vix, the representative of a changing society. At this time features of various cultures – Bronze Age, Scythian, Greek – gradually coalesced into a new pattern: the Celtic. This process is not clear-cut. The men of Mont Lassois and the Swabians who mounted guard on the mud-ramparts of the Heuneburg may or may not be called Celts. What encourages us to do so is the fact that their culture is already strongly marked by features that can later be seen in Celts that have, as it were, academic credentials. Against this there is only the suspicion, albeit difficult to overcome, that such a warrior-people could hardly have entered into history by setting up trading-posts. We would naturally expect these moustachioed and wood demons to make a less peaceful entrance.

This is just what they did. The 'European market', which had for over two hundred years given the men of the Danube valley and Bohemia, the Alps and northern France a wealth hardly known since the Bronze Age, was suddenly destroyed by tribes who seem to have felt that this business was not their affair at all. At the same time their battle hordes appeared for the first time in northern Italy. What caused these troubles is a question that once again can be answered only with hypotheses; one has been put forward by Livy.

At the time of king Tarquinius Priscus, Livy says, the Bituriges were the leading tribe among the Celts. One third of Gaul belonged to them and the land was so rich that its king, Ambigatus, reckoned that it was barely possible for him to reign over such large numbers. He therefore sought to free his kingdom from this burdensome superfluity, and besides he was very old. He made known that he would send his two nephews Bellovesus and Sigovesus, an enterprising pair of lads, towards whichever lands, by the flight of birds, the Gods indicated as their home. So many were to accompany them that the influx would be irresistible.

The birds took off, the priests did the interpreting: Sigovesus was given the Mittelgebirge in Germany, while 'Bellovesus was granted a much more favourable route by the gods, that into Italy. He now collected all men who could be spared by their peoples – Bituriges, Arverni, Senones, Aedui, Ambarres, Carnutes, Aulercii – set off with a large force on foot and on horseback and reached the Tricastin' on the lower Rhône.

'Now in the west the Alps lay before him' – more properly, Haute Provence. As these mountains seemed to be barren, the force initially joined up with Greeks from Phocaea who were at that time founding Massilia and having some difficulty with a tribe living there. They finally went, anticipating Hannibal's route, over the Alps. Like the Carthaginians they staged their first battle on the Ticinus (Tessin), except here they faced not Romans but Etruscans. Having won the battle, they settled and founded Mediolanum (Milan). Other tribes followed, as both Polybius and Livy tell us.

Livy's description is not completely confirmed by archaeologists. Milan, they say, was founded a century before the Celts' irruption and Tarquinius Priscus, one of the legendary kings of early Rome, also lived long before this invasion, at the end of the seventh century BC. Moreover the centre of Celtic unrest was not France but the region of the Heuneburg. There, in around 520 BC, villages began to be burned, ramparts torn down and hidden stores plundered. From the upper Danube a wave of destruction spread to the valley of the Rhine, on to eastern France, reaching the Rhône valley and finally northern Italy. The whole network of market-places and trade-routes that had arisen in the previous centuries was torn apart. Ligurians and Greeks armed themselves for a life and death struggle, as had the other potentates threatened by this migration.

In Mastramele was erected a giant protecting wall, nearly a mile long and made of hewn stone blocks. The little village near La Pègue, which already overlooked an outpost of the northern intruders, was destroyed. But the Etruscans, whose land according to Livy was one of the goals of the wandering hordes, seem to have adapted to the new situation. They gave up, for almost a century, their trading links with the inhabitants of Provence, and began instead to send their wares over the Alpine passes into Germany and thence to eastern France via the Rhine and the Moselle. Wine-dealers such as the cuckolded Aruns of Clusium may at that time have discovered the Celts as new direct customers. For the invaders of the Golfe du Lion (called by Strabo 'the Gallic Gulf') commerce on a large scale was over for the rest of the century. The Celts had done everything to justify their later bloodthirsty reputation, for the whole area they had crossed now lay in ruins. Meanwhile the Hallstatt culture flourished.

Graves in the field by the salt-mountain dating from after the great invasion contain fibulae, a sort of ornamental safety-pin known to have existed in the early and middle Bronze Age. Many of them had loose, dangling metal clappers. All of a sudden we find a preference for rattles of all sorts – possibly a Scythian fashion. The swords of those days must have been fashioned by smiths who understood bronze-casting well but were less proficient when it came to iron-working. They dissipated their gifts in particular on magnificent hilts made of a copper and tin alloy. One fine example has a strong ivory pommel, the trapezoid shape of which is accentuated by inlaid plaques of amber. Cattle also seem to have played a decisive part in economic life. At Hallstatt alone were found five representations of horned domestic animals. The finest of these embellishes an ornamental bronze vessel. Scholars think that it may have served the same purpose as the Crater of Vix.

The old Alpine cattle can hardly be compared with their modern descendants. They were quite close to the Ur-cow, though they were already being selected according to certain breeding characteristics. Their owners laid particular stress on a white blaze on the forehead, no doubt as a target for the sacral weapon that was to kill the animal in ritual sacrifice. But this practice did not prevent profane use of the herds. The word alp – the source of the name not only for the European range but also, in Swiss dialect, for the high summer-meadows and dairy farming known in Austria and

Bavaria as *Alm* – is of Celtic origin. It went over into Latin and was later re-adopted. It has from that time been the custom to celebrate the first day of May, when the cattle are driven up to their pastures.

Little as the rich, salt-trading dairy-farmers of the central Alps were involved in the Celtic invasion of northern Italy, they did feel its effects to some extent. The rising trade with Etruria encouraged their Celticization, for they now dealt directly with the warriors from the Danube basin who had settled on the Po and in South Tyrol. This can be seen from finds which date from around 500 BC. The Hallstatt culture at the time consisted of two great regions; one in the west showing increasingly clear Celtic features; and an eastern one in Carinthia, the north Adriatic and Yugoslavia, affected by their cousins the Illyrians and the Veneti. Only now did the three peoples originally from Bohemia begin to separate distinctly; though there was never complete separation, there being Celtic elements in Illyrian art and Illyrian ones in Celtic.

However even at this stage concepts such as Celtic and Illyrian would still have to be used with caution, were it not for an event in the middle of the first millennium BC that experts, according to temperament, consider 'miraculous' or merely 'enigmatic': the rise of a new culture in the western Hallstatt region. Only its existence justifies our now talking unambiguously of 'Celts'. Philologists, normally the most important authorities when it comes to separating one people from another, confirm this in their own way. They believe that the warriors who terrified Rome and Greece belonged to a group of tribes who for a long time spoke related dialects; but only at the end of the sixth century BC did they fuse into a larger unit, thereby promoting the development of a common language. If they are right – and it is hardly to be doubted – this also means that henceforth all the conditions were met that nineteenth-century Europe regarded as the criteria of nationhood. Herder and Fichte believed that a people demonstrates its historical identity through its own native culture. The process through which this emerged was thought to be identical with the coalescence of a people. However the French, among them Ernest Renan, believed that the 'nation' was a 'daily repeated plebiscite'; anyone who accepted its values might belong to it. Overlooking the contradiction between these two views and taking them instead as twin halves of a single whole, it may be helpful to apply them to the Celts. Their various peoples must at some stage have decided to merge; this decision was later sealed by the creation of a new culture. The question then remains as to what led to this decision. To answer it we must persist with hypotheses and the sparsest evidence.

EIGHT

Head-hunters, Artists and Entrepreneurs

All economic development can be seen as a continual diminishing and
devolution of the privileges of birth.
Friedrich Ebert, *Inaugural Address of the President of the Reich*

A monarch has the advantage over an ordinary head of state that he
can make political capital of the fruits of his loins and enlarge his
domains more effectively by cleverly arranged marriages than
another ruler can by war. This was the case in the Hallstatt era.
Archaeologists have established that in widely separated communities a similar style often prevails. Thus there are astonishing
similarities between objects found at Mailhac in southern France
and in the seats of a Spanish and a Bavarian monarch. Jean-Jacques
Hatt explains this as follows: a ruler on the Danube gave his son in
marriage to a princess in the Languedoc, thus joining her possessions to his. As her inheritance included domains south of the
Pyrenees, three different courts became involved in a single
gambit. They would then co-ordinate their interests, trade and
politics, acquire goods from the same sources and, for heraldic
reasons, decorate their weapons with the same ornaments. There
was nothing at all unusual in this. Feudal lords have always seen
the basis of their power less in their nation than in their clan, and
have therefore sought to bind its members together as closely as
possible. It was by this means that the Habsburgs brought a great
empire into existence, and it is reasonable to compare the era in

which their house rose to greatness with that of the Princess of Vix and the Junker of the Heuneburg.

Jean-Jacques Hatt's 'European market' was a system of little states similar to those that in the Middle Ages ruled the area between the Baltic and the Mediterranean, sometimes competing, sometimes collaborating. But just as these feudal possessions were gradually whittled down in the course of a struggle lasting centuries to make way for modern nation-states, so the Hallstatt kingdoms must have succumbed to men's refusal to respect the zones of influence that a few sovereigns had artificially established. In fact the storm that swept them away would strike us as a series of senseless civil wars, unless it is interpreted – to pursue the analogy with modern European history – as the outcome of internal troubles, indeed as an outburst of revolutionary character.

With the goods that were taken north from Marseilles, new ideas may have penetrated the hinterland of the Mediterranean coast, ideas about whose nature it is obviously idle to speculate. However they could have sufficed to give a new generation an unfavourable picture of their own circumstances, to breed discontent and eventual unrest. Older lords who could or would not adapt to the new mood were overthrown; young men – in the main, noblemen – took power and established themselves through fratricidal struggles. It is conceivable that national, and even Pan-Celtic, notes were sounded in these quarrels. The tribes from France, Swabia, Bavaria and Bohemia had become acquainted with each other in the days of the trading princes, and had learned they were a community with similar customs, views, way of life, language. They grasped that they belonged to a single great people. Now they wanted to take over a suitable region for themselves. That their momentum carried them over the existing boundaries is not surprising. More recent peoples have done as much: the French after the Revolution, the Germans after their wars of unification.

Livy and Strabo borrowed mythical models to explain the abrupt Celtic advance. All they could imagine were kings who would send their superfluous population over the border, princes in rivalry or, as with Polybius, an unmotivated explosion of battle-lust. The thought that the blond warriors appearing in northern Italy and later in Greece could be representatives of a people that had just found its identity and was carried away by the discovery did not occur to them, although it is an obvious explanation, and becomes all the more probable when we consider the economic background to the Celtic troubles of the fifth century BC.

A technological revolution had taken place in the soot-blackened smithies of the day. In the last years of the Hallstatt epoch iron-working advanced so far that pre-historians reckon that the European Bronze Age ended with the opening of this era. Iron could now be properly worked not just as a material for prestige-objects such as weaponry, but also for everyday utensils. What the Hittites had managed to achieve even before 1400 BC now lay within the capacity of craftsmen in the Alps and on the Seine. They knew how to drop oil or water on a glowing piece of metal to harden it – perhaps, as in the Arab east, preferring blood, because in the process it produces phosphorus. They had learnt how to weld iron bars together, from which tough blades would then be hammered (a process later called damascening), and to inlay various metals into one other – bronze strips were shaped into animals or other patterns and pressed into pieces of iron into which a negative impression had previously been struck. By the early Middle Ages the Europeans had forgotten this art and it was, like damascening, re-imported from Damascus and the East.

More important than such artistry was of course the fact that, with iron-ore, there was a raw material accessible virtually every-where. Five per cent of the earth's surface is composed of it and even today the soil of western Europe contains about twenty-five thousand billion tons. With the capacity for iron-working it was no longer necessary to use the long trade-routes over which British or Slovak tin had to be brought. Iron thus threatened the monopoly of a few dynastic houses over the far-flung communications network. In the smithies they were acquiring a native competitor. That affected them not only in the markets but in another area in which they were no less vulnerable. The anvils produced, among other things, wheeled ploughs with iron shares, which made possible the farming of the heavy fertile valley soil. Parallel and deep furrows served as irrigation ditches and drained off the superfluous water. There was an end to the days when grain-farmers could cultivate only dry and mainly stony slopes or plateaus, and one of the oldest conflicts of mankind re-appeared: between Cain and Abel, agriculture and stock-raising, farmer and cowboy.

Men with earth-breaking tools occupied the fertile meadows and pushed the roaming herd-drivers to those barren fields that had been their domain. This could not happen without much quarrelling and fighting, even rebellion, because since nomadic times cattle had been mobile capital, a pillar of aristocratic wealth. Dealings with cattle had sharpened men's commercial instincts. The

ERA		CULTURE	PEOPLE
Up to 4000BC		Early Stone Age	
4000-1800BC		Late Stone Age	
Bronze Age		Passage-grave	Indo-European
		Tumulus	
		Early Urnfield	
1000BC		Late Urnfield	
Iron Age	Hallstatt era	Hallstatt	Rise of the Celts and Illyrians
	500BC		
	La Tène era	La Tène	Celts
	15BC		

The pre-history of the Hallstatt era

great barter-places almost all emerged from cattle or horse-markets, the trade-routes from paths over which cattle had been driven. A man controlling both could count on hordes of warriors, who were easily recruited from adventurous and mobile shepherds. This hegemony was now called into question. A new and strengthened class wanted greater rights from the older class, and economic sense was entirely on its side.

The iron goods made possible not only more intensive agriculture but also rationalized cattle-raising. Inexpensive scythes could cut the grass so it could be stored in barns; in many regions a change could be made from summer to winter wheat. Cattle that no longer needed to be constantly driven over long roads could now put on flesh; cows kept in an enclosure or in a stable could give more milk. The land and the soil became more valuable, villages grew into towns, organized states became conceivable and could have been set up, the more so as in the new society classes began to emerge. Besides the professional warriors there were farmers, artisans and traders. The Druids formed something like an intellectual caste, whose members must have been capable of fulfilling the tasks of judges, priests and poets.

But it is doubtful whether the Celts did take the final step towards a greater community. All we know is that younger rulers put together new thrones out of the ruins of the old powers, that they built cities, set up industries and throughout were no doubt able to rely on the national (more properly, tribal) feeling that had meanwhile developed. The existence of this new consciousness can be attested only if we follow Herder's or Fichte's conception of things. If we accept their debatable argument that where there is a culture, there will be a people, and vice versa, the rich art of the La Tène era may be seen as testimony to the existence of a new, rising Celtic nation.

La Tene is a shallow area at the northern end of the Neuenburg Lake in Switzerland. Early in 1858 the amateur archaeologist Colonel Schwab brought up almost two thousand finds: swords, spears, fibulae, tools. Many of them show signs of decoration such as scholars had never seen: stylized tendrils entwining almost naturalistic animal figures. That these ornaments were of Celtic origin was, from the beginning, clear to almost everyone. That they belonged to an as yet unknown culture only a few bold interpreters dared suggest.

A specific search for further objects of the 'La Tène style' brought a rich reward over almost the whole area the Celts had inhabited. It was shown that the style had developed in the area between the Meuse, Neckar and Main, and had spread quite rapidly. Experts were soon describing it as the first 'independent artistic achievement of any significance north of the Alps', in

Pörtner's words, since Ice Age art. The era in which it flourished begins around 450 BC and ends, at least on the Continent, around 50 BC. It marks the apogee of the history of the European head-hunters and an examination of it reveals curious phenomena.

'Greek ornament,' says Paul Jacobsthal, one of the main interpreters of the La Tène style, 'uncovers the abstract laws underlying the world of plants. In Celtic bowls and shield-fittings, by contrast, organic nature is present in a quite different sense: here we are reminded of the flowering of spring, its lush blossoms, the bowels of nature.' Jean-Jacques Hatt supplements this: 'The originality of Gallic art consists in a tendency towards, on the one hand, stylization and, on the other, an expressionism that gives its representations of human beings, animals and gods a fantastical and disturbing character. This art is the very opposite of Greek and Roman humanism and rationalism.'

It differs, of course, from Mediterranean classicism in another respect as well. While the Greeks of the fifth and the fourth centuries BC equipped their monumental temples in part with gigantic statues, the Celts toyed with small, even tiny, forms. Their artists produced figures of human beings and of gods which were, at most, of average human height. The smiths covered tiny surfaces of pots, sword-sheaths and ornaments with a maze of lines, animal figures and faces. Details were not merely suggested but chiselled out on an almost microscopic scale. If they wanted to have a column of warriors defile along the sides of a bronze vessel, they would depict them in such detail that we can see whether their coats have fringed or straight hems. Outstanding torcs contain masks smaller than a thumbnail, with fully modelled faces – arched eyebrows, goggling eyes, bulbous noses and mouths turned down sarcastically at the corners. Such filigree work could hardly have been done with more precision by jewellers working with magnifying glasses. They revelled above all in endless arabesques, arches, curves, performing every imaginable variation on each motif.

They seldom bothered with the effect of two contrasting surfaces, preferring to fill in whatever could be filled in, as if horrified by bare metal. All their figures are enclosed in a rich network of tendrils, allowing play of light and shade only on a miniature scale. They seem to strive ceaselessly inward: into hollows, the womb, the belly, or, as Jacobsthal conceives it, into the very bowels of nature. Everything they created is redolent of the senses. Many of their works are pleasing to the eye, but also evoke a desire to possess them, the more so as most of them could be effortlessly carried away. Others are like windows, through which we can see, as it were, into the world of the Celts. They tell stories, as for instance the Gundestrup Cauldron and a sword-sheath found at Hallstatt.

On the latter, riders in checked clothing are following a group of foot-soldiers and, unmoved, trample into the dust an enemy lying on the ground. The other figures, in garish trousers and smocks – the colours suggested by varied hatching – are holding a wheel. It might be a windlass with which miners help one another out of the shaft, or the sun, or a symbol of rebirth. But on the sides of the Gundestrup Cauldron, found in 1880 in a Danish peat-bog, the whole pantheon of the Celts, worked in silver, looks down on us. A god with antlers sits in the position Buddha recommended to his disciples for meditation – legs crossed, right foot resting on the left calf – amid a veritable menagerie of mythological animals. In one hand he holds a torc, in the other a snake with a ram's head; flowers blossom around him; a little figure rides through the air on a dolphin. The seated god is thought to be Cernunnos, lord of the Underworld. Another panel depicts Teutates, moustachioed, with side-whiskers, beard, and hair carefully curled over the forehead (each individual hair can be made out); he is holding in both hands men wearing a kind of knitted garment. On a further panel, a powerful figure looks on as, to its left, a helmeted man fights and, to its right, defeats a monster. This is thought to be identifiable as a mother-goddess. On the interior panels of the bowl, where Cernunnos sits enthroned, swarm winged, bird-headed quadrupeds with eagles' claws, crosses between horse and lion, giraffe-necked bucks and grinning snakes. There are even elephants with rhinoceros hides.

The most delicate scene shows a graceful maiden with a horned helmet. She crouches near the sky-god Taranis; her shapely arms and legs are revealed by a tight-fitting mini-dress which looks as though it could have come from the boutique next door. The most hideous scene is a ritual sacrifice such as the priestess of Vix might have conducted. A man is hurled head-first into a cauldron while sinister warriors look on. Trumpeters, whose instruments are taller than a man and end in open animal jaws, provide musical accompaniment: a tableau that recalls the visions of Hieronymus Bosch.

The blood of any Greek that saw it would have frozen in his veins. But we might class it somewhere between Gothic gargoyles and the surrealist paintings of Max Ernst. In any event the Celtic style sometimes seems astonishingly modern. In Jacobsthal's words: 'It anticipates rhythms and formal principles that do not return or take effect for centuries.'

La Tène art developed as did each succeeding style: classical and romantic or baroque phases alternated. Eras in which clear lines and sober motifs predominate are followed by wild outbursts of formal experimentation. Between 400 and 350 BC clear Scythian motifs can again be found in Celtic art. During the next hundred years, however, a classical tendency was dominant. The craftsmen controlled their urge to allow ornamentation to proliferate, sometimes even leaving empty spaces between decorative motifs. The result is a clear, calm style of great elegance.

The Gundestrup Cauldron seems, in comparison with the work of this period, almost primitive, though it itself came from the late La Tène period, after 120 BC. We might assume that its creators, as modern artists sometimes do, consciously went back to imitate an earlier style, or that they no longer had the power to develop new forms. But it is also possible that such stories could be related only according to traditional rules, that the attempt to banish demons was a sacred task.

The vessel itself could quite easily have belonged to the equipment of a ritual sacrifice. It is certainly large enough: fourteen inches high, twenty-eight inches in diameter, it weighs nearly twenty pounds. The figures on its sides seem to come from the Celts' own version of hell, their collective subconscious. Here dwelt other beings as well. At Roquepertuse in Provence was found a Janus-head which, bald, cold and albino-white, stares into the light as through the putrefying fumes of a knacker's yard. From Noves in the same area came a stone animal – rampant, its front paws on the severed heads of two slain men, while the arm of a third dangles from its hideous jaws. Today this monster stands in the Musée Lapidaire at Avignon. It may be seen for two francs but it can give only a feeble impression of the nightmares that probably engendered it. Though this may help the visitor with his night's sleep, it is unsatisfactory because the description of such terrors was taken particularly seriously by the Celtic artists and because in them we may perhaps find a key to their nature. On the surface, which is what we see, La Tène art is of course brilliant, refulgent and technically perfect.

The Celts of that time completely absorbed Mediterranean techniques and elaborated them with great sophistication. Not only could they inlay metals but, long before the invention of the necessary rolling equipment, they were also capable of producing the finest iron. They even seem to have mastered the casting of soft iron, a technique once thought to have been perfected only in the later nineteenth century. As tin was relatively expensive they invented a sort of brass, for which instead of zinc – unknown to them in its pure form – they used the mineral carbonate of zinc. They could also cover copper objects with tin and may have been the first in the whole world to silver them over with mercury, for they were able to produce and distil this extremely poisonous element with the sureness of touch of experienced alchemists. Furthermore they could boil ornamental glass, coloured and white, and knew how to enamel.

Their weaving and dyeing techniques must also have been highly developed. Men wore close-fitting trousers and pullovers, obviously sewn; women, freely-flowing cloaks of the same material. The colourfulness of their cloaks and jackets that so impressed Diodorus can also be found in the human figures of the La Tène artists. The fact that the most significant work they left behind came not from sculptors and architects but from smiths implies that even after the introduction of intensive agriculture they retained their dislike of all property that tied a person down. Everything they owned could at any time be easily and rapidly removed, and they put their wealth into movable goods, such as precious vessels, ornaments and weaponry. They never trusted the peace that occasionally befell them, always remaining like nomads, ready to move even when they had for long lived in fixed settlements and towns.

They also devoted much care to the manufacture of weapons. Their magnificent helmets could be more easily imagined adorning the head of a Pyrrhus or a Eumenes than on some nameless moustachioed chief. The chain-mail of Celtic princes, judging from the stone representations we have, could have stood comparison with those of the High Middle Ages. The swords of the La Tène era are evidence not only of a highly developed sense of formal beauty and functionalism, but also of changing tactical conceptions.

Around 450 BC these swords were, as in the Hallstatt period, relatively short and pointed: large daggers for stabbing if the lance-attack got bogged down in hand-to-hand fighting. One hundred and fifty years later the swords could also be used for cutting, as in the Bronze Age. At the time of the great battles in northern Italy the Celtic sword was used only for cutting. It was rounded at the end and the swordsmen seem to have relied on the shock of their first attack, striking at the enemy from their horses or, in infantry action, trusting to their superior height. How this was later to be turned against them, Polybius has shown. His assertion that the blades of Celtic weapons were of such inferior material that they bent after the first blow can be explained by the fact that only the cutting-edge was of costly steel, while the rest of the weapon was of poorer metal. Commanders were no doubt better equipped. It was certainly no cheap sword that was carried on to the battlefield in sheaths such as the one from Hallstatt; and Brennus must have thrown a richly ornamented ceremonial broadsword on to the Roman scales.

This is also true of the shields. The finest surviving examples – such as the 'Battersea Shield' in the British Museum – are masterpieces of the smith's art, large enough to cover a man from the knee to the chin. They were rectangular or double-trapezoid in shape, sometimes with bosses or kidney-shaped indentations in the centre. But the common soldier must have had only a leather-covered board for his protection and was thus naturally inferior – especially when his *furor* made him abandon all caution – to the legionary, who carried a tall, broad and arched *scutum* of Roman design.

Altogether the Celts' greatest error seems to have been that they relied too much on natural superiority and never undertook the hard work of exploiting and organizing their resources. Creating the La Tène culture was easy, mere child's play for them. In less than one hundred and fifty years – in about four generations – it reached its peak. But they manifestly failed in the attempt – if indeed they ever made it – to set up one or more large states; although on a smaller scale they did here and there create what they never managed on a larger scale.

The old trade-route between the mouth of the Rhône and the area
north of the Alps was almost completely restored by the early
fourth century BC. Greek influences again began to be superimposed on the Etruscan ones that had prevailed in the later
Hallstatt period. Marseilles and neighbouring cities such as Nikaia
(Nice) became once more a focal point for the tribes living in
Provence and southern Germany. The Celts themselves now advanced towards the Mediterranean and became accustomed to
living in towns, as for instance on the hill of Nages.

Nages is a little Provençal village, a few miles west of Nîmes. It
has houses of quarry-stone, a little railway station, relaxed *boule*-
players in the shade of the great evergreen oaks. If you ask for the
Celtic settlement, they will nod nonchalantly in its direction. What
one finds on the great plateau above the village makes up for the
difficult climb. Walls between two and five yards thick, faultlessly
assembled without mortar from unhewn rock, dominate the wild
maquis. Massive semi-circular bastions occur at intervals and in
front of it is a labyrinth of little dwellings, jostling one another, of
which only the foundations survive. Sometimes you can see that a
house was often separated from another only by a narrow passage,
sometimes barely shoulder-wide. You have the impression of
sitting in the ruins of a giant ant-hill, nestling on both sides of the
rampart, so that it is hard to distinguish between what was *extra
muros* and *intra muros*.

The *maquis* makes it difficult to make out at a glance how large
the settlement was. Archaeologists have laid bare only a small
segment, but believe the surrounding wall was over half a mile
long. Why the settlement was established here is easy to see. From
its walls there is a fine view over the plain in which Nîmes lies. It
was at once castle, look-out post and place of refuge. If war came
men could flee with all their herds to the plateau and stay there for
months. But the town above Nages is not a Celtic foundation. It
must have been created by Ligurians. They had first fought, then
co-operated with and finally intermixed with the invaders from the
north. At the end of the La Tène period their hill-town was one of,
in all, twenty-four settlements around Nîmes. The old Nemausus
was then a centre of the Volcae, a people to which, as Strabo
supposes, the Tectosages belonged.

The remains of Entremont, another of these hill-towns which
have come to be known by Caesar's name of 'oppidum', offer a

rather more profound insight into the lives of its inhabitants. High above Aix-en-Provence, it has a more regular ground-plan than the ancient ant-heap of Nages, which was repeatedly built on. Its streets meet each other more or less at right angles. There were subterranean drains that led into the open through the ramparts, a bakery with a brick-kiln with fine walls, and a rectangular temple. Here too the dwellings themselves were tiny, containing the bare necessities of life but no trace of comfort. Life must have gone on in the open air, on the mighty, three-tier rampart (again of quarry-stone and constructed without mortar) and under the beautiful old oaks that must have shaded the oppidum. That it was Celts who lived here is shown, as in all their settlements, by the skulls with nails driven into them that were found among the ruins, by the niches in the wall from which these skulls grinned and by the door-beams hollowed out to accommodate such trophies.

A stranger sauntering through Entremont must have believed that he was in an inhabited ossuary or, so long as there was still flesh on the bones, in an execution-yard. And yet it was also a little town, with children playing and women hanging out their washing in front of the houses. But the imagination fails when it comes to putting these details together into one picture, and it is hard to believe that in such surroundings modest metal-workers could create the objects of La Tène art, which at least to some extent had aesthetic pretensions. But so it was: the beautiful and the hideous went hand in hand. This must have been difficult for the neigh-bouring Greeks to understand. For all the economic benefit that the inhabitants of the Marseilles region could get from them, the Celto-Ligurians were very difficult partners, the more so as oppida like Entremont had full control over the trade-routes.

But where Hellenes and Celts had closer contact, there developed cities of bewitching simplicity and wholly agreeable character, particularly when a third element was introduced, the Iberians.

Near Ensérune, north of Narbonne in the Languedoc, a settle-ment of the late fifth century BC was excavated that must have been built by men consciously adopting Greek architectural principles and trying to realize them with their own methods. They imitated the chessboard pattern of towns like Miletus or Piraeus and sup-ported the roof-beams of their houses with pillars taken from Doric and Ionian models – though this does not necessarily mean they gave up using them to carry barbarian trophies. Admittedly the Celtic inhabitants of the Languedoc seem to have been more anxious to adapt than the rough descendants of Nordic invaders and resident Ligurians. This was because they had intermingled with the Iberians, a people living on both sides of the Pyrenees.

Strabo reports that they were proud, arrogant and easily provoked, but also musical and rather frivolous – the last because the women apparently held the men's hands while dancing. Curiously they also did not drink wine but great quantities of beer instead. They liked great banquets and were skilful metal-workers. On the Iberian peninsula, which had continually attracted peoples with the gold and silver in its mountains, they must early on have come into contact with representatives of the great Mediterranean cultures, particularly the Phoenician. Though they always fought hard against invaders, contact with these cannot have been fruitless. They became cleverer, more civilized, more adaptable, and hence must have passed on part of their experience to the Celts, who were always anxious to learn. This put a stamp on their joint creations that distinguished them from the men of the old Ligurian region. As we shall see, its inhabitants too did not in the long run resist the spirit emanating from Marseilles and other Greek towns.

Near Saint-Rémy-de-Provence, at the end of a ravine cut into the bald, sun-baked rock of the Alpilles mountains, the Ligurians had a sacred grove that is so beautiful as to beggar description. It is a spring, in the shade of trees clinging to the rock, and was probably dedicated to the water gods. The Celts later became associated with it and worshipped their own Cernunnos, who was depicted, as on the Gundestrup Cauldron, seated in the lotus position. Still later came the Greeks, and the temple precincts became first a Nymphaeon, wherein the gods of these three peoples lived peaceably together as equals, and then a small town, as different from the rough hill settlements of Nages and elsewhere as a tea-rose from a dog-rose. White, stuccoed houses bordered the narrow road to the spring. Steps led up the slope. The water, over which the spirits presided, was drained into canals and basins; and there were bathing-places, colonnaded courts and fortifications as well.

Glanon, as the Hellenes called the place, seems to have been a meeting-place for merchants and middle-men; here they negotiated, got to know one another and took the waters, all the while watched over by the gods. That the Greeks set the tone and the form of the place is beyond doubt. The natives acted as pupils, looking on and learning, trying to absorb how and what men thought in more civilized lands, what products, manners and customs were in vogue there and what styles prevailed. Both sides must have profited from this. As the Greeks were too weak for imperialistic gestures, the Celts needed to have no fear of being exploited; and since both were mainly concerned with long-term trade, the Greeks had no fear of being attacked for the sake of a little plunder, though this may sometimes have happened. Glanon developed into the most captivating blossom on the frail stem of a Greek-Celtic culture whose rudiments already existed and which might have developed further but for its premature extinction.

As early as 150 BC Italian merchants began to interfere with the Greeks' business and gradually to expel them from the southern French markets. Trading-houses such as those of Marcus Sestius or Decimus Aufidius – their names survive in the stamps on the handles of wine-amphorae – delivered wine from the Campagna and made huge profits that astonished Posidonius's successors. They seem to have used the juice of the grape much as fur-traders used fire-water in dealings with Red Indians. They were, besides, more practical and hard-headed than their Greek competitors. Probably these Italians already knew Glanon, but the little town became Roman only after Rome had conquered Provence in the second century BC, after which it became Glanum. Even at the apogee of Greek-Celtic collaboration southern France as a whole was only a tiny part of the vast area that the La Tène culture people had meanwhile conquered. They also lived further north, on the Marne, the Danube, the Main and in the Alps, in a style not very different from that under Europe's most brilliant skies.

Oppida could soon be found wherever the Celts settled, in Yugoslavia as much as in Austria, Bohemia, southern Germany and, of course, France. We even know the names of some of these settlements: at least that they usually ended in *briga* (hill), *dunum* (fortress), *magus* (plain) or *nemeton* (sacred place). Thus Lugdunum, 'the castle of the god Lug', was Lyons (Loudon and Laon in France are also derived from this name, similarly Leyden in Holland and Liegnitz in Silesia), Namneton (Nantes), Noviomagus

(Speyer), Cambodunum (Kempten) and Boiodunum (Passau).

In old Gaul over ninety such place-names have been identified. These lay, like Nages and Entremont, mainly on hills; they had developed out of old places of refuge but had become much more than this by the later La Tène era. Bibracte, in old Burgundy, the most thoroughly investigated of all the Celtic oppida, gives impressive evidence of this. The archaeologists, who began to dig in 1867 on Mont Beurray near Autun and worked for four years, laid bare a community that was not only surrounded by a rampart three miles long but was divided up in ways that would be familiar to modern town-dwellers. There was an 'industrial estate' occupied by craftsmen, a superior quarter for the rich and a market-place that in Roman times was surmounted by a forum. The manufacturing district was not, as is usual nowadays, placed in an outer suburb but formed the very heart of the settlement. Along a street leading from the main gate to the town centre was a series of huts of various shapes and sizes, smithies, weaving-centres, saddleries and, it may be assumed, the shops in which these products were offered to passers-by. The whole thing must have been like an eastern souk, for in bazaars too you can frequently buy goods fresh from the work-bench or kiln.

In the residential quarter it was more quiet. The houses were very simple constructions, expertly built on foundations of quarry-stone, the outer walls coated with mud; but there was also, though not until Roman times, a great villa with an atrium and no less than thirty rooms. The walls had been erected by a technique as typically Celtic as the moustache or the enemy head over the front door. A thick frame of wooden beams was filled with pieces of stone and covered with unmortared stone on the outer walls, in such a way that the ends of the transverse beams remained visible. Caesar called this construction the *murus gallicus* and suggested that it had many advantages 'because the stone gives protection against fire and the timber against wall-breakers. As the woodwork is joined with internal cross-beams of at least forty feet, it can be neither broken through nor torn apart.'

In Germany a gigantic Gallic wall was found near Nonnweiler in the Saar, the so-called 'Huns' ring' of Otzenhausen, together with other, smaller, constructions, such as those at Finsterlohr in the Tauber valley and on the Heuneburg. Their inhabitants later gave up Mediterranean mud-brick building for a technique better suited to the country. All these pale, however, in comparison with the most recently discovered Celtic town, found in 1955. What it was called, no one knows. It is named after the village of Manching, with some seven thousand souls, near Ingolstadt.

It is not exhausting though one would not be averse to a beer after walking right through Munich from one end of the old town to the other, from the Isartor to the Karlstor. But in Celtic Manching it would have been, for Bavaria's capital would have fitted four times into the oppidum on the Danube. Its wall was over four miles long – almost twice as long as that of medieval Nuremberg. It covered an area of some four hundred hectares, three times as much as Bibracte.

However it would not have seemed much like a city to a modern visitor. He would have begun his walk of one and a half miles in a great meadow within the defences that formed a five-hundred-yard-wide green belt around a residential and industrial quarter. This was a hive of activity. There were goldsmiths, bronze foundries, iron and glass works, potteries and trading houses. The inhabitants of old Manching made hartshorn handles for knives, rings of saprolith, a coal-like substance, set amber, struck gold coins, the so-called 'rainbow-keys' found throughout southern Germany, manufactured millstones from imported porphyry or basalt, and raised pigs, goats, cattle, dogs, poultry and two kinds of horse, a breed of small pony and a larger one, able to carry armed men.

The iron-ore was taken from the Danube marshes beyond the town gates and also smelted there. For working it would then have to be brought into Manching. Bronze, tin, gold, silver and many other materials were imported: saprolith, porphyry and basalt from the Bohemian region, amber from the Saar, wine, stored in clay jars, from southern Italy. Manching must have been a trading-centre with contacts in the furthest corners of Europe and with its own high-quality output to contribute.

Among the finest pieces found there is a yoke-fixture through which the reins of a horse's harness were passed; it is decorated with two bull-heads and two bird-heads, faultlessly cast in bronze. Among the most remarkable was a block of purple-violet unworked glass, the production of which required knowledge that even in the Middle Ages was a closely guarded secret of Byzantines and Venetians. It was at that time part of the treasury of oriental art-secrets, but the La Tène Celts had already been able to produce highly coloured glass. They could not of course blow it. They were content to cast rings of this breakable material and decorate them with glass threads in other colours. It must have been a much sought-after decoration.

Manching has not yet been exhausted; it will take archaeologists years – even decades, if we count the work of evaluation. What experts can now say after several excavations is however astonishing enough. They believe the place may have been the chief town of the Celtic tribe of the Vindelici, who were settled in Bavaria, and that the task of setting up the town was undertaken by some powerful prince early in the La Tène era. This ruler must also have had a remarkable understanding of the surrounding world. In contrast to most founders of oppida, he did not choose a hill as the site but a slight, flood-free elevation in the marshy Danube valley. This had a double advantage: on the one hand, it could control the ancient trade-route which led up from Hungary and joined at Manching a further north-south one; on the other, the marshy country gave protection from attack.

To secure his aims he invested substantial funds. A farmstead in the wall-builders' path was simply torn down, two streams and a river were joined up and diverted so that they formed a moat around part of the wall. The wall, ten feet high, must have consumed whole forests, tons of nails, mountains of chalk-stone, an immense number of working hours and – not only in accidents – human lives. Archaeologists were able to uncover at least one example of a child of about six years of age being walled into the foundations, as a sacrifice to the gods.

All these details naturally make one wonder who this ruthless town-builder was. Which Celtic prince was able to recruit thousands of men for such a gigantic undertaking and then at least ten thousand citizens to live in it? What kind of a man was this who could span the entire continent with his commercial network and even strike his own coins? We shall probably never know the answer. The town, significant as it was, is mentioned by none of the classical writers; even its destruction around AD 15 was deemed worthy neither of a note nor of an inscription on a triumphal arch by the Roman generals. We do not even know who conquered it and can only deduce from the split skulls that it came to a violent end. If a military airfield had not twice been built on its site, in

1936 and 1955, we might not have known to this day that an oppidum of this size existed on the Danube.

During the construction of the first airfield, archaeologists made only a few accidental finds; but when it was being modernized they managed, after a great campaign, to get in before the bulldozers and save what there was to be saved: the image of a Celtic town. Since then diggers of the Frankfurt Roman-German Commission assemble in Manching nearly every two years to extend the knowledge they already have, while above their heads the war-machines howl up into the skies.

The most interesting bit of information that we owe to the diggers of Manching is that in the La Tène period principalities emerged whose rulers clearly resumed the practices of their Hallstatt predecessors, though on a higher level of development. In the town on the Danube marshes, next to the craftsmen's quarter, an area was found that consisted not of small dwellings but of large courts with unusually large houses. Almost all were only six yards wide, but between thirty-five and eighty yards long; some were partitioned into little rooms.

What purpose can such uneconomic constructions have served? As dwellings they hardly seem practical and the Celtic retinue houses found elsewhere, as in the Goldberg near Nördlingen, were not narrow tunnels of this sort. There remain three possibilities: stables for large cavalry-units, barracks or factories. The last assumption turns out to be right. In two of the yards containing the long houses – many more have not yet been excavated – such quantities of sacks, tools and pieces of iron were found as to suggest that it was not single smiths but groups of them who, employing mass-production techniques, worked the material from the furnaces in the peat-bog into bars and then manufactured tools. There also appears to have been a large carpentry workshop, organized on similar lines, and a further area for textile and leather-working – in other words a clothing factory, a large saddlery or perhaps also a place where shoes could be made.

All this may seem somewhat fanciful – but only at first glance. The factory – more exactly, manufacturing – is the logical culmination of a process that began with the development – on the basis of iron – of an artisanate who no longer produced primarily luxury goods for a small and wealthy clientele but mass-articles for a large number of less well-off customers. Where pioneers of new economic processes stake their existence on cheap manufacturing, they soon recognize that further rationalization is possible if workers complement one another, each undertaking only those tasks he can best manage. In the nineteenth century this was recognized by the founders of modern mass-production, men such as Samuel Colt and Henry Ford; the Greeks knew it as early as the La Tène period. Xenophon described the division of labour in his day: 'Here a man lives only from sewing the shoes, there another only from cutting them. . . . The simpler the process, the more successful it is.' This must also have been understood and practised by the Celts. They certainly lacked neither technical skills nor a sense of reality. This was even appreciated on the Mediterranean.

The Celtic invention of the barrel replaced the wine-jug north of the Alps. Their two and four-wheeled chariots were among the most perfect and elegant constructed at the time, and the utensils they manufactured looked so alike throughout the great area between the Carpathians and the Atlantic that we have to conclude that there must have been great factories in the oppida working to much the same specifications for axes, pots, hammers and pick-axes.

Nor were minerals exploited by the Celts only on a small scale. Not far from Manching, at Karlskron, a foundry with sixty-two smelt-furnaces was excavated, though hardly more than a dozen can have been in use at any one time as these primitive furnaces could not be used for long periods. Small foundries seem to have existed in virtually every Celtic town, for slag-heaps and remains of pig-iron have been found wherever they once flourished. The same was true of salt. All the German and Austrian places with 'hall' in their name – Hallein, Schwäblisch Hall or, of course, Hallstatt – were at some time inhabited by Celts. *Hal* was their name for salt, and they naturally produced it on an increasingly large scale. Archaeologists have shown that near Bad Nauheim, in a field two miles long and several hundred yards wide, there was one oven after another. Clay jars with a capacity of up to two hundred and fifty litres have been found in the surrounding area. In these the salt was preserved. Once the required degree of concentration was reached, the contents would be poured into smaller jars and then put into the ovens; what remained was a salt-cake that could easily be stored and transported once the jars had been broken. This shows clearly how good the Celts were, and not in Manching alone, at organizing their industry and suggests that at the height of the La Tène period their settlements must have hummed with economic activity. Behind the *muri gallici* could be heard not only the yelling of savage warrior-hosts but also the hammering of smiths, the clattering of looms and the squeaking of grindstones. Out of the turbulence of the fifth century BC had emerged a society in which warlike features mingled with highly capitalist ones.

The successors of the Hallstatt princes seem to have been not only representatives of a new social class but also supporters of new economic forces. They created an industry whose products could no longer be marketed by old methods. The lords of the 'European market' had made their money out of capital in highly concentrated form: gold, silver, amber, luxury goods from European and Greek workshops; this was also true of tin and bronze. A few waggon-loads yielded vast profits if they reached their destination safely.

But with mass-articles it had to be otherwise. They could not be taken in isolated speculative expeditions from one place to another but, to provide a decent return, had to be entrusted to a properly functioning trading network, within which they could regularly reach their selling points. This again required not only safe roads but professional organization to deal with the despatching. Single entrepreneurs like the lord of the Heuneburg could not, with the limited resources at their disposal, manage both factories and the regular despatch of their output to all corners of the globe. Their successors could; in a market like that of the La Tène period specialists worked with specialists. This also had social consequences. Smaller entrepreneurs had the chance to connect their limited knowledge, capacity and means with the business of a greater one and thereby to increase their profits. A sort of middle class must have grown out of this. There is some evidence of this at Manching: on one side were the large factories but next to them, grouped around the east-west axis of the town, were the forges and houses of the lesser craftsmen, who perhaps undertook the finishing work or simply dealt with those products that it was not profitable to make on a large scale – pincers, files, borers (for the factory workers), as well as made-to-measure shoes and ceremonial weaponry.

What the relationship of large to small was – whether as serfs or vassals or merely the dependence that all suppliers have on their contractor – we cannot of course know. Reports from Gaul in the last century before Christ suggest that both were applicable. There were both slaves and also citizens who had won considerable freedom from those lords who had risen to power during these turbulent times. The laws of capitalism may thus have some limited relevance to La Tène society. Wealth, together with power and influence, had become concentrated in a few hands. The Celtic *stater*, divisible down to one twenty-fourth of their value and decorated with highly abstract symbols, linked all markets between the Danube and the Seine in the most practical way with the Mediterranean world market.

The Celtic mentality seems to have responded to all of this. The Celts had always sought wealth in palpable form; Romans and Greeks alike said that they loved money and even that they were passionate businessmen. How this attitude affected the attempts of political leaders to create large, tightly organized states is another question. Highly developed competitiveness and the desire for private profit seldom go together with clear-headed statesmanship; in fact they seem to have been responsible for the division of the people of the La Tène era into smaller and smaller groups, many of which were probably economic units.

This did not harm the Celts so long as they lived undisturbed lives behind the protection of the Alps and were strong enough to send their plundering hordes again and again into the civilized states of the Mediterranean region. But later, when Rome had set up her own power on a stable basis and was herself about to advance into those regions from where her terrifying enemies had come, it was clear that this physically large and numerically strong people, for all their military efficiency, had nothing but courage with which to confront the legions; and this was not enough. It would have needed organized power to repel the armies of the Roman emperor. As we shall see, it was just this that was lacking at the decisive moment. A survey of the La Tène era thus leaves a somewhat ambivalent impression.

Out of revolutionary disturbances had emerged a culture whose members spread almost in one movement over the greater part of Europe. Around 300 BC there were Celts in France, Spain, Switzerland, southern and central Germany, Bohemia, Hungary, northern Yugoslavia, Romania, Bulgaria, England and Ireland. They probably gave the Rhine its name, as well as the Main

(Moin), the Neckar, the Lahn, the Ruhr, the Lippe, the Isar, the Inn and the Tauber (Dubra, meaning simply 'water'). South Germany alone they must have settled so intensively that it is difficult to find a single region in Bavaria or Württemberg that does not have its 'Celtic fort'. From here they also went off towards Rome, Delphi and Asia Minor. The young lords who had pensioned off their predecessors seemed to be on the point of subjugating at a stroke virtually the whole of our continent. Had this been a concerted effort, it could have created one of the greatest empires in European history.

Then the storm ebbed; the might of the sudden onslaught subsided, and there remained a group of industrially oriented peoples who clearly lacked the capacity for political integration of either the old Hallstatt princes or brilliant commanders such as Brennus and Aneroëstes. A sort of moneyed aristocracy took the old nobles' place. It must have formed in the hinterland while – strange though the idea may seem – the last Insubres, Boii and Gaesatae were still fighting the Romans in northern Italy. Down-to-earth business instincts on the one side, naked *furor* on the other; two sides of the same coin.

This ambivalence also characterizes the art of the La Tène era. Beneath its brilliant surface lurk forces, fears and notions that are seldom mastered, merely exorcised. The creators of the torcs and sacrificial vessels, the richly ornamented helmets and exquisite sword-sheaths, were not as independent of their gods as were the Greeks: they were delivered to them body and soul. But this is not surprising. The Christians took almost two thousand years to transmute the worst of their fears into frozen concepts; the Celts did not have a quarter of that time at their disposal. They remained too close to their barbarian roots and had long been subject to rule by others before they could sublimate what oppressed them. When they managed this there emerged from their old myths some of the finest works of European literature. To achieve this later maturity, they had in the La Tène era also to overcome the tension between two powerful spiritual poles. On the Mediterranean they had links with the rationalistic culture of Greece, but on the eastern borders of their territory they were always in contact with peoples, such as the Scythians, who incorporated Asiatic traditions. Both influenced them: shamans on the one hand, worldly intellectuals on the other. Even the Druids seem to have been a product of this division.

They had not only to master and balance influences from both west and east; they also had to provide the integrating force that the princes lacked. That they played this substitute role, and thereby became the focus of powerful spiritual energies, lends our picture of the Celts another dimension; entirely characteristic, though unreal. As they were mentioned only fleetingly by the Greek Celtographers, it is now essential that we consider the mysterious 'oak-sages' once more, this time in greater depth.

NINE

The Mastery of Death:
Deities and Druids

> Doubtless every culture, visible or invisible, is impelled by its own conception of death.
>
> André Malraux, *Antimémoires*

The curtain rises. We look upon 'the sacred grove of the Druids'. In its centre stands the 'oak with the Irmin pillar, at the foot of which is a Druid-stone that serves as altar. It is night. Distant fires glimmer through the bushes.' The scenery, if well painted, could hardly be more imposing. As expected, the stage now comes to life: 'to ceremonial music, the Gauls enter, followed by a procession of Druids'. Orovist, their chief (bass), sings:

> Climb up to the hill, Druids
> Look through the dark branches
> And see if in silvery light
> The new moon will appear
> If in the firmament
> Its renewed face appears
> The Druid grove will resound
> With thrice the sacred brass.

This elicits from the chorus the question: 'Does Norma break the mistletoe in the sacred grove?', which Orovist ceremonially confirms. In the next scene but one his daughter (soprano) takes this parasitic plant, with the aid of a golden sickle. After the aria that she sings while doing this, celebrated primadonnas seldom have to wait long for shouts of 'encore'.

Norma has today disappeared from the repertory of the great opera-houses – this may be regrettable, musically, but less so for the cultural history it purports to reveal. Vincenzo Bellini, who wrote the work in 1831 for a first performance in La Scala, Milan, probably knew little more of Celts and Druids than what he could glean from an ordinary encyclopaedia, but he knew a usable libretto when he saw one. So when Felice Romani provided him with the story of the tragic love of a Druid's daughter for an officer of the Roman garrison he jumped at the chance – all the more willingly as the author had incorporated all the details that a public hungry for romanticism generally expected: oaks, the moon, Celtic Sarastros and even the Germanic Irminsul from Westphalia. His hunch had been correct. *Norma* was a huge success, particularly in England, where designers replaced the mysterious grove with a model of Stonehenge. Everyone was convinced that this imposing monument was the work of Druids.

In general the educated layman in the nineteenth century had a fairly exact picture of the Celts' white-bearded priests. The very mention of them raised a slight thrill. They were the embodiment of a retrospective Utopia. The rich would have miniature megaliths erected in the gardens of their country houses; Sir Rowland Hill even had a man dressed up in Druidical garb who was supposed to emerge mysteriously while his guests were admiring his private Stonehenge. Others took it more seriously, founding Druidical orders of which they of course appointed themselves the head – and calling into existence secret religions, some of which still have adherents. These were a catch-all for everything that seemed sufficiently Celtic and archaic: moon-worship, midsummer festivals, the Holy Grail, exorcism of devils, phallic worship.

Some of these cults were even exported. In 1872 a Druid society was founded in Germany, modelled on the hundred-year-old British order of the same type, and it amalgamated later with others to form the International World Lodge of Druids. Its members passed through two grades, 'Perception and Knowledge' and 'Understanding of Art and Will', and then had to pass a third, in which 'Resolution and Will' was taught and practised. At the head of the hierarchy stood the 'High Brass Chapter', the members of which led – and lead – the whole organization of 'groves'. The

Druid order survives to this day. Its members adhere to the ideals of humanizing mankind, international peace and brotherly love.

What was in the head of the young Winston Churchill when in 1908 he accepted membership of the Albion Lodge of the Ancient Order of Druids at his birthplace, Blenheim Palace, is more diffi-cult to guess. On the surviving photograph of his initiation-ceremony he does manage to look deeply stirred. But the false beards of many of the brothers in the order hide a suspicious grin. They appear to be taking the whole thing as a joke. But it was not that. Ideas of what the Celts could have known of God, nature, death and the hereafter have preoccupied people on the most varied intellectual levels – doubters, dreamers and scholars alike. In one of his writings Gerald B. Miller, for instance, who has con-fessed to membership of ancient British witchcraft societies, ex-presses his longing to know what the Druids believed and taught, as if they had the key to some supernatural reality. In 1945 Ernst Jünger discussed with a Breton who had fought on the German side whether it was not better to confide the secret of nuclear fission to an order whose members were, 'like the Druids, distinguished for their non-profane knowledge. In which case physical power would be surmounted by spiritual power.' All this suggests how far the few facts that we know about the Celtic priests have grown into a whole mythology. Unsatisfied curiosity provoked rumours that were often fantastic. Misteltoe plays a disproportionately large role in this, because a Roman writer associated it with the Druids.

On the sixth day of every month, wrote that competent collector of facts the Elder Pliny in his encyclopaedic *Natural History*, the Celts held a great feast. White-garbed Druids would climb to cut off the mistletoe 'with a golden sickle' and lay it on white cloths. Then two white bulls would be sacrificed. What this might have meant has been discussed from every angle. The most plausible and the most obvious explanation is that mistletoe was used for medicinal purposes. If pressed when fresh one could obtain a juice containing cholin, acetylcholin and viscotoxin, all three of which, when injected intravenously, can for a time reduce excessively high blood-pressure. Moreover the pain of malignant ulcers can be eased with crushed mistletoe leaves.

The belief that it can also protect men from lightning and sor-cery is probably no more than a distorted interpretation of the

secret knowledge of early medicine-men. Thus in the saga the
most cunning of all the German gods, Loki, killed the shining
Baldur with a mistletoe-spear. Pliny believes that the Druids were
no more and no less than very clever nature-healers. Apart from
mistletoe there were, he reckoned, two other medicinal herbs,
which he calls 'samolus' and 'selago'. The one had to be plucked
with the left hand; in taking the other, it was necessary to stretch
one's right hand through the left sleeve of a white robe. He also
talks of an 'anguinum', a magic egg the size of a small apple. It was
said to contain snake-poison, and to have served its owner well
before a court of law or on other public occasions.

Samolus and selago have to this day not been identified, and
anguinum has also been the object of fruitless speculation. We can
again only suppose the Druids – or some of them: what Strabo
calls the 'vates' – were in effect natural philosophers who pro-
foundly understood at least vegetable but probably also animal
remedies and poisons. That they collected the ingredients of their
medicine according to particular rules and only in particular phases
of the moon is by no means unusual for a period when men believed
that all the powers of nature work together. Older farmers and
gardeners to this day assert that sowing should be done under a
waxing moon, harvesting under a waning one, and moreover that
it is not harmful if poisonous plants are picked up with only the left
hand, the *sinistra*, which was the more suitable for dangerous
work. The Druids combined such magical and poetical practices
with sober and precise computations.

In 1897 at Coligny in Burgundy fragments of a bronze tablet of the
last century BC came to light. Put together they constituted what is
still the longest known document in the Gallic language. It contains forty different words written in Latin script – for philologists,
a magnificent find – and was a calendar. In deciphering it, it
became clear that the Celts worked in units of sixty-two lunar
months, i.e. the period between each new moon and the next. One
of these months would contain thirty days, the next twenty-nine,
which gave half-months of fifteen days, or one fifteen-day one
followed by a fourteen-day one. Each day was counted, as is today
still the practice among the Jews and Moslems, from moon-rise to
moon-rise, with the result that it was not always exactly divided
into twenty-four hours. The year that emerged from all this was

eleven days shorter than the 365-day period the earth takes to go round the sun.

This created a problem common to all calendar-makers who base their calculations on the moon. If they ignored this annual time difference, sooner or later March would occur when the leaves were already turning brown and June would be in winter. To compensate, they would have to do some juggling. Stone Age man set up the giant constructions of Stonehenge and Carnac so as to get at the astronomical facts necessary for solar and lunar time to be synchronized. For a short time in the fifth century BC the Greeks, who also calculated according to the phases of the moon, established a complicated system of dividing up time. The geologist Meton of Athens had worked it out. It was based on a nine-year cycle of twelve ordinary and seven leap-years: the average of 110 twenty-nine-day and 125 thirty-day months resulted in a mean solar year. The Coligny calendar was rather simpler, but arrived at by a similarly ingenious method. The twelve-month periods were balanced out by two of thirteen months. In the end the period of five solar orbits emerged, fairly exactly calculated. The disadvantage that not every year within such a sixty-two-month cycle would be as long as the others was overcome in a rather charming way.

The additional month had no name, so each of its days was called in numerical order after one of the twelve regular phases of the moon. Within the leap-year this gave something like a miniature image of two and a half normal years. In addition each unit of time had to be given its particular significance. The Coligny calendar's thirty-day months were characterized as favourable, whereas in the twenty-nine-day ones men were advised to walk cautiously. Moreover, particular days in the good months were less good, and not all the bad days in the bad months were unmitigatedly bad.

To a man accustomed to living by the clock and the deadline all this would have seemed confusing. But we can hardly deny that the Celts' way of dividing time was more poetic than our own. Almost every day had its own character. This arrangement, for which the Druids must have been responsible, reveals them as men who could give their considerable scientific knowledge a lyrical embellishment. Caesar says as much, noting in the *Gallic War* that the essence of Celtic secret knowledge was encoded in verses; a man who wished to know them completely had to memorize them for twenty years. 'They think it sinful to write down what they know'; they could have done so, for 'in public and private writings they used the Greek alphabet.'

This detail has also reinforced the tendency of those who admire the Druids to see in them an order that possessed considerable stores of esoteric wisdom and knew how it had to be handled – with care. Modern Celtic scholars are, however, more detached and explain the Druids' practices with theories that may strike us as surprising.

Bryan McMahon, historian, scholar of folklore, teacher, a well-known poet and much else besides – the kind of man that can probably exist only in Ireland – likes to test his favourite theories in practice and to retail them with all the skill and timing of a seasoned performer. He told me: 'Whenever I meet an Indian I take him to one side and hum the first lines of an Irish folk-song. Then I ask him to continue the melody as he likes; and, believe it or not, almost every time he will sing it to the end as if he already knew the song. Isn't that astonishing?' He leant back and the dying embers in the hall of the Listowel Arms Hotel in Listowel, County Kerry, threw his features into relief against the gloom of a dull, rainy day. Then he continued: 'For me it is an indication that Indians and Irishmen have a common past; that, as I put it in one of my plays, "We Celts came from the mysterious east".' Bryan McMahon must be aware that with this story he is going over ground that other scholars have already ploughed, for this theory is no longer a sensation.

The late Myles Dillon, formerly Professor of Celtic at the University of Dublin, cites a whole series of further astonishing parallels between the culture of the Aryan Indians and that of the Irish Druids. His main contention is that in both cases there was a distinct class of scholars; the Brahmins in India, the highest representatives of the four-part caste system (below them came the Kshatriyas, the warriors; the Vaisyas, the men of commerce; and the Sudras, the workers and peasants); while in Ireland there were the 'wise men of the oak'. Dillon reckons that the Brahmins and Druids should be equated because they carried out their profession – teaching and study, poetry and law – in a similar way. There is evidence that this was so.

Thus the principles by which justice was administered were

similar, indeed identical with those of India. There a father with daughters and no sons could order one of them to take a man of his choice and produce a legal heir. Beyond the Hindu Kush, such a girl would be called *putrika* (she who takes the son's place) and in old Ireland *ban-chomarba* (female heir). But who if not the Continental Celts can have told the Irish what was going on among the eastern descendants of the kurgan people? Dillon notes further similarities: in both cultures there were eight different forms of marriage, from arranged marriages, marriage by purchase and love-matches to kidnapping – though this was illegal. In both cultures there was a strict distinction between inherited and earned property and when contracts were drawn up there was an exact statement as to who was to provide what guarantees before obtaining what he wanted. In the one case it was the Brahmins and in the other the Druids who administered these principles.

All this, Dillon says, suggests that the Celtic Druids indeed represented the same tradition as the Hindu Brahmins. The class to which they belonged could, if we count Indo-European priests as its forefathers, already have been in existence for a millennium and a half by the La Tène era. It is understandable its memory has persisted so stubbornly and that its representatives still hold the power to fire the imagination. Sagas containing the exploits of these Celtic sages are themselves a kind of historical document, though unfortunately keys to them are often lacking. At any rate three things are clear: the Druids were doctors, they studied the heavens and they understood law. But there was more to them.

If we continue to feel our way along the parallels between India and Gaul, sooner or later we sense that the Druids were also political leaders, just as the Brahmins clearly stood above generals and warriors. However, conditions in Asia were more distinct than in Europe. Caesar confirms that there were in Gaul only two classes 'that enjoy importance and respect . . . that of the Druids and that of the knights', but he does not say the scholars were superior to the military. A Platonic state in which the nation's affairs are directed by philosophers does not seem to have existed among the Celts. Instead, a medieval structure prevailed; a dual headship of the community, temporal and spiritual.

The sword was borne by chiefs with grandiose names such as Dumnorix ('king of the world') or Anextlomarus ('great protector'). The sickle – often equated with the bishop's crook, for want of another emblem – was borne by men of an organization of ecclesiastical nature. Once a year all 'wise men of the oak' would meet at the 'navel of Gaul' – presumably at the site of the Benedictine abbey of St Benoît, near Orléans – to discuss their affairs and settle quarrels. The leadership of this 'council', Caesar says, lay in the hands of a man who 'has the highest prestige among the Druids'. He must have been similar to an independent prelate because his colleagues stood, at least *de jure*, above all parties and were immune from the chieftains' interference. Druids did not 'usually go into battle. They pay no dues like the others, and are exempt from military service or similar obligations.' Moreover, they seem like their old Irish colleagues, the *filid*, to have had no territorial boundaries.

Such considerable privileges were of course purely a matter of power – the more so as secular rulers were much less favoured by custom and law. In the first century BC they often had attached to them the so-called *vergobrets* (those who execute the law), much like elected magistrates' officials, who converted the orders of authority into practicable decrees. Elsewhere, oligarchies of influential landowners had pushed back single rulers. This promoted the emergence of shifting coalitions between interest-groups; it furthered party interests and also nepotism.

Caesar even says that each family had two opposing groups. But this may have been only what he could see: it is more plausible to visualize 'clans' jockeying for influence and privilege, as later in Celtic Scotland. All the tribes of this restless people could fall apart into a multitude of subordinate groupings, the smallest of which was the extended family. The Druid class was a source of cohesion in such confused circumstances. To young people it must have appeared the very essence of order and permanence and many, as Caesar says, thus 'voluntarily apprenticed themselves to it or were sent by their parents and relatives'. There was due importance attached to the choice of their chief. According to Caesar, if there were several equally worthy contenders the matter would be settled by the votes of the Druids, and sometimes by their weapons, for obvious reasons.

In the councils of St Benoît not only the affairs of single tribes or clans would be decided, but matters of concern to the nation as a whole. At most the *majestix* ('Majestix' being the king in the French comic saga of Asterix) had to decide – or merely help to decide – on wars, dues, the division of land and booty; but the *miraculix* or Druid would lay down what was right and what was not. They ruled over past and future, healing, the course of the seasons and the secrets of nature; they were university, church and court of the realm all in one. It is thus possible that the more powerful rulers sometimes tried to interfere in their affairs, to get them over to their own side, to corrupt or sway them. Some may have succeeded, but probably not for very long. The golden sickle was mightier than the sword. The Brahmins too outlived their Rajs, at least as an institution, as did the Popes of the Middle Ages their imperial challengers.

With all this in mind, we may assume that the Druids were the authentic and most important representatives of the Celtic people, the embodiment of all that was unique to it. This inevitably suggests two other questions. What was their role in the confusions of the early La Tène period – indeed did they give rise to them by promoting a national revolution? Secondly, what gave them such immunity from attack, other than their secret political skills? The first must remain an open question; but the second can easily be answered. The Celts, Caesar says, 'were to a great extent religious'. From a political viewpoint, creeds, like ideologies, are the best way of ruling men.

In all public and private quarrels [Caesar asserts] the priests alone judge and decide. They fix punishments and rewards, where crimes or murder have been committed or boundary and inheritance disputes arise. If a private person or persons fail to respect their decision they can exclude the men involved (where need be, the whole tribe) from public worship. This is for them the worst punishment imaginable. Those thus excommunicated count as godless criminals; all men must avoid them and eschew any talk with them, lest the infection be passed on. If they try to get in touch with them, they forfeit justice and honour.

That famous Greek collector of quotations, Diogenes Laertios, who lived towards the end of the second century AD, has revealed how these verdicts were formulated. He says that a Druid announced: 'We teach that the gods must be honoured, no injustice done and manly behaviour always maintained.' St Patrick, the patron saint of Ireland, is said to have been told by a heathen Celt whom he questioned about his basic principles that these were: 'Truth in the heart, strength in the arm, honesty in speech.' Both answers are cast in a common mould. They show a preference for tripartite division and epigrammatic expression that seem typically Celtic. This suggests that the Druids spoke both laconically and to the point. The rhythm made their utterances quotable and memorable. Such a verdict might be as ambiguous as it was precise, but it would have the ring of real authority.

Verdicts such as those quoted by Caesar could of course be pronounced only in a society whose highest authorities were enthroned in the skies. A man condemned somewhere on the Danube could easily have slipped into a gathering several hundred miles to the west, say in Brittany, had he not been oppressed by a feeling that he was being observed by some celestial secret police. These did make up a substantial force. Researchers into the maze of Celtic traditions have dug out 374 names of deities, 305 of them appearing only once, implying they were only local gods. This still leaves a contingent of sixty-nine. We may ask what a fugitive would have to fear from them: bewitchment, evil spells, lightning striking out of a clear sky, sudden sickness, or punishments that would not take effect until the hereafter? A possible answer cannot be found in the Celtic pantheon because the Druids left no myths. There is no literary elaboration of their spiritual world. If we wish to know more we must look to the central point that Diodorus touched on with his Pythagoras theory and ask what their attitude was to the gravest of human problems, death.

Religion is among other things a way of reconciling people to the fact that some day they must die, whether by the promise of a better life beyond the grave, rebirth, or both. Sometimes death can successfully be portrayed as a sacrifice, an abandonment of life for the sake of others, for a better future, a more beautiful kingdom, or for the world itself. The Druids seem to have regarded both as different sides of the same coin. As judges, Caesar shows, they condemned murderers to death not because they had killed people but because 'if a human life is not given for a human life, the ruling gods cannot be appeased'. They were not taking revenge but merely redressing the balance, in an entirely consistent way.

'If a wrongdoer escapes them, they will even slaughter the innocent.' Life for them was clearly something to be transferred from one vessel to another as soon as the complicated earth-heaven relationship had been disrupted. Since not only murder would arouse the gods against those they had created but other crimes as well, it

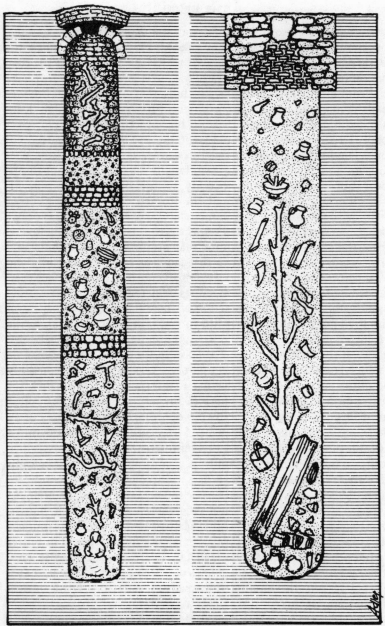

Cross-section of two ritual burial shafts in the Vendée

was vital – 'for reasons of state', as the Romans said – to stage occasional ritual sacrifices, not preceded by any trial. Then the basket-like colossi were set up, in which, as Strabo tells us, men and animals were burned together.

From all of this we might conclude that for the Celts life was expendable; but that would be illogical. It is more likely that death seemed to them the lesser evil and life something that could never really be forfeited, for it would go on beyond the grave. Indeed not only Diodorus appreciated this but Caesar as well, as did the poet Lucan. The Druids, Caesar says, taught that 'souls do not disappear but wander from one body to the other'. Lucan in his *Pharsalia* – a verse epic about the Roman civil war – addressed them with the words: 'If we understand you aright, death is only a pause in a long life.' Maybe he was right; if so, did the belief come from the Indo-European source that produced the Brahmins and the Druids? Or was it chance that lands as far apart as India and France produced a belief in metempsychosis? Does the fact that, according to Scythian custom, crests depicted eagles, wolves, bears as ancestors reflect the conviction of these people that the spirit of the dead goes through many life-forms, human and animal, as the Hindus believe? If so, do the Russian steppe-people form a bridge between the cultures of the Far East and the Far West?

Such conjectures may open up only a vast new field for possibly pointless speculation. But having made them, we must look for such pointers as do exist. There is, for instance, the report culled from Posidonius that Celtic men would have their throats cut so that they could follow their prince into death, and of course into a new life; or one can suggest a novel interpretation of the sacrifice scene on the Gundestrup Cauldron, according to which one column of warriors is marching towards sacrifice, while the second, reborn, rides away. This would not be too perverse an explanation, as it makes the sacrificial vessels receptacles within which human existence was transformed and explains the offering-up of human life as the exchange of one form of existence for another. The wheel that appears not only on the Hallstatt sword-sheath but also on a striking number of La Tène works of art could be considered as a symbol of rebirth. Finally, the severing of enemy heads makes another appearance in this context.

Head-hunters who had turned the hunt for trophies into a cult may have had at least two additional motives for their barbarous

1 Ornamental dagger-hilt from the sixth century BC, discovered at Hallstatt. The style is characteristic of the Illyrians as well as the early Celts.

2 *Left:* The terrifying
mythological man-eating monster
found at Noves in the Rhône
valley. The two severed heads
would appear to indicate that
their sculptors were Celts who
still practised the ritual of head-
hunting.

3 *Right:* Gallo-Roman carving of
the Celtic god referred to as Dis
Pater by Caesar, who thought him
comparable to the Greek god
Chronos.

4 Gallo-Roman stone relief of a
sacrificial bull found at the
Château de Maraudi near Vaison.
Such ritual sacrifices were
common to nearly all the
Germanic peoples, including the
Hittites and the Celts.

5 *Above left:* A final resting place: the sanctuary at Hallstatt. The local inhabitants claim that their medieval burial ceremony can be traced back to ancient Celtic tradition.

6 *Left:* The Roman ruins at Glanum near St Remy-de-Provence. An ancient meeting place for the Celto-Ligurians and the Greeks from Marseille.

7 *Above:* 'The Dying Gaul': a very striking sculpture with the characteristic flowing hair, moustache and torc of the Celt. This is a Roman copy of one of the statues which adorned the altar to Zeus at Pergamon. These depicted a victory of the Hellenic forces over the vast and formidable race of Celtic Galatians in Anatolia.

8 The megaliths of Carnac in Brittany. The original purpose of these
mysterious rows of stones is unknown. They could, however, support the
theory that a West European culture once existed during the Neolithic
Age which resembled those of the Near East.

9 *Below:* The Janus-heads found near Roquepertuse in Provence –
historical evidence that the Celts were fond of depicting their gods as
either dual beings or triads.

10 Foundation walls of a dwelling in the Celtic-Ligurian settlement of Nages at Nîmes. The houses are sometimes separated from one another by passages of no more than a shoulder's width.

11 *Below:* Entremont, overlooking Aix-en-Provence, is one of the twenty-four oppida which were discovered in the area from which the Volcae tribe originated. The quarry-stone ramparts date from a period before the discovery of the Gallic Walls.

12 The magnificent silver Gundestrup Cauldron, discovered in a Danish swamp. The Celtic design probably dates from the La Tène period.

13 *Right:* Details of the Gundestrup Cauldron.

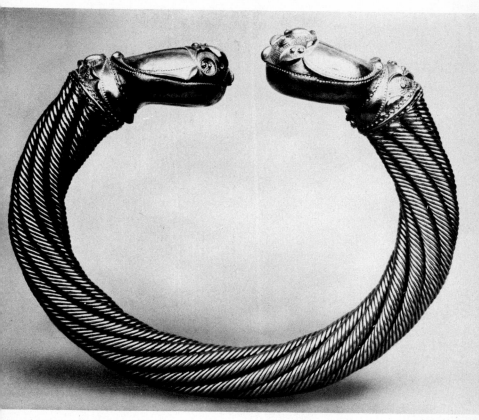

14 Left: A bronze flagon. One of the chief treasures of Gallic art.

15 Golden torc from Snettisham, Norfolk. One of a series of torcs found during ploughing at Ken Hill, Snettisham in 1948–50.

16 Walls of a dwelling in the oppidum at Entremont. Skulls of defeated enemies were displayed in the niches.

17 *Below:* The Mound at Vix near Châtillon-sur-Seine. In the Hallstatt period it was the site of an early Celtic settlement. The Crater of Vix was discovered at the foot of the hill.

18 Celtic coin with the head of Vercingetorix.

19 Below: An attempted reconstruction of the Heuneburg, an early Celtic settlement on the edge of the Swabian Alps. An unusual feature is the loam brick wall on the east side with built-in bastions, which indicates an architect from the Mediterranean.

20 Gallic farmer of the period after 50 BC. It is possible that he belonged to the colonies which were expelled by the Roman landlords against whom they led several uprisings. The cowl he is wearing is characteristic of Celtic dress.

21 *Below:* Irish Ogam stones at Killarney, which served as tombstones. The inscriptions, which consist of dots and dashes, were always engraved on the edges.

22 The Atlantic coast of Ireland. The Anchorites sailed from this point to suffer bloodless martyrdom in the solitude of the rocks and islands.

23 *Below:* The Cloister of Glendalough with the Kevin chapel and the round tower. One of the spiritual centres of the Celtic Church.

24 The West Cross at Monasterboice. The elaborate design and lavish decoration, typical of the art of the La Tène era, can be clearly seen in the high crosses of Ireland.

custom: the conviction that the collected heads of their enemies would magically increase their own powers; and the belief that, decapitated, an enemy would not be able to return from the hereafter, whether as a reborn man or as a spirit. If the Scythians are seen as the eastern pole of their culture, the second motive seems more appropriate to the Celts. The Scythians also cut the heads off their slain foes; moreover their Shamans seem to have conceived of death in much the same way as did the Druids. This allows us to infer certain things about both, and it perhaps explains many of their practices.

Shamans, according to Mircea Eliade, one of the leading European religious historians, came to office by vocation or appointment. In either event they needed a summons that came to them in dream, ecstasy, trance or vision. They themselves might even die in the process and then experience a return to life. It happened in this way: inner voices urged the young adept to seek the solitude of the forest; there he encountered apparitions that made him behave as if he were going mad. In a dream, he experienced his own dismemberment. Demons cut off his head, pulled out his eyes, hunted him down through flames; later he went up to heaven, on a pole or a tree, and only from there would he come back down to earth.

When he finally left the woods, his clothes were torn, his face bleeding, the hair on his head matted. 'Only after ten days,' says a Russian ethnologist who has studied the phenomenon in Siberia, 'does he again manage to stammer out some coherent words.' What had happened was, so the experts say, nothing less than the disintegration of profane man in the 'psychic chaos' of madness and the birth of a new personality. He underwent 'phases of mystical death and resurrection' that Christian saints also sought to undergo, though they were usually inspired by the New Testament account of Good Friday and Easter.

Such phenomena would seem to reflect a pattern basic to all religions, in their primary aim of overcoming death. A man who had overcome it, as the Shamans did, who had gone to heaven as a kind of scout and returned, must be so superior to his fellows that he could thereafter lead them and even sacrifice them. Whether the Druids' authority came from a similar source we do not know, although Mircea Eliade considers this possible. As even Stuart Piggott, an expert who generally admits only proven facts, accepts

Eliade's view, it may be regarded as at least close to the truth. Both
scholars base themsleves on some obvious parallels between the
Celts and the Scythians. They take into account that Shamans and
Druids dealt with the problem of death in almost the same way, no
doubt having in mind the rumour that there was in old Gaul a
doctrine of resurrection founded on mystical experiences. That
there too magical practices were carried on is well known to them.

An example may be found in the well-attested custom of going
naked into battle – no doubt partly because the warrior was, quite
simply, too hot. Bodily heat is, however, regarded in many religions
as a sign of sacral power and of unlimited spiritual freedom. The
Indian Yogi becomes hot through meditation and it is said of
Buddha that he 'burnt' in spiritual rapture; the Moslems of
Pakistan are also convinced that a man in communion with God
will begin to 'seethe'. Indo-European languages contain a whole set
of words to describe this 'extreme heat': among them the Latin
furor and the German *Wut*. These in their original meaning implied not only a wild raging but also great strength, which the
Romans may have been aware of when applying the word to the
Celts.

Young warriors of the tribes that succeeded the kurgan peoples
were accustomed to, as it were, charging their batteries in ritualized
initiation duels before going into their first action. They would
emerge as glowing as the hero of the old Irish saga, Cú Chulainn,
of whom it is said that he had to be put successively into three tubs
of ice-cold water before he was cool enough to don his clothes
again. A detail from Livy's *Annals* that has already been mentioned
seems to belong in this context. The 'dancing leaps' with which the
Celtic prisoners took up their weapons before entering the duels
that Hannibal had arranged may have struck Livy as the expression
of battle-lust, but in reality they were part of a ritual. By working
themselves up into fiery ecstasy, they had already overcome death
before the battle began.

But if the Celtic Brahmins used these techniques too – which
may be assumed – they were much more than the scholarly 'wise
men of the oak' that many of their historians have made them out
to be. They took part in mysteries that may seem sinister to us,
leading a people that saw no frontier between the human and the
infernal, practised ecstatic rites, self-abasement, orgies, blood-
sacrifices, made head-hunting sacred out of religious conviction

and indeed possessed the shamanistic traits that centuries-old reports ascribe to them. Their gods were just as they were themselves.

The god Lug who gave his name to Lyon, Liegnitz and Leyden was one of the greatest of the sixty-nine major deities. In Irish sagas he is depicted as the very essence of the noble warrior. His equipment included a golden helmet and breastplate; he wore a green cloak, 'on his white skin a shirt of silk', and golden sandals. He seems to have liked ornament as much as the Celts themselves, and – a quality later ascribed to him by the Roman historian Ammianus Marcellinus – he was exceptionally cleanly.

But this brilliant exterior concealed a more complex character. Lug was no simple bully, no Mars in Gallic dress, but a magician who could practise all the useful and decorative arts. He could play the harp, write poetry, build houses, forge iron and also, with the help of magic, win battles. An Irish king into whose service he had entered, kept him as a valuable piece of property. He let Lug make preparations for wars but forbade him to take any part in them, for fear that this priceless helper might be slain. However, Lug stayed on the field when one of the encounters he had set up took place. Limping around and muttering spells, his hat pulled down over one eye, he walked among the warriors. He could not prevent the king from being killed, but he restored to life all the other warriors who had been mortally wounded by dipping them in a magic well. Finally he himself took up arms and challenged Balor, the champion of the enemy side, to a duel. Balor said: 'Lift my drooping eyelid so that I may see the boaster who insults me.' In reply Lug hurled a stone that struck his eye – indeed so hard that it came out of the back of his head. Balor, a giant, seems to have been Lug's grandfather.

To kill him the god could also have called upon not only his infallible sling but also his magic javelin or some other magic weapon: evidently his arsenal was well equipped. The ravens that always flew around him, sat on his shoulder and whispered information into his ear served as spies, messengers and birds on his coat of arms. When Lyons was founded, swarms of them were said to have come down from the sky. Taking these features together, a remarkable picture emerges. The brilliant hero in his gleaming golden armour has raucous birds fluttering around him; he has a limp; he covers an eye when he wishes to remain anonymous; he kills his grandfather; and he practises unheroic magic. It is natural to identify him with a better-known god, Wotan. He too was accompanied by ravens, had an infallible spear, discovered the runes and thereby acquired magic powers. He too hid his empty eye-sockets beneath the rim of his cap, but he was on horseback a brilliant warrior, who fought against giants.

Such similarities allow us to surmise who Lug must in reality have been. Wotan, whom the northern Germanic tribes took into their Valhalla as Odin, is regarded by mythologists as 'the great Shaman'. Nine nights long he hung on the tree of the world and there, like every prospective Shaman, underwent his own death and resurrection. Moreover his name indicates that he was 'lord of fury' (*Wut*), the magic heat that inspired warriors. The Celtic god must have been related to him. But Zeus as well, one of the oldest of the Indo-European gods, belonged to this breed. He too defeated a Titan in order to come to power – his own father Chronos – and was capable of varying kinds of magic. We may conclude that he and his two cousins originated from a situation in which the descendants of the kurgan people began to depart from an older tradition. Rulers of the sky, with whom men can no longer identify, were abolished and forgotten. In place of the ruling giants who, like Chronos, had possessed the characteristics of omniscient and kindly fathers, young men of action were called into existence, warriors and magicians, throughout the whole region between Indus and Atlantic – in other words, among the Celts as well.

Caesar, who instinctively but not unjustifiably compared the gods of the Gauls with those of the Romans, mentions a father of the gods, a *dis pater*, whom 'the Celts reckon to be the father of their tribe. They say they have learned this from the Druids.' There is no reason to doubt his assertion. This celestial patriarch may have been a Chronos who was replaced, as in other religions, by a trinity – to begin with at least. Among the Germans such a trinity existed with Wotan/Odin, Donar/Thor and the god of war Zin/Tyr; among the Celts these were Teutates, Esus and Taranis.

Of these Teutates was the most powerful, the oldest and the most sinister. He was appeased by blood-sacrifice and had other names such as Albiorix, 'lord of all', and Toutorix, 'lord of the tribe'. He was considered to be the inventor of all the arts and was regarded by the Romans both as a Celtic Mars and as the equivalent of Mercury. His mortal counterpart would be one of those rulers who created industrial empires in the Hallstatt period by methods both warlike and commercial. He also had shamanistic features, and it is not clear whether he should be identified with Lug.

Esus, the second of the trinity, was not so clearly different from Teutates that an individual picture of him can be attained. His animal was the bull; in a picture from Roman times he is shown with three cranes flying above him. He too seems to have favoured human sacrifice; the victims were however not slain before his altars, but hung on trees, like the adepts of many of the shamanistic rites. They did not of course experience death purely as a vision; they actually did die. Esus is sometimes identified with the Cernunnos who is depicted on the Gundestrup Cauldron. He was supposed to be the ruler of the underworld, though that did not prevent his worshippers from considering him to be the god of plenty and occasionally portraying him with a sackful of coins.

Taranis, finally, differs from his colleagues in that, like Zeus, he controlled the skies with thunder and lightning, though without renouncing human sacrifice; he preferred burnings.

Whether this trinity really occupied the status ascribed to it by analogy with other schemes, indeed whether it even existed in the form described, cannot be stated with any certainty. We can be relatively sure only that the trinity served the Celts as model for their version of a greater whole. They liked to depict their heavenly rulers as triple or double-headed figures. Their pantheon strikes us, however, as a disordered jungle only because we do not see it, as we do the Greek or German pantheon, through the eyes of genealogically oriented men of letters but, so to speak, in its natural state.

In all the polytheistic religions the gods live like men with demonic powers. They are born, get mixed up in incidents both dark and racy, and ceaselessly propagate. The soil from which they grow is the human imagination. New perceptions, new situations, new circumstances required new interpretations of the world, which then provoked new celestial configurations. Men labour endlessly at achieving a harmony with heaven: it is a philosophizing in images, a kind of collective poetry. Even wit could be used in the context of immortality, something Lucian of Samosata confirms, although his work cannot be wholly trusted. In Gaul, he says, he had seen a picture of a native Heracles depicted just like the Hellenic one, but he was a far from heroic figure. His face was full of wrinkles 'as nut-brown in colour as are the faces of old sailors in our country'. But there is a still odder element in this painting; 'This old, bald-headed Heracles is pulling a great crowd of people towards him, all tethered at the ears.' Their chains are attached to his tongue, 'which had been bored through for the purpose'. A passing 'philosopher' reveals to the observer, after he has spent a long time puzzling over this, what it means: 'We Gauls ascribe eloquence not to Mercury, as you Greeks do, but to Heracles, who is much stronger. That we have depicted him as an old man should not surprise you, for among all the talents eloquence is the only one that does not show its complete strength until old age.'

Whether this was invented by Lucian, who earned a great deal of money as *rhetor* in Gaul, or was in fact a Celtic caricature, it is impossible to say. We know only that eloquence was as highly regarded by the Druids' pupils as bravery in battle; and we must suppose that by this time not all the Gallic gods were taken completely seriously or believed in blindly. One of them, Smertrios, had to defend a sacrificial animal against the dogs of Taranis, who wanted to take it over without cause: in other words, the gods tried to cheat each other. Sucellos was depicted with a little barrel that he carried on a pole – it might of course also be a hammer, but it seems to indicate that he was a drinker and that you were closest to him when drunk. In the forest one had to be on the look-out for Artaios, for he assumed the form of a bear. All these beings midway between animal and man, demon and wise father, represented various attempts to get hold of the truth and to interpret the world – and this goes for the Belenus in whose name little Asterix usually swears. He was compared by the Romans to Apollo; a God from subterranean depths but none the less embodying the clear light of reason.

Much can be read into this labyrinth of divinities. If we are to systematize it we must above all remember that these celestial beings grew up with their terrestrial creators. The energetic immortals of the Indo-European period had for long waged a battle against the more peaceful spirits whom the subject peoples of Europe worshipped; and from this they emerged in greater strength. Their greatest victory seems to have been the discovery of rebirth. Once the war was won, Lug – of whom it is supposed that he died and then rose again – rose to the head of the divine hierarchy. He merged with or dislodged Teutates. Thus began the apogee of the Druids. Sense had been made of death; but what of birth?

It might be assumed that only males were involved in a religion so intensively concerned to take the sting out of mortality. The promise of resurrection does seem to deprive life of its singularity and women of their maternal dignity. The work of bearing children becomes a mere function within a closed system. The Druids could thus have as their motto the words of the apocryphal gospel of the Egyptians – 'I have come to undo the work of woman' – and perhaps this does describe their attitude. In many religions male priests have made hostility to the body into a latently anti-female dogma, though they never managed to make it a general principle – not even the 'wise men of the oak', if indeed they ever attempted to do so.

Among the oldest members of the Celtic pantheon were powerful goddesses, often grouped, like their male counterparts, in trinities. The Romans called them *matres* or *matronal* and asserted that the highest honours were paid to them, including human sacrifice. They also mention hunting-goddesses such as Arduinna, to whom the Ardennes owe their name; Belisama, whom they identified with Minerva; Damona, who was portrayed as a cow; a patroness of horses called Epona, to whom they themselves later set up altars; and Nemetona, who was considered goddess of war. Besides these there was in old Ireland and in Gaul as well a Mother called Brigit, who even gained admittance into Christian hagiology as St Bridget.

All this merely re-emphasizes that divinities are a projection of the way things are in the world. Here below there were men and women who fell in love and got married – why not in the mythical kingdom above? Celtic gods sometimes had very powerful women at their sides. If the males ruled, as was usual, the sky and the clouds, the females ruled the soil and fertility; it was thus tempting to regard the falling rain as the fruit of their unison. Lug, too, had to fit in with this scheme since every year, on the Lugnasad, or 1 August, he would enter into a kind of marriage with the earth goddess. It was an old and, in part, Indo-European inheritance. The earth-spirits of the Stone Age peoples had married the sun gods of the kurgan people, otherwise their existence would have been impossible. In fact despite their apparent inferiority the latter turned out to be the stronger. We might even be inclined to think that respect for Mothers increased in proportion to the Druids' concern with powers beyond the grave; more simple souls would be unable to fathom the symbolism in male images and sought refuge in the wombs of goddesses. Some Ancient writers have indicated as much. In times of danger the Celts, they noted, relied on their women as on strong comrades-in-arms. Ammianus Marcellinus says that a whole horde of enemy warriors could not withstand a single Gaul if he had his wife to help him: 'As a rule she is blue-eyed and quite terrifying, particularly when her neck-muscles swell up, when she grinds her teeth and bares her huge arms. If she strikes out and kicks, it is as if a catapult had shot out four blows at the same time.' Evidently life with the goddesses of such women was no bed of roses.

But we can assemble only a mosaic of their cults. The most interesting aspect is the tradition that at one of the Celtic feasts a felled tree would be carried round and then, presumably, buried. This might be taken to mean that the myth of the god Attys from Asia Minor (in Phoenician, Baal) and his beloved, the Mother Cybele (Aschera or Baalat), had reached Gaul. The day of this beautiful boy's death – he died and rose again – was celebrated in Rome with a pine, for he was supposed to have bled beneath one and the pine-cone, perhaps for this reason, was a symbol of eternity. The inhabitants of western Europe may have learnt about this from the Galatians.

Another piece of the mosaic is the rumour preserved in sagas that there were also Druidesses; a third, the little that we know of the priestly Princess of Vix; a fourth, Strabo's curious note on an island of virgins in the Atlantic; and finally, the fact that there were in Britain Celtic queens – to whom we shall return – who gave the Romans a great deal more trouble than their male counterparts. Where such matriarchal features are evident, it is conceivable that there were also special cults that represented the feminine element in the Celtic faith. Archaeologists can neither confirm nor dispel these assumptions. They have however managed to reconstruct one of the places in which male and female priests worshipped the gods of Gaul. It was a tortuous process; and Wessex was the first port of call. Here it was established that Stonehenge, contrary to all popular belief, cannot be related to Celtic cults. The second port of call was in southern Germany.

In the regions south of the Main the 'square fortifications' still popularly called 'Celtic forts' have long been known. They are simply walled compounds, their gates opening to east, west or south, but never north. A good two hundred and fifty were discovered in the foothills of the Alps alone, though there were also some in eastern France, on the middle Seine and even in Portugal. They were, understandably, thought to be small fortresses or places of refuge, until the so-called 'ritual shafts' were discovered: three in the most famous example alone, that at Holzhausen on the Starnberg Lake. Between seven and forty yards deep, they contain all kinds of junk. They might have been rubbish dumps or collapsed wells, but this hasty supposition was also wrong: what man would bury his rubbish forty yards under the earth? Then it was discovered that one of these mysterious holes concealed a cult-pole, while another contained 'traces of decomposed organic substances such as flesh or blood'. This pointed to their having been places of sacrifice; though it still seemed possible that they were wells.

A reliable picture did not emerge until French archaeologists had discovered further shafts in the Vendée. They brought up the remains of a cypress trunk twelve feet long, pots, plates, jugs, antlers and the figure of a goddess. The experts remembered that in many sagas from Wales, Ireland and Brittany reference is made to ponds or springs into which votive offerings were thrown, that even Posidonius's successors reported the Celtic custom of burying treasure in holy places, and that the Frankish historian Gregory of Tours had mentioned rural feasts in the Cevennes where animals would be sacrificed and thrown into a lake. Stuart Piggott raised the question whether it was by chance that the famous finds of La Tène were taken from the waters of the Neuenburg Lake.

The answer he hit upon was that, like the Greeks and Romans, the Celtic faithful had believed that they could get in touch with water and earth spirits through wells and springs. To further this aim they would sink shafts, fill them with gifts for the subterranean deities, including animal and human sacrifices, and then carefully seal them up. Nor was it unheard of that men would help themselves to the buried treasure – most gods approved of speculation with their capital. The tree of Le Berard in the Vendée seems to confirm the horrendous sacrificial scene depicted on the Gundestrup Cauldron. It is an uprooted tree-trunk that the sinister warriors are carrying to the priest, who is pushing a man into the bowl.

Though the sacrificial bowl may have been the portable equivalent of the ritual shaft, the tree was also part of the cult of Attys and Cybele. The motifs, including both resurrection and Mother worship, intertwine in various ways and allow of just as many interpretations. Only one thing is certain: the 'square fortification' developed out of the oak-shaded *nemeton*. At first such a grove would be bounded by palisades, traces of which have been found in Holzhausen, later by a wall and ditch. Within the sacred square there were already primitive, temple-like structures, rectangular cells surrounded by an arcade.

From these simple huts emerged in turn round, oval and even polygonal shrines, of which one hundred and eight have been found in France alone. Sometimes they were also colonnaded or surrounded by moats, but they were seldom over ten yards square and do not always seem to have been properly roofed. One of the most impressive is at Roquepertuse in Provence. It had wooden gates, the lintels of which contain the usual skull-niches, and five steps leading up to it. Others, such as that within the vast Goloring near Koblenz, seem to have been topped by massive wooden staves: all the sacred places must have resembled a forest of such staves, on which the skulls were hung. Trees were also regarded as an embodiment of the divine, which suggests another way of interpreting the tree-trunks that were employed in some of the rites.

In Gaul and Galatia the oak above all was venerated; in Britain the yew; in Ireland the rowan. Trees supported the firmament and opened a path to the gods for the apprentice Shaman, and not only among the Celts. In the sacred grove of Dodona near Epirus rustled the oracular oaks of Zeus; the Germanic north was dominated by the Ash of the World, Yggdrasil; and even Felice Romani was on the right track when he located the Irminsul in Norma's druid-grove, for it must have been none other than a stylized tree.

The Celts gave their gods human shape only when, at the end of the Hallstatt era, they came under Etruscan influence. Their wood-carvers now created the idols that Lucan describes as 'grim-faced god-images, coarsely hewn from rough tree-trunks, bleached by the weather'. They must have grinned from the branches near shaded springs. A collector of primitive art would be happy to display those that have been found, which is a great number. But these simple figures mark only an early stylistic phase. The more contact there was with the Mediterranean world, the more naturalistic the Celtic sculptures became; and stone was now also used as a material. But the idols remained as terrifying as ever.

The life-sized heroic figures that Fernand Benoît excavated in Entremont could be mistaken for the output of a provincial Roman sculptor if some of them did not unmistakably show to what religion they belonged. The left hand rests on a severed head, while the right holds up a lightning flash. The employee of the Granet Museum in Aix-en-Provence with whom I looked at these figures told me that the heads under the heroes' fingers represented their death, which is why the eyes are closed, while the lightning represents the light by which they go through the graveyard night. This struck me as too symbolical. But this is not to dispute that the statues of Entremont are an attempt to depict that constant preoccupation of the Celts: what happens when life comes to an end? In the years after 58 BC they had every cause to ponder this with particular intensity. From Rome emerged a man to whom we owe the most detailed descriptions of the Gauls and their priests. He did not come to study the natives of France, but to conquer them; and his name was Gaius Julius Caesar.

TEN

The Coming of Caesar

They say that legionaries are being recruited in the inns on the Tiber for the war in the west, which is now to be conquered. The land is called Gaul.

Bertolt Brecht, *Das Verhör des Lukullus*

A young man whose ambition and appetite for life were larger than his purse could have done worse than pick a political career in the Rome of the first century BC. The more so if his qualities included a first-rate intellect, a certain laxity in moral matters, a keen eye for human weakness and the cool head of a professional gambler.

Caesar had all of these qualities or acquired them in the course of time. The career that he made for himself in the first forty-two years of his life was correspondingly successful, though also erratic and adventurous. By 58 BC he had been high priest, staff officer, finance minister, military governor, senator and consul in turn. He had repeatedly had to flee from his political foes and had married three times, studied in academies, had countless love-affairs, fought in the front line, led campaigns, been involved in intrigue and, more than anything else, got himself into debt. Circumventing laws he regarded as inconvenient and looking on the state as a *res privata* – a purely personal matter, namely his own – had become a habit. Nor did he draw any distinction between foreign and domestic policy. Wherever he invested his energies, whether in Rome or in some distant theatre of war, it was all part of a single game. The moves he managed to set up would have been worthy of a Grand Master in chess, despite – or rather because of – the essentially simple principle underlying them.

It was vital for him to have a secure base for the expeditions he undertook to subject, or still unconquered, foreign lands, and immediately to invest at home the capital – fame and fortune – that he acquired there. As long as he lacked both, and particularly money, he was forced to find on the one hand a financial backer and, on the other, a man whose unchallenged popularity could divert a fall in his own. The first he found in Crassus, probably the richest man in Rome, and the other in Pompey, one of the most successful generals of this republic which had long since risen to world power. He intended first to harness this unlikely pair to his own purposes and then to reap their inheritance.

The first thing he did was to join them in the so-called First Triumvirate. Only when this power bloc – at bottom, a purely personal agreement between influential men – had been established could the ambitious Caesar set about reducing his deficit in prestige and money by a spectacular enterprise abroad. With the help of the votes that the Triumvirate could assemble in the Senate, he had himself appointed governor of the province of Gallia Cisalpina and subject Illyria. This post suited his intentions in two ways. From rich northern Italy considerable income flowed to Rome. Part of this could be diverted into his own pockets. Moreover, he saw the chance of advancing on some pretext or other from northern Yugoslavia into the Danube region, which he would duly conquer and gain a triumph and due military glory. But fate was to deal him an even better hand.

Before his departure the consul in Gallia Narbonensis, the southern part of Gaul that Rome had already conquered, died; Caesar, the newly appointed dignitary, was given this office as well. That brought within his reach the richest of all possible prizes: the rest of Gaul. To conquer it was Caesar's immediate thought. He had already had dealings with Celts in Spain.

The Iberian peninsula, at least its former Celtic parts, had fallen to Rome in the Second Punic War. Publius Cornelius Scipio, called Africanus Major, had cleared the last pockets of resistance by the western Phoenicians and succeeded in presenting himself to the natives as their liberator from foreign yoke. The goodwill did not, however, last for long. When the Romans made no move to evacuate the country again, the inhabitants launched a guerrilla war, in which the legionaries once more had to face the *furor* of barbarian attacks and got a first-hand opportunity to verify the old reports about the Gallic terror.

Spain had been widely Celticized since the early La Tène period. In the great changes at the end of the sixth century BC strong tribes from the north had not only penetrated the French homelands of the Iberians but also crossed the Pyrenees. From the intermingling of the two peoples emerged the great barbarian group that Ancient geographers describe as the Celtiberians. Later they discovered within this area the Galicians as well, in the extreme north-west, the Lusitanians in modern Portugal and, along with lesser tribes, the Vaccaei. Only in the south and east of the peninsula did older peoples manage to preserve themselves from interbreeding.

Diodorus's picture of the Celtiberians reveals many of the features he also discovered in the inhabitants of northern Italy and France. They were, he says, cruel and hospitable, brilliant iron-smiths and formidable warriors. They marched to battle singing and sang as they attacked. They were as proficient on horseback as on foot; they had weaponry and clothing much like the Gauls', wearing trousers, woollen cloaks and plumed helmets. They specialized in surprise attacks for plunder; a lightning advance out of the hills was followed by equally rapid withdrawal into the undergrowth or the rocks, as the Romans would repeatedly learn to their cost.

In 197 BC, nine years after the fall of Carthage, the tribes of the south and east rebelled against the garrison; somewhat later the Celtiberians also rose up. The guerrilla warfare tied down one hundred and fifty thousand men and soon produced its own out-standing heroes. One of them was the Lusitanian shepherd Viriatus who set up his standard in 147 BC and – a commander of chivalric stamp – soon attracted so many warriors as to be able to engage the Romans in open battle. He destroyed an army under Vitelius and forced on his successor a peace-treaty that was highly unfavourable to Rome. The pro-praetor did not ratify this treaty but sent more and more troops against the rebels. When they, too, were defeated, he turned from iron to gold. A relative of Viriatus's was bribed and the guerrillero was stabbed from behind.

But Spain was not thereby pacified. Numantia, on the upper

Douro, near modern Soria, developed into a centre of bitter resistance. For fourteen years every attack launched against the walls of the exposed hill-town failed. Its defenders, Celtiberians of the Arevacian tribe, gained such a fearsome reputation that Roman soldiers refused to fight them. To settle the problem the Senate was finally obliged to send in the best general it had at that time (134 BC). Scipio Aemilianus, a friend of Polybius's, who bore the name Africanus Minor because he had destroyed Carthage, arrived with no less than sixty thousand legionaries to combat the four-thousand-man garrison of Numantia. Even then he did not feel strong enough to attempt an attack; instead he proceeded with a siege. After a further sixteen months it was to bring him scant booty. The last half-starved inhabitants of the place burnt their houses and then killed themselves. As in Tunisia the general entered a set of smoking ruins; and, like Carthage, he had it razed to the ground. The Celtiberians seemed finally to have been broken, although under the surface the old hatred of the treacherous occupier smouldered.

In 77 BC, half a century after the destruction of Numantia, it burst into flame again. Having fled to North Africa from his political enemy Sulla, now dictator in Rome, the Roman general Quintus Sertorius was invited to lead the discontented Lusatians, whom he led against his former colleague's armies. Not only a brilliant strategist but also a talented agitator, Sertorius was able to unify his following so that Rome could defeat him only by calling on her best general. At that time it was Pompey, Caesar's later ally. But he too could not rely on the sword alone. Instead he had Sertorius assassinated, like his predecessor Viriatus, and mopped up the now leaderless Lusatians. This of course did not suit Caesar at all.

The praetor, a sort of middle-ranking consul, had in 61 BC so damaged his already tarnished reputation by his adulterous affairs that he needed a chance to recover. Spain seemed the right place for him. It had been assigned to Caesar as a province; but since Pompey had already fought so successfully, to avoid being put completely in the shade he had to arrange some heroic spectacle of his own. With contempt for the existing laws, on his own authority he raised the strength of the troops under him and once more attacked the shattered Lusatians. Then he attacked Galicia, the last refuge of the Celtiberians. They were unable to resist; their capital

Brigantium (probably named after the Brigantes, who also lived in England and gave their name to Bregenz in Austria) was stormed and their country annexed as a province. Spain was now finally Roman, and it was Caesar who had conquered it.

That sufficed to silence his critics and to ensure him the highest rank that the senate could give. In 59 BC he became consul. However the prize that he brought was of benefit not only to the Roman exchequer but also to his own financial circumstances – though it eased them for only a short while. Within a year, in 58 BC, when he was setting about the absorption of the next province, his debts were again so great that in order not to fall completely into Crassus's hands he had to try to make some money out of Gaul. This was to bring in more than the Spanish enterprise had done; but it also brought complications.

Rome was no mere robber-state that allowed its generals to go off on plundering expeditions of their own with Roman armies. If a foreign country was annexed, there had to be sufficient strategic or legal grounds for it. Thus Rome had occupied northern Italy because the Po valley had been the refuge of aggressive Celts. It had sent its legions into Spain because Hannibal's bases had to be destroyed so long as he himself stood on Roman territory. And in 125 BC it had annexed a broad strip of land along the Mediterranean coast of France and turned it into the province of Gallia Narbonensis because a link between Italy and Spain was needed. Even if Rome did not conquer, it did not return what its legions had taken. But it was impossible to maintain these principles in the remainder of free Gaul. Gallic land had never been moistened by Roman blood, and the inhabitants nowhere threatened Rome's interest. The new proconsul therefore had to be on the constant look-out for some reasonably convincing pretext for war. He began to observe the country with care.

What he saw was roughly this: the innumerable lords of innumerable tribal principalities had for some time not matched the picture the Romans had long ago acquired of the Celts. Severed heads still grinned down from the door-beams of their houses, but the occupants now seemed considerably Romanized or Hellenized. They preferred trade to war and constituted a wealthy elite, ruled by popular assemblies and Vergobretes. Among their tribes were the Arverni, Aedui and Sequani, the three most powerful, followed by the Allobroges, Helvetii, Senones, Carnutes, Veneti, Pictones, Treveri, Nervii, Menapii, Vangianes, as well as the Usipetes, Eburones, Tencteri, Sugambri and Ubii, who were long thought to be German. These were only the more important for, all in all, Strabo believed that there were about sixty different groups among the Celts, each with its own name. How large the greatest of them was can be seen if we halve Caesar's propagandist figure for the Helvetii (360,000) and reckon that many of the sixty tribes probably numbered only a few thousand souls. All Gaul is unlikely to have had more than four or five million inhabitants, though for Rome this was by no means a negligible figure.

Based in Gallia Narbonensis, Rome's representatives had to play off one great tribe against another so as to keep the political balance between them. Thus at the end of the second century BC an attempt by the Arverni to take the leadership of the country was frustrated by diplomatic methods. Similarly the proconsular officials tamed the princes of the Sedui by addressing them as 'brothers' or 'cousins' – an empty name that was taken as a great compliment. Above all Rome profited from the incapacity of the Celts to unite in political association, from the fascination exerted by a more advanced culture, and from the princes' love of money. On the other hand Rome, because of some of these characteristics, could never be quite sure of them. This was displayed in 61 BC in the case of Dumnorix of the Aedui.

A successful financier, Dumnorix had suddenly decided to become politically active as well. To this end he mobilized his 'clients', the thousands of men dependent on him economically or by allegiance. With this updated version of the old retinue-system, he began to make trouble for his brother Divitiacus, the reigning Vergobret, whenever he could. It does not seem to have been an unusual procedure. Rich princes' sons, Caesar reports, had often mobilized up to ten thousand men and thus been able to put pressure on popular assemblies and on courts. He also says that these followers were ready to accompany their chiefs, if need be to the death. They are to be seen as bodyguards, whose members were inspired by the old ideals of male comradeship. These were probably the young homosexuals described by Diodorus. Dumnorix seems to have used them very effectively.

He so intimidated Divitiacus that in 60 BC the latter travelled to Rome, became acquainted with Cicero (who thought he was a

Druid) and shocked the Senate with his tales of mysterious con-
spiracies. The 'revolutionary minded' prince, he said, intended to
take power not only over the tribe, but over the whole of Gaul. To
this end he had made an alliance with the Sequani, who on their
part had come to a further accord with the German Suevi; in
return for the cession of land in Lower Alsace, they were now
ready to serve Dumnorix and his comrades as auxiliaries. However
threatening this might seem in Gallic eyes, the Senate regarded
it as a conspiracy among savages and on this account could not
decide to intervene militarily or diplomatically. Caesar inevitably
regarded things in a different light. Here was a chance for him to
interfere in the affairs of Gaul, provided they continued to develop
in the way he desired. He was not kept in suspense for long.

In the very year the proconsul took office, the Celtic Helvetii
came to feel the effects of the Sequani's policy of alliance. Suabian
hordes began to make inroads into their own territory, which ran
from Lake Constance along the Jura down to Lake Geneva. These
ancestors of the Swiss, who had shortly before emigrated from
Baden into modern Switzerland, were so troubled by this that they
decided simply to enter France. 'When they felt ready for this,'
Caesar wrote, 'they set light to all of their towns, twelve in all . . .
destroyed their grain-supplies with the exception of those that they
intended to take with them, so that if ever they were tempted to
return, they would the more resolutely press ahead against the
dangers.'

On 28 March 58 BC they set off, allegedly with 360,000 men,
60,000 carts, 24,000 draught animals – a veritable migration,
though not on a grand scale. At Geneva they meant to cross the
Rhône and make a short journey across the territory of the
Allobroges, which already belonged to Gallia Narbonensis. Their
goal was the homelands of the Aedui between the Saône and the
Loire. Dumnorix had invited them. Caesar saw his chance. When
the Helvetii asked if they might cross Roman territory he not only
refused, but barred their way with all the troops he could muster.
However the battle that he may have hoped for did not take place,
for the Helvetii changed their route and crossed the Jura directly
into free Gaul. Dumnorix eased their path through the lands of the
Sequani. Caesar had been deprived of his opportunity. From now
on he had to embroider the facts a little.

He made out that the Helvetii had returned the invitation of the

Aedui with murder, rapine and other crimes; as proof, he offered
the Divitiacus party's plea for assistance. These documents simultaneously allowed him to justify to the Senate the raising of new
troops in northern Italy. But he did not wait for an answer before
attacking. As soon as he had reinforced his troops sufficiently he
thrust into Gaul, met the Helvetii at Bibracte (Autun) and
defeated them in a battle that gave brilliant evidence of his military
gifts. He admits that it also cost him high losses, though only with
the parenthesis that 'as we were fixed for three days because of the
wounded and the need to bury the dead, we could not pursue the
enemy'. He himself claims to have destroyed no less than a round
quarter million of the enemy. Two-thirds of their men, women and
children were said to have remained on the field, which must, even
taking into account the results of a few preceding skirmishes, have
meant veritable mountains of corpses around the circle of Helvetian
carts. He ordered those that remained to go back to their old home,
which saved the future confederation, though to this day the
Swiss have failed to name him as their national hero.

The Aedui, if we are to believe Caesar, behaved cleverly.
Divitiacus in particular is said to have pleaded his people's cause so
well from then on that Caesar felt justified in doing as he wanted in
France. He had done himself a good turn in that the Senate now
saw no possibility of further obstructing his progress as Roman
Patronus Galliae. Because of these manipulations posterity finds
his own account of the matter unreliable; his descriptions have the
fatal ring of cabal and melodrama. Long sections read as if they had
been retouched to suit the tastes of readers who conceived politics
as above all a game of intrigue, and it is impossible to take some of
the other passages about the bellum Gallicum entirely seriously.

The famous first sentence, 'Gallia est omnis divisa in partes tres'
('Gaul is divided into three parts'), betrays the hand of an accomplished stylist. It is simple and of textbook clarity: it sets the scene
for the reader as if it were a bowling alley. In one of the three parts
of Gaul, that north of the Marne and the Seine, lived (skittle
number one) the Belgae; in the second part, south of the Garonne,
were the Aquitani; and in the third – the king-pin – lived 'the
tribes that are called in their own tongue Celts, and in ours Gauls'.
Reading this, we are already awaiting the ball that will come and
knock these down one after the other.

But the triple division hardly squares with reality. Archaeologists know that in the area that Caesar ascribes to the Aquitani, Celtiberians were settled, a people already well known at the time to geographers, and under their own name. Moreover they believe that the north Gallic areas alleged to be inhabited by the Belgae were in fact characterized by a La Tène (Celtic) culture. On this third people Caesar adds information that may not have been available when he wrote the first part of his account: it appears in the second part and may have been based on hearsay. He states that a king of the Celtic Reni, who lived on the upper Meuse, told him that 'most Belgae were originally Germans and had in the dim and distant past come from across the Rhine'. Strabo confirms this, half a century later, with the words: 'Next to the [Belgian] Treveri there lived the Nervii, a Germanic tribe' (whom Caesar also included among the Celts). Tacitus also says as much. Modern scholars make little of these three pieces of information and philologists are fairly certain that the tribes living in northern Gaul were Celtic-speakers and thus not Germans.

What did Caesar suggest they were? The obvious and certainly not wholly incorrect supposition is that he just did not know. He had to rely on spies, scouts and not always trustworthy accomplices: he simply had to accept such information as he could come by. But here his primary concern must have been to present the Roman public with an easily comprehensible situation. This is particularly clear when he deals with the Germans, his fourth skittle. With unobtrusive artistry he characterizes them as successors of those Cimbri who had been defeated at Vercellae by his uncle Marius, honoured on this account as the third founder of Rome. He describes them as 'monstrously tall, brave and skilled in arms'. Gauls who had had to fight them had not even been able 'to bear the sight of them' or the fiery gaze of their eyes. He also gives the impression that they belonged to a very numerous people and that the rest of their tribe lived on the far side of the Rhine.

This last point is of particular importance. If Gaul was an area whose interests Caesar, at the behest of Divitiacus and his comrades, was supposed to be guarding, he must have felt obliged to fight all who sought to disturb its peace from outside. That could be used against the Belgae who, if they were Germans, would have little right to be living on the left bank of the Rhine, in what are now the Benelux countries; it was even more true of the Suevi, with whom the Sequani and their friend Dumnorix had allied. His plan thus became obvious. He had made a bogeyman of the Helvetii and defeated them; now it was the turn of all peoples who could be categorized as Germans, and of course their accomplice, the unruly Aeduan prince. This sparks off two more related questions. Was Divitiacus's brother really a traitor? Did the Gauls really fear nothing more than an attack by the hordes from across the Rhine? To answer these we have to consider a third question. Who were these Germans anyway? As Strabo had already discovered, it was not easy to say.

As regards this question of definition, it seems clear that the Teutones and the Ambrones cannot be classed as Germans but rather as Celts or cousins of the Celts. On the other hand the Cimbri probably came from the northern region where the highly developed culture of the Bronze Age had once flourished. They were at least forerunners of the tribes with which the Gauls now had to contend.

In the early or middle La Tène era there must have been a development in Jutland, on the Baltic and North Sea coast and around the lower Elbe similar to that undergone by the Celts. Peoples that had adapted to the harsh climate developed a common language and possibly some kind of national consciousness, but above all an iron industry that enabled them to establish a solid economic basis. Correspondingly the population increased. Graveyards in those parts that, in the early La Tène era, comprised only a few dozen graves, grew to become vast cemeteries by the first century BC; villages flourished; Germanic trading princes, offering much better steel than the Celts, got in contact with Roman civilization and acquired a taste for its luxuries. When finally their native domains could no longer contain them, these. northern Brennuses turned south to gain new lands.

Their first encounter was of course with the Celts, who had settled as far north as modern Westphalia. How they dealt with them – whether peaceably or by force – is not recorded. Both are possible. For one thing the Germans were so little different from the Celts that even considerable scholars rely on Strabo's formula for distinguishing them: they were rather blonder than their southern cousins. Moreover the many parallels between the Germanic and the Celtic gods suggest that there must have been a time when these two peoples mingled and influenced one another. Some time in the later La Tène era this must have turned to war.

The Siegerland inhabited by Celts was at this time deserted –
which suggests that its occupants must have moved south. In the
region between the Teutoburger Forest and the Westerwald, tribes
such as the Cheruscii were identified; to this day we cannot tell
whether they were Celts or Germans. From the Fichtel mountains
to the Hunsrück were built a series of fortifications which most
investigators have seen as a kind of Great Celtic Wall against the
invading Germans.

The largest example is the Steinsburg near Römhild in the
southern reaches of the Thuringian Forest. It has a treble protecting ring, the walls of which were almost seven miles long and up to
twelve, and in some places even eighteen, feet high. The Hunnen-
ring of Otzenhausen and an almost equally massive site on the
Donnersberg in the Palatinate also belong to this network. Taken
as a whole it tends to contradict the argument that the Celts were
incapable of large scale, co-operative enterprises. At all events, its
existence shows how dangerous the Germanic tribes had become.

The line of fortifications, which secured a stretch of the border
roughly two hundred and fifty miles long, was probably built as
early as the second century BC. But as in Caesar's day (the mid-first
century) the Suevi had already settled in Alsace and were threatening the Helvetii, they must in the interim have broken through the
Celtic defence system and forced its founders to face the attackers
with means other than the sword. What these means were, we can
only speculate. It is nevertheless interesting that according to
Caesar the leader of the Suevi spoke Celtic quite well and bore a
name that did not sound purely Germanic; there was also at this
time another Ariovist in Britain, a famous Celtic eye-surgeon. The
two peoples may have begun to influence each other quite rapidly.

The Suevi, who came from Holstein and the Baltic, were not in
fact a tribe but a sacral association to which, Tacitus says, the
Langobards, Marcomanni, Quadii and Senones also belonged.
Once a year delegates of all of these sub-groups met in a sacred
grove and celebrated 'a hideous and mysterious religious feast
which was inaugurated in the name of all with a human sacrifice'.
At other times the Langobards sacrificed slaves to their goddess by
drowning them in a lake; and ritual shafts were also known among
them. The Celts may have found many of their customs so familiar
that they had no difficulty in collaborating with the Suevi, even if
only because there was no way of getting rid of them. It seems

justifiable to assume that large areas of southern Germany, from
the Main to Lake Constance, were during Dumnorix's time
already controlled by Germans, and that the earlier inhabitants
simply had had to put up with it. This however shows Divitiacus's
brother in a quite different light from that in which Caesar portrays
him.

A Gaul considering the overall position of his people would
necessarily perceive that he and his countrymen were between the
jaws of a giant pincer-movement: from the north and the east,
Germans were encroaching on their fertile and beautiful land; from
the south the Romans were exerting pressure. To weigh up which
was the more dangerous would be senseless: both could take what
they wanted and they had shown it – the Romans in Gallia
Narbonensis, the Germans in Alsace. The only real question for
the Gauls was which of the two was the lesser evil, Caesar or
Ariovist, and which would be the better ally? That many rich and
powerful Gauls chose Rome comes as no surprise. The Mediterranean was a profitable export-market for them, and for centuries
they had been in close contact with its inhabitants; the superiority
of Mediterranean culture was patent.

The broad mass of the people could, however, have felt equally
drawn to the Germans. In their customs and military prowess
lay values that the Celts still cherished. The warriors surging in
from the east would have appeared as a kind of super-Celt – blond-
maned giants with their hair sticking up, capable of the most intense
furor. Young noblemen of Dumnorix's type probably reacted in
this traditionalist spirit, as no doubt did the priests. Caesar, in his
somewhat dismissive account of the Druids, gives some suggestion
of this. The division ran right through Celtic society, and perhaps
even through the hearts of many individuals. This is a justification
for Dumnorix. Anxious to rely on the Germans, an excessively
ambitious politician maybe, but he was certainly no traitor. Nor of
course was his brother Divitiacus.

To decide finally which of the two was in the right could only
be done by someone who turned this situation to his own advantage, as Caesar seems to have appreciated. In order to portray
Dumnorix and his Sequanian friends both to contemporaries and
to the Gauls as collaborators, he had to defeat the Suevi, for if they
had won, they could of course have written history their way. It

helped Caesar that in the Sequani's lands Ariovist behaved not as an ally but as a conqueror. He asserted his claims to land with violence and by taking hostages. He thus fell out of favour with this people who had earlier invited him in. With a clear conscience, and with the support of Divitiacus, Caesar could thus present himself as defender of the interests of Gaul.

The Suevian, however, inevitably saw through this. He declared – with an open cynicism that Caesar always denied himself – that it was 'the law of war that the victor should rule the defeated as he liked. The Romans are also in the habit of behaving at their own discretion towards those they have subjected and not according to the precepts of others.' This sounded much like the message that the Roman envoys had heard from the Celts 332 years before, before Clusium. It meant in effect that the Celts had not been taken in. They saw that the Romans wanted Gaul as much as they did; let it therefore fall to the stronger. Ariovist is described by Caesar as intolerably arrogant, but he seems also to have had a certain stylishness – though not enough to defeat the Romans in the field.

Just before the autumn of 58 BC there was a battle – one assumes it was near Mulhouse in Alsace – between the invaders from the south and those from the east. It ended in a complete overthrow of the Suevi. Caesar's self-imposed task in Gaul ought to have been fulfilled. He did not however withdraw to his starting-point in Gallia Narbonensis. Instead he confirmed Ariovist's suspicions and stationed troops in the lands of the hitherto independent Sequani between the Saône and the upper Rhône. Thus Dumnorix could now say that he had been right all along; but it was no use to him for Rome had already won. Only his brother's plea restrained the proconsul from executing the prince at once. Instead Caesar put Dumnorix's entire retinue under observation and later tried to take him to Britain. Can this young man be labelled a collaborator? History, despite Caesar's attempt to retouch it, provides an ambiguous answer. Five years later, when his star again seemed to be setting, it was the turn of Divitiacus's adherents to ask themselves if, by their policy of friendship with Rome, they had not been betraying their country. The fraternal quarrel in the Aéduan princely family house was only an excerpt from the tragedy of Gaul. Caesar was still its stage-manager.

After the victory over Ariovist he went to his north Italian headquarters to 'preside over justice' and, though he does not say so himself, to deal once more with his Roman affairs. He could be quite certain that sooner or later there would be a new opportunity for further conquest in Gaul. By the following spring it came, supplied by the Belgae.

After the events in Alsace and Burgundy the tribes living in northern Gaul realized that Caesar was anything but a liberator from alleged oppressors. As he himself admits, they feared 'that the Roman army would march against them after conquering the whole of Gaul' and therefore formed a coalition, though the consul adds in the same breath that they 'rose against the people of Rome'. This tactical lie is understandable, for Caesar had still somehow to invent a plausible enough justification for his campaigns of conquest for the benefit of the Senate. It was particularly difficult to find such pretexts for the enterprise against the Belgae, and this forced him to adopt the above-mentioned publicity campaign.

As there was no foreign power behind them, he had the king of the Reni lead them at least in the general direction of the Germans. Because he wished to strengthen his own troops he described the Belgae as a particularly savage and extraordinarily numerous people. In reality they were not nearly as strong as Caesar suggested and as their warriors liked to persuade themselves. The Belgae failed to cross a strongly fortified line that Caesar had set up on the Aisne marshes; incapable of supplying a besieging army for a long period, the separate tribes split up again and went their own way – into destruction. The Romans first defeated the Suessiones, then the Bellovaci and finally the Ambrones. None of these groups was, on its own, able to put up serious resistance.

Only the Nervii and the Atuatucres demonstrated once more that Gauls could still fight. The former gave battle on the Sambre, near Maubeuge, and Rome won only because of Caesar's personal courage and cool-headedness. The latter he himself admits could trust only in the courage with which they opposed him and in their physical strength: 'Indeed the Gauls generally scoffed at the Romans' small stature in comparison with their own height.' This again recalls Polybius's description of the Celts, but it was quite differently interpreted by Caesar. The Atuatucres, he believed, 'are descendants of the Cimbri and the Teutones'. He did not miss the chance to present himself as a second Marius, though this was no longer at all necessary.

All in all the reports of the successes of the year 58 BC amounted to a run of victories the like of which the Senate can seldom have heard. The whole of Gaul seemed more or less to have succumbed; and for the heads of the Roman state this was enough to forgive Caesar all his earlier flouting of the law, and to make him

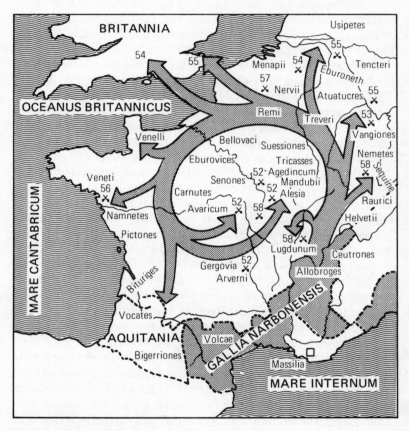

Map 8   Caesar's advance through Gaul

forget that they themselves had never really wanted to conquer. There was a fifteen-day jubilation, 'an honour', as Caesar remarks, 'that hitherto no one has had'. He was right. Ordinarily a victorious general would be given no more than a five-day celebration for his victory; only Pompey had had a ten-day celebration, after his successes in the east when he brought under Roman control the still unconquered portion of Turkey, together with Syria and Palestine. Now Caesar was points ahead of him, which could be dangerous. It gradually dawned on the somewhat corpulent veteran what an ambitious climber he had linked himself with in their joint venture, the Triumvirate.

But Pompey was not Caesar's most difficult problem. In spring 56 BC both he and Crassus were persuaded to renew and continue the old association; both also became consuls. Caesar himself was assigned Gaul for a further five years; yet this land now turned out to be anything but the easy prize its conqueror had imagined. He did succeed, once he had finally discarded the mask of *Patronus Galliae*, in occupying Brittany and Normandy; but in the Valais his legate Sulpicius Galba wore his teeth out against the Gaesatae or their successors. Over the next few years the other Celtic tribes set off one rebellion after another and forced Caesar to pay a second time, and more dearly, for each rapid victory that he had won before. Caesar was faced with difficult times.

Surrounded by a staff made up less of military experts than of *habitués* of the Roman scene, he dashed from one corner of Gaul to the other, seldom on horseback and usually in a litter. He dictated virtually without stopping; and several secretaries wrote down his words. Messengers tore the letters from their hands and rode off, towards Rome where the eloquent Cicero, once Caesar's enemy and now his ally, had to be maintained with gifts of money, or towards Brittany where the Celtic Veneti had seized Roman requisitioning officers. This sometime playboy, in not particularly good health, was in these years transformed into the gaunt figure of legend which has gone down into history. He worked day and night and would be scribbling away at his desk long after his exhausted adjutants had gone to bed. He sat alone by the smouldering camp-fire, lost in worries, plans, new intrigues. And yet he could still call a passing NCO by name and ask about the wound he had received in the last battle.

But however nerve-racking, discouraging or depressing this life must at times have been, he never lost his nerve, was seldom in a bad mood, was seldom given to authoritarian ways, and always listened politely to the good or less than good suggestions that were made to him. He even pursued his studies in the few leisure-hours he had, took from his travelling library what the Greeks had writ-

ten of the Gauls, polished his despatches to Rome until they had
attained that form of refined simplicity in which he later published
them, and even took an interest in the theory of correct usage.
What was superficial in him – his frivolity and gambler's arrogance
– melted away in these years until nothing remained but the spare
figure of a gigantic will. Like a wolf he held Gaul, which almost
threatened to slip from his grasp again, tight between his jaws and
defended his prey with attacks that were ultimately always more
dangerous than whatever hatred or armed force his enemies could
muster. 'Nowhere,' writes the Göttingen historian Alfred Heun,
'was Caesar automatically given the chance to bestride the
world. . . . It was in Gaul that he took the first steps.' In fact Caesar
as proconsul was pushed into the tragic role of Sisyphus. He fulfilled it with brilliance, and every attempt by the Celts was met
with a still bolder one.

The rebel Veneti, relying on a strong fleet and British auxiliaries,
were defeated by an armada whose ships were built by soldiers on
the Loire. The Aquitani he overran at the first attempt, for they too
had tried to shake off the Roman yoke; when, shortly afterwards,
the Tencteri and Usipetes crossed the lower Rhine he not only
drove them off but pursued them. Via a bridge that his sappers
threw over the river which he himself declared to be Gaul's frontier – probably at Neuwied – he became the first Roman to push
into the lands on its right bank, though he did not remain there for
long. The enterprise served only as a shot across the bows.

All these campaigns, battles and expeditions would have been
enough to fill a whole year for an ordinary man, but they seem only
to have stimulated Caesar to do more. Once he returned from
Germany he declared that he wanted 'rapidly to cross into Britain,
as I knew that in almost all Gallic wars our enemies had had help
from there' – which makes the Channel-crossing sound like a
pleasure-trip. As the year 55 BC was to show, it was anything but
that, even though it was little more than an armed reconnaissance
expedition. When it was over, it was none the less greeted by
thunderous applause.

Rome celebrated her proconsul's boldest venture to date with a
triumph lasting no less than twenty days. The enthusiasm was
understandable. To the inhabitants of Italy, Britain seemed almost
at the edge of the world. That the eagles had been set up there
seemed to confirm all that the early prophets had foretold of

Rome's greatness. However, Caesar was to learn that he could be less sure of his conquests than ever. He went again to England in the following year, and defeated a strong army under King Cassivellaunus; but before this happened there emerged in Gaul enemies who represented a far greater danger than Dumnorix had ever done.

ELEVEN

The Vain Struggle of Vercingetorix

The Latin word, *Gallus* means both 'Gaul' and 'cock'. It was Vercingetorix who gave the first cock-crow.

Gaston Bonheur, *Notre Patrie Gauloise*

The first Gallic noble to oppose Caesar was also among the first to pay for it with his life. When Dumnorix refused to take ship for Britain he was surrounded by horsemen; as he tried to draw his sword, crying 'he was a free man and the son of a free people', he was hacked down.

Caesar justified this murder with 'the conviction that the man had not behaved reasonably in my absence'. It was from his point of view an irrefutable argument. As before, Dumnorix represented the heart of the resistance against Rome. He would certainly have tried to promote the rising agitation among his countrymen while Caesar was in Britain for the second time. But his call for freedom, stifled by spears, did not go unheard. The first to take it up was the Treverian prince, Indutiomarus. He collected his followers with the aim of plunging into the Ardennes to begin a guerrilla war against Rome. But as, like Dumnorix himself, he represented only half of the twin leadership that characterized the epoch, Caesar was able to frustrate the enterprise without using force before he left for England. He turned to Cingetorix, the ruling Vergobrete of the tribe, and ordered him to restrain his hot-headed son-in-law. Cingetorix, who believed that a successful war of independence was neither possible nor desirable, bowed to the command and forced Indutiomarus to swear loyalty to the proconsul. Indutiomarus reluctantly obeyed, but he had no intention of keeping his oath. Moreover he was not the only one who had decided on rebellion, as Caesar was to discover on his return from Britain in the autumn of 54 BC.

He had just disbanded the expeditionary force and assigned his legions their winter-quarters in various parts of Gaul when he was informed that the Eburones, neighbours of the Treveri, had tried to attack a camp of his subordinates Sabinius and Cotta on the middle Moselle. In itself this would have been a quite unremarkable report from Gaul's unruly border country, except that it concerned a tribe that had no particular reason to rise against Rome. The Eburones had been liberated in the Belgian war from the yoke of the Atuatucres and were effectively doing better under proconsular rule than in the past. Moreover they were much too weak to put up successful opposition. What had caused them to attack? Sabinius and Cotta also wondered. They sent to Ambiorix, chief of the Eburones, to ask for an explanation. The answer they received must, on first impression, have struck anyone who knew conditions in Gaul as unbelievable. Ambiorix said that 'he himself was not naïve enough to suppose he could defeat the Romans with his weak forces alone', but his own people had forced him to attack the camp as they did not want to disobey 'a common resolution of Gaul'.

This struck a new note. What could be meant by 'a common resolution of Gaul'? Did it mean that the many tribes of the country, splintered and quarrelling, large and small, had got together in a sudden 'conspiracy'? Could these fighting-cocks possibly constitute a team? Caesar's scepticism on hearing this news is understandable, but his officers took it more seriously. Made anxious by the constant attacks of the Eburonian cavalry, depressed at the barren, rainy country, the war council of their units resolved to ignore orders and return to the nearest large legionary camp – which was just what Ambiorix wanted.

Just two miles beyond their safe, fortified camp, in a valley that was too narrow to be crossed in proper formation, the Romans learnt how he intended to use his 'weak' forces. Horsemen suddenly emerged from the thickets and rushed like lightning on the least protected parts of the narrow column, the supply-units. Cotta and Sabinius met this situation as they had learned to. They ordered the baggage to be abandoned and a square to be formed. Ambiorix was not in the least impressed. Since he, as Caesar admits, 'certainly did not lack sense' and was thus a great deal more than a hot-headed Celtic warrior, he shouted to his men that the plunder was as good as certain and that they should take no risks and merely shoot from a distance. This command was obeyed. Not until the Romans in their frustration undertook sallies did the Gauls attack, surrounding the cohort that had advanced and annihilating it. These salami-tactics were kept up for so long that one of the legion's officers, Quintus Titurius, lost his nerve and offered to negotiate.

Astonishingly, Ambiorix accepted this proposition, though with an ulterior motive. As soon as the Roman delegation had approached and laid down their arms, he had them surrounded and hacked to pieces – a breach of law such as Caesar had sometimes practised. When the soldiers remaining in the square saw this, they realized there was no hope and made ready for the end. Between dusk and dawn they were slain in a bloody massacre, almost literally to the last man for only 'a few escaped from this battle, and by mountain paths they came through the forest to the legate Titus Labienus in his winter quarters to relate what had happened'. Now Caesar realized that Ambiorix had not altogether been a victim of his own imagination when he maintained that there was 'a common resolution of Gaul' to defeat the Romans. A single tribe on its own would never have had the courage for such a great act of provocation. There was indeed, behind the little Eburonian chief, one man at least who could mobilize much stronger forces than he: Indutiomarus, Cingetorix's recently reprimanded son-in-law.

Immediately after the Gallic victory over Sabinius and Cotta, Indutiomarus, who must in the meantime have arranged to outmanoeuvre his father-in-law, advanced against the heavily fortified headquarters of Caesar's deputy Tullius Cicero. The outcome was no mere ambush but a full-blooded siege.

His troops erected a wall nine feet high and a ditch fifteen feet deep around the whole legionary camp. They built mobile siege-towers, brought up grapnels to tear down the palisades and arranged for testudo formations just as the Roman sappers did when working on an enemy strong-point. 'All of this,' says Caesar, 'they had learned from us in the previous years.' The attack they quickly launched also showed how well they had absorbed Roman lessons. With their own *ballistae* the Gauls hurled glowing mud-balls and burning spears on to the straw-covered winter-quarters of the legionaries. When half the camp was in flames they brought up their siege-towers, though these seasoned campaigners forced them back in hand-to-hand fighting. However the position of the beleaguered garrison steadily worsened.

Help in this dire situation came from the pro-Roman Nervian, Vertico. He sent off a slave who – 'moving unsuspected, as a Gaul among Gauls' – was to ask Caesar to bring relief. The message arrived and he acted upon it at once. After assembling his troops, as many as he could muster, he raced within four days from the Atlantic coast to the Treverian lines, re-manned the half-demolished camp and then, with calculated coolness, enticed the attackers so close to the palisades that they could be scattered by a sudden sortie and chased back into the woods. But Caesar did not for a moment entertain the hope that the situation had been settled. For the first time since he had taken office, he did not winter in friendly northern Italy and instead resolved 'to remain personally with the army'. Roman affairs would have to wait; Gallic ones were more urgent.

Apart from his army Caesar's most powerful weapon in the battle for the country between the Atlantic and the Rhine was, above all, the disunity of the Gallic princes. This was revealed again and again by such combinations as Divitiacus versus Dumnorix or Indutiomarus versus Cingetorix. These Caesar consciously exploited. He assisted rulers of subject or allied tribes to gain power that they had not known for years, supported these mainly elderly princes against popular assemblies and younger competitors alike, and made them attend at regular intervals the meetings at which he listened to their opinions and complaints and passed on his own commands. Any prince who failed to attend would count as a deserter and have to reckon with a visit from Roman forces. That he was thereby insulting the pride of the lesser chiefs and other notables who set such store by their independence Caesar seems to. have appreciated, but he accepted the risk. Counting on a few reliable people struck him as more practical; and he created a steering mechanism that was efficient, though it did not suit the Celtic mentality.

The Gauls were a people governed less by reality than by their own picture of it. They still lived with the notion 'that they counted for something among all peoples because of their [old] warlike reputation', imagined themselves to be invincible warriors, descendants of the men who had once set Europe trembling. To have to bend to the rule of a people whose capital had once been burned by Brennus seemed, at least to the younger elements, intolerable. The thought of their own disgrace and of Roman hegemony made their pride smart more and more; and this wounded pride turned them into Pan-Gallic nationalists and resistance-fighters.

All this pent-up emotion was to be directed, given the conditions of the time, not only against the external enemy but also against the established Romanophile system among the Gauls themselves, which to the new men seemed corrupt. The question whether a man who collaborated with the Germans should count as a traitor now lost its meaning to such an extent that Indutiomarus, who was certainly a Gallic patriot, felt no compunction in summoning the men from beyond the Rhine to march into his occupied homeland. The only 'collaborators' he knew were those who worked for the Romans, and many of the native notables were to experience this to their cost in the next few months. A prince of the Carnutes – a tribe who lived north of the Loire – whom Caesar had restored 'to the former dignity of his fathers', was murdered by his fellow-tribesmen. The Senonian king, Cavarinus, who lived on the lower Seine, escaped by only a hair's-breadth from a similar attempt on his life. Indutiomarus gave the retrospective sanction of popular law to this feuding when, at a meeting of rebels, he declared his father-in-law to be a traitor and confiscated his property. This was no longer merely guerrilla tactics but a revolutionary act. He raised the lid still higher when he declared war not only on collaborators but also on tribes such as the Remi who refused to join the rebellion.

Following the laws that seem to obtain for all such mass uprisings, a people's war thus came very close to being a civil war. Only those who supported the common cause counted as friends; all others were enemies – one of the most horrible situations in which a people can find itself. However Indutiomarus must at this stage have represented the feelings of a large number of his fellow-countrymen. We can tell from Caesar's brief description that he was a powerful speaker, a warrior who shrank from no risk or cruelty, proud to excess and inspired by a hatred that stemmed partly from the Romans' having restricted his noble privileges to the benefit of other noblemen. He was a typical Celt in that he confused boldness with lack of judgment, in that his pride often turned into arrogance, logic into wishful thinking.

Had he and his like been sober realists they would have combined much earlier, abandoned part of their privileges and thrown them into a common national enterprise. But it was almost too late for that. They were in the situation of de Gaulle after the German invasion of France, but without the backing of a third power such as de Gaulle had in England and America. For the *maquisards* of Gaul had little enough with which to oppose the Roman soldiers. They did have men intelligent enough to imitate their enemies' military techniques; they had horse and foot in great numbers and terrain favourable to guerrilla warfare, with woods, ravines, marshes and fog-bound nights. But all of this together counted for little when one compares the opposition: iron discipline and the genius of one of the greatest generals in history.

The Celtic hordes were contending with a machine that functioned at the press of a button. Caesar's men were not so much soldiers as military technicians – each one a palisade-builder, a bridge-builder or a trench-digger, as well as a soldier. Indutiomarus was in the end to be routed by these 'bulldozing legions', as the French writer Gaston Bonheur calls the Roman units, and of course also by his own light-mindedness. When in 54 BC he rode, bored, away from a Roman outpost that had not at once succumbed, the defenders pursued him and cut him off. 'His head,' Caesar laconically observes, 'was brought into the camp' – a suitable end for a Celtic warrior. Ambiorix's failure was equally appropriate: when Caesar had defeated him several times he disappeared into a forest a year after the death of his ally, 'protected only by four horsemen whom he would trust with his life'. He had become an outlaw, as if the Druids had excommunicated him. Those resistance-fighters whom Caesar did capture were in turn condemned and executed, 'according to the customs of their ancestors' – that is, with hideous tortures. One of them escaped this fate by poisoning himself with yew berries before the executioners found him.

Caesar, it seemed, could now breathe freely. Indeed he closed his despatch for the year 53 BC once more with the formula: 'I travelled as usual to northern Italy to hold assizes there . . . Gaul being peaceful.' But was it?

A force that had undergone the fearful blows rained on Ambiorix and Indutiomarus ought to have asked itself whether it would not do better to accept its fate and lay down its arms. But a people in rebellion reacts differently, even when it is as unstable as the Gauls were. The leaders themselves must have wondered how they were to maintain a struggle that so far had brought only severe losses and bitter humiliation. What had they to oppose a technically superior enemy other than brute force and cunning?

The answer they hit upon was not an original one. Weak peoples in all ages have defended themselves against strong intruders by poisoning wells, destroying roads, burning down houses and leaving the enemy nothing but a devastated countryside, stripped of all resources. In the older military textbooks the method was known as 'Parthian tactics', which entailed a combination of self-destructive sabotage and guerrilla attacks. The experts are unanimous that these methods must be applied only in regions that are not too well endowed with towns, villages, roads and industries. Gaul in the first century BC was certainly not in this category.

A *maquisard* leader who had resolved on a scorched-earth policy would have to demand considerable sacrifice from his countrymen, and it is difficult to imagine a people attached to their possessions allowing this. But what the Gauls possessed could easily be carried away and buried in some inaccessible spot; herds could be driven to some remote meadow and corn supplies could be laid up somewhere. Only the women and children would have to be left to the enemy – a difficult decision.

The freedom-fighters considering these possibilities in 52 BC seem none the less to have taken this decision. They had found a new leader. He was called Vercingetorix and as a man was just that: *ver*(over)-*cinget*(warrior)-*rix*(king); a man who could lead, persuade, motivate men to great deeds. The French regard him as their first national hero, which rather distorts the historical picture. Amid the halo of legend he figures as a youth who, impelled by the noblest of motives, unfurled the standard of resistance once again; this is no doubt an exaggeration.

Celtillus, Vercingetorix's father, had attempted in 80 BC to unite the people of Gaul and subject them to his sway; his bid was foiled with Roman help. It seems that his people, the Arverni (who lived in the Auvergen, which bears their name), for some reason believed that they had a mission to become the leading power in old Gaul or that they had once had this role before. This suggests that Vercingetorix sought not only to regain freedom but to defend his house's claims to hegemony over the whole country. Beyond that, he can have been no blue-eyed Parsifal. His readiness to turn whole towns into ruin and ashes and to sacrifice others, even neutrals, for his own purposes reveals him rather as a fanatic; though a milder man would hardly have been able to stand up to Caesar for any length of time.

Caesar was equally ruthless. During the ten years of the Gallic wars, Plutarch estimated he must have destroyed eight hundred towns and villages and killed or enslaved three million men. Vercingetorix could not rival this bloody record, though he did his best. His suggestion of destroying all settlements 'not protected by fortifications or their natural position' was hardly 'unanimously' adopted by the war council, for more than two hundred and eight Biturigian villages had already been burned and, as Caesar says, 'the same was happening with the other peoples. Everywhere, fire was smouldering.' But then it turned out that the prophet of scorched earth had driven his followers too far. When the question arose of sacrificing Avaricum, one of the land's finest cities (modern Bourges), to his dream of liberty, 'the Bituriges threw themselves at the feet of those present', begging them to spare their chief town. Under protest, Vercingetorix had to give way. That he did so earned him a severe defeat – or so it seemed.

Avaricum lay on a hill at the confluence of the Yèvre and the Auron, which flow together from there into the Loire. It could be reached only by a narrow causeway and its fortifications caused Caesar to speak in praise of the *murus gallicus*. Even for troops as experienced as the legions, they seemed to present quite a problem.

Caesar, who had advanced on Avaricum when he heard that Vercingetorix meant to retain it, brought to bear all the technology at his disposal. Since the settlement was surrounded by marshes and rivers, he could not cut it off from the outside world by a wall, as current practice dictated. He therefore had set up on the narrow causeway a ramp which was to be high enough to reach the top of the wall. He also held *vinae* in readiness, a kind of wooden hut on rollers, which would be moved up to give cover to the attackers. In

1943, when the French were again preoccupied with their relationship with foreign invaders, the French archaeologist Matherat excavated such mobile gangways from a bog near Brevil-le-Sec, north of Paris. They clearly belonged to the standard equipment of Roman sappers.

All these preparations were already suffering from Parthian tactics. As no supplies could be had in the region of Avaricum, Caesar had to have them brought up from the lands of the friendly Aedui and Boii. But so reluctant was their support that his soldiers were forced to eat Gallic cattle – not that they had any scruples about it, but steaks were not part of their usual diet; Roman legionaries were unable to survive without bread.

Vercingetorix too had his problems. His main forces, in position below the town and the besieging army, accused him of doing nothing to relieve Avaricum by attack. They were on the verge of mutiny. To justify himself and to make clear once more that nothing could be gained by wild onslaught, he produced Roman prisoners, taken when they had left their units in search of food – Caesar contends otherwise. Vercingetorix maintained that the Roman army was being 'worn down by hunger' and added that he had 'seen to it that no tribe in the country would give them refuge when they retreated'. He could not have provided more graphic evidence of the effects of his scorched-earth policy.

But Caesar was not going to capitulate to hunger. Foot by foot, the ramp approached its goal. Even with rumbling bellies, his sappers were able to frustrate all the attempts of the defenders, well-versed in the art of mining, to undermine the siege-works or to build up their own bastions so as to be able to fire down on the siege-towers. Burning brands, boiling pitch, pointed shafts were hurled down; these the Romans side-stepped as best they could. Not even the cold or the constant drizzle could divert them from their task. After twenty-five days their ramp had progressed so that its front end touched and overtopped the walls of Avaricum. Only now did the garrison decide to give up and flee to the marshes at the bottom of the hill on which the town stood. But before they could do this, Caesar, once more in heavy rain, pushed forward his mobile gangways and attacked. It was a massacre. 'Full of rage at ... the troubles they had had during the siege, the legionaries spared neither women nor children nor old men. Of forty thousand inhabitants [an exaggeration] only eight hundred escaped.'

Vercingetorix observed all this without lifting a finger. He had always felt that it was senseless to defend Avaricum; now he had been proved right.

As even the most stubborn of the resistance-fighters were bound to appreciate this, the defeat brought him an unexpected victory. The Romans had taken the town; an important one true enough, but also one that had already been written off. Vercingetorix had managed to execute a plan: a barbarous one, but one whose logic was now clear. A resigned Caesar wrote in his despatch: 'We believed that [Vercingetorix] was able to foresee and appreciate things in advance because, from the beginning, he had wanted Avaricum burnt down.' It had been a Pyrrhic victory for Caesar and his troops.

Immediately after the battle for Avaricum, in the late spring of 52 BC, the occupiers must have seemed so demoralized and discouraged that even the hitherto Romanophile Aedui got the impression they would not last for long. They therefore tried to bring their people rapidly to safety under the banner of the *maquisards*. Convictolitavis, successor of the Divitiacus who now disappears without trace from Caesar's despatches and thus from history, suddenly declared that his people too 'was free and born to rule'. Vercingetorix, however, already felt himself king of rebel Gaul. His messengers sped across the whole land, winning men to the cause, explaining his policies and bringing in new recruits from all sides.

Caesar, on the other hand, grew more and more painfully aware of this hectic activity. On all sides he saw his troops engaged in battle or ambush; on all sides hitherto friendly tribes now refused him assistance and obedience; and the supply position became increasingly difficult. But he hoped as before that all these adverse circumstances could be rectified at a blow. He resolved to attack Gergovia, where Vercingetorix had just staged a grand review of his forces; it was the chief town of the Arverni and is thought to be near Clermont-Ferrand. He had never calculated less correctly. The eyrie above the fertile valley of the Limagne was even less accessible than Avaricum, for it lay on the crest of a rising chain of hills, whose edges the Gauls had only had to protect with a wall ten feet high in order to be completely safe. None the less Caesar commanded that a *coup de main* was to be attempted.

It almost seemed to succeed. His soldiers were already at the gates when the Gergovian women appeared bare-breasted on the ramparts and begged the legionaries not to subject them to the same fate as the women of Avaricum. Then, and only then, did Vercingetorix appear with his own strong forces – which were, as usual, stationed away from the fort – and unleashed an attack that was bound to defeat the Romans if only because their units could not operate in proper formation on such mountainous terrain. By the evening Caesar noted that he had lost thirty-six centurions and seven hundred ordinary soldiers. For the first time since he had taken office in Gaul he had been forced to leave the field to the enemy. It so discouraged him that he thought of 'withdrawing to northern Italy' again, giving up the enterprise as lost. He seemed to have reached the lowest point in his career. The Aedui, who had now finally settled the question as to who was a collaborator, now deserted him. Their countrymen were already dreaming of re-taking Gallia Narbonensis itself.

Amid all this jubilation Vercingetorix seems to have been the only man who kept his head. He must have been pleased that in an assembly at Bibracte he was formally confirmed in the position he had long held; but he had no intention of taking unforeseeable risks on that account. As before, he hoped for further and final victories, less from great, decisive battles than from scorched-earth tactics and endless pin-pricks in the soft underbelly of his enemies: their supply-lines. Unfortunately he was after Gergovia less able than ever to convince his hot-headed followers that this was the right course. The grotesque situation which resulted is clear from the last great joint undertaking by the *maquisards*.

Spies had told Vercingetorix that Caesar meant to withdraw initially into Gallia Narbonensis, to clear the passes into northern Italy that were blocked by the rebel Allobroges. His columns, flanked by hired German horsemen, were supposed to be on the march already. It seemed a perfect opportunity for ambush and decisive victory. Vercingetorix did not rate it as highly, for he knew how fast the Romans could form up, even in the least favourable circumstances, and switch to the counter-offensive. But presumably he could not say this out loud. Thus, partly to keep intact his people's conviction that they were invincible and partly to avert disaster, he persuaded them that forcing the Romans to abandon their baggage would be a severe blow to their morale. What he hoped to achieve is obvious – the Gallic attackers were to be protected from running straight into Roman spears.

But that was just what took place. In the grip of their *furor* the Celts forgot all the rules of prudence that had been hammered into them, took on whatever stood in their path and thus threw away in one day the fruits they had so painfully garnered in the costly guerrilla warfare. Caesar, quick as ever to react, seized the chance he was offered, allowed the attackers to charge as far as the legionaries' wall of shields and then, manoeuvring with parade-ground precision, took them in a deadly pincer movement. From then on it was the same old story. Celtic swords were broken on Roman lances, Celtic rage on Roman discipline. When the quick victory they had hoped for was not achieved, discouraged horse-men made off in all directions. Vercingetorix had been right again; but it was not much use to him now. Caesar left his supply-units on the battlefield under the protection of two legions and with three thousand men followed the retreating enemy to the walls of Alesia, alleged to have been built by Heracles. Here the Celtic leader had taken refuge with his forces. He was not to know that for posterity three towns would mark his career: Avaricum, Gergovia – and Alesia, which was to be the last.

The French have debated for many years where exactly Alesia was. Some believe it was Alaise, a little place in Franche-Comté; others argued the cause of the barely larger Alise-Sainte-Reine on the lower Seine, near the Vix hill. But since Napoleon III was among the supporters of the latter, and since he had the means to have his opinion archaeologically verified, it was the Queen of Heaven, the *Sainte Reine*, that finally won the argument. An archaeological expedition between 1861 and 1865 brought up, near her village, the remains of an unusually bloody battle: bones of humans and horses came up, with weapons, various pieces of equipment, pieces of pottery and innumerable Gallic coins. Most important of all, traces were discovered of a ditch eighteen feet wide, with other remnants of fortifications. This cleared Caesar of any charge of exaggeration in his description of the battle of Alesia and confirmed that Vercingetorix's place of refuge had been con-quered more by the spade than by the sword – a mark of respect for the Gallic resistance.

Caesar now meant to use even the slightest opportunity because things had gone, so surprisingly, in his favour. With memories of

Gergovia still fresh, he resolved not to storm the oppidum on the isolated Mont Auxois, but instead to cut it off with a wall that would completely surround it – a plan that seemed lunatic. Field-surveyors reported that the planned construction would be ten miles long. The 'bulldozing legions' none the less started work.

Vercingetorix did not just sit and watch all this but made sallies whenever he had the chance and at the same time organized relief. He ordered all horsemen to leave the place while the Romans' wall was still incomplete. They were to go to their own tribes and mobilize auxiliaries. He himself would stay until the new forces arrived. It is not easy to detect his reasons. Did he, given his low estimate of his people's fighting capacity, really imagine that an organized attack on Roman walls could succeed? If so, would he not have done better to lead it himself? On the other hand, a general could not desert his men and, according to Caesar, there were still eighty thousand of them. Besides Vercingetorix probably speculated that the Gauls would fight much more resolutely if they had to liberate him, their elected commander, from enemy encirclement. Only one thing is certain. With his decision to stay Vercingetorix helped to build up the pedestal on to which legend would elevate him – national heroes never run away.

Caesar thought in different terms. He had the encircling walls constructed with manic perfectionism. The eighteen-foot ditch that Napoleon III's excavators later found was extended and behind it a second, double one was filled with water from the nearby Oserain (traces of this too were found). Then came a series of cunningly placed man-traps – 'iron calthrops, wholly buried' – and carefully concealed holes in the ground, four feet deep, containing pointed staves that would impale anyone who fell in. The soldiers coined the not unsuitable name *cippus*, which means both grave-stone and pointed pillar. Far behind these front-line defences there was an encircling wall, roughly nine feet high, topped with tin and breastworks: 'I had the whole construction provided with towers as well, at intervals of eighty feet.' But this was only half of what Caesar had planned. Parallel to it there was a second, similarly protected wall, with its barbed front turned not towards Mont Auxois but towards the hinterland. It was fifteen miles long. Caesar thus not only closed in the town but himself and the siege-army as well. He constructed something like a five-layer cake, consisting of *circumvallatio* (outer wall), the troops manning it, then *contra-*

vallatio (inner wall), no-man's-land and then the Gallic heart, Alesia (see map on p. 196).

It was, all in all, one of the maddest constructions ever made by a commander, but there was method in it. Caesar was pushing his luck to the limit, staking everything he was, everything he had – including his life – on one gamble. But he was a master of the now-or-never and knew that Gaul might still be lost if he let go of Alesia.

Some thirty days after work had begun on the great wall Vercingetorix and his men felt the first effects of the new tactics. Supplies were running short. A council of war met to discuss the situation. There were three proposals: to surrender, to make a sortie, or to wait to the bitter end. Critognatus, one of the most fanatical enemies of Rome in this group, suggested a fourth: when the Gauls had had to defend themselves against the Cimbri and were themselves enclosed, they had 'lengthened their lives with the bodies of those who were too old to fight, and had not surrendered to the enemy'. This cannibalistic expedient was now, he felt, the right one to adopt.

We do not know how his speech went down; if it was indeed made (Caesar's report is of course based on hearsay) then it does honour to Vercingetorix that he swept the argument aside. But he could not prevent a measure that was hardly less cruel. The women and children, the old and sick – all the non-combatants – were ordered to leave Alesia so that there would be fewer mouths to feed. How they were to break through Caesar's ring, no one told them. They got only as far as the *contravallatio* and then begged 'in tears, insistently, to be taken on as slaves and given something to eat'. But the legionaries, who could not make too great demands on their own food-supplies, rejected them, as ordered. They must have died one by one somewhere in the obstacle-studded wilderness of no-man's-land, with both armies looking on. However much this inhuman interlude may have discouraged the Gallic garrison, the mood rose sharply when, beyond the Roman wall, there finally emerged the relief force which their messengers had alerted. According to Caesar, it was a large army.

Forty-one Celtic tribes, he maintains, had sent no less than 8,000 horsemen and 250,000 infantrymen. This must be a great exaggeration, but even a considerably more modest figure would have justified the preparations he had made. Only now, with the five-

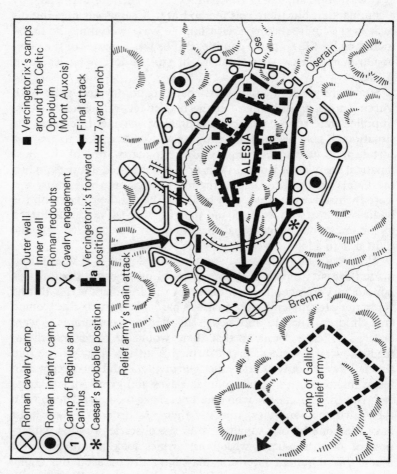

Map 9   The siege of Alesia

layer cake becoming a six-layer one, did the point of the outer wall become apparent. Without it, the troops posted round Mont Auxois would have had to be pulled out and thrown against the relieving army; this would have given the garrison the chance to break out and take the legions in the rear. Caesar was spared both only by the double wall. But the position remained strange enough. An army of forty-one tribes was besieging an enemy, who was himself besieging; the focus of the battle was not the town in the middle but the vast construction encircling it. Caesar had all the advantages on his side. He did not have to attack the oppidum and he could repel all attacks on his own walls by concentrated fire and occasional sorties. In this way his soldiers saved in blood what they had spent in sweat – at least theoretically.

In the day-to-day fighting it rapidly became clear that the whole enterprise, despite Caesar's enormous efforts, was balanced very finely indeed. When the Gauls, who had kept in contact by signalling over the Roman lines, opened their first joint attack, the legionaries were heavily pressed. The second attack, at night, was worse still. Most of the warriors who stormed down from Mont Auxois were felled by the hail of bolts and staves from the Roman artillery, tumbled in rows into the *cippi*, were maimed by mantraps or drowned in the double moats. All attempts by the relieving forces to fill the moats with fascines were foiled. But the Romans were just as hard pressed. They had to fight in a dozen different places at once, felt that they were in a trap and were unnerved by 'the loud yelling that sounded in the rear of the attackers'.

The Celts could still arouse dread, but it was not enough. Germanic cavalry squadrons, the proconsul's new favourites, threw them back to the palisades of their own camp. Their attack on a legionary strong-point beyond the wall was bloodily repulsed. Caesar's bold gamble paid off. He had counted on the limited staying power of his opponents, their incapacity to organize or sustain a long siege and, of course, that Vercingetorix's food-supplies would run out before his own. This point was reached on the fifth day after the arrival of the relief army. The war council again met in Alesia, this time with two proposals before it. Vercingetorix declared 'he had not begun this war because of his own difficulties but for the common cause. As fortune was now deserting him, he could offer only the following alternatives: either he should be executed or delivered up alive, to gain the Roman's good graces.' The assembly decided on the second course of action. Vercingetorix's monument was almost complete. He donned his finest armour, mounted his best horse and rode to the Roman camp, where he prostrated himself before Caesar – at least, so legend has it. There is nothing of the kind in the *De Bello Gallico*. To the whole dramatic scene Caesar devotes only one short sentence: 'Vercingetorix was handed over.'

Caesar's account breaks off suddenly after the description of the battle of Alesia, and rightly so. The siege had brought him victory over Gaul. In the next two years he had only to put down a few local rebellions and secure what he had won. He did so with calculated leniency. The Aedui were again graciously accepted as allies of Rome. All other tribes had to submit to a relatively generous Roman administration. Their tax burden amounted to an annual four million sesterces, equivalent to coins weighing forty-five tons of silver. Four thousand Gallic volunteers were taken into the army as an independent legion; some notables were even attached to Caesar's personal staff – which later prompted the Romans to compose the mocking lines: 'In his triumph Caesar led Celts even into the City Hall. They took off their trousers and donned the purple stripe' (the mark of senatorial status). There were, however, fugitives from Roman pursuit, and not a few of them at that.

So many Gauls must have streamed into southern and western Germany between 52 and 50 BC that an unmistakably Celtic flavour was again imposed on the area's culture. At Hradiště, near Stradonice in Czechoslovakia, former citizens of Bibracte and Gergovia, who had gone a long way east, even seem to have set up their own oppidum, for many finds in this region are virtually identical with those from central France of the time.

The news was unrelievedly bad for the Druids above all and, of course, Vercingetorix in particular. The 'wise men of the oak' were forbidden to practise their cult, which is unusual for the Romans generally did not suppress other religions but instead took foreign gods into their own pantheon. Caesar dragged Vercingetorix along with him until finally he could be executed in his triumph in 46 BC. He himself survived his foe by only two years. In the interim he made his most adventurous play for power, one which he had been forced into. After the death of Crassus and the murder of Clodius, Pompey had risen to supreme power in Rome and branded his former ally as an outlaw. Caesar, with a victorious army expanded by Gallic and German troops, then crossed the little river called the Rubicon that flows into the Adriatic south of Ravenna. That he quoted a line from the playwright Menander, 'alea jacta est' (the die is cast), shows his extreme cool-headedness as well as his gambling streak. He had displayed it at Alesia, and he did so again on the river between Gallia Cisalpina and Italy. Both times he won a huge prize; first Gaul and then an empire, though assassins were to exact payment for it.

None of the Roman historians says how the news of Caesar's victories and of his death were received by the Celts outside Gaul. Northern barbarians do not appear again in their pages until Tiberius and Drusus, Augustus's step-son, who invaded Germany. Their earlier conquests in the Alpine and Danubian regions scarcely seem to have made any impression on the historians; to find out how they went we have to make do with a few brief and scattered references and with archaeological evidence. Thus the *De Bello Gallico* mentions a prince named Voccio, one of Ariovist's brothers-in-law. To judge from an oppidum on the Magdalensberg near Maria Saal in Carinthia, he seems to have ruled the Celtic-Illyrian mineral-rich mountain state that the Romans called Noricum. But he did not mean to play the role of Vercingetorix, rather that of Divitiacus.

His predecessors – in view of Rome's interest in their mines of gold, iron, silver, lead and salt – had formed an alliance with the Senate that opened the native metal forges to Roman entrepreneurs. For princes who had already collaborated closely with the Etruscans this was the obvious thing to do. When in 15 and 14 BC Tiberius and Drusus approached to complete the annexation of Noricum to the empire, Voccio – or perhaps his successor – opened the borders and at once announced that he would exercise sovereignty jointly with the Romans. But it is on the whole unlikely that his fellow-tribesmen in the remainder of the Alps, its foothills and the Danubian area behaved in the same way. The split skulls of Manching and its destroyed ramparts indicate that there was severe fighting. So does an inscription on the triumphal arch of Emperor Augustus in the pass of La Turbie near Monaco. The last lines read: 'These are the defeated people of the Alps; Trumpilini, Carnuni, Venoti; . . . Ambisontes . . . ; . . . Verusii, Velnani, Suetri.'

Tribes could only be described as defeated if they had put up resistance beforehand, though there is no way of proving that they did so.

Of the Ambisontes we know only that they lived in the Pinzgau in Salzburg and were neighbours of the Tauriscii to the south and the Alauni to the east. Their chief town was an oppidum on the Biberg near Saalfelden, their kings minted coins and their workshops produced goods that may be compared with the finest of the La Tène era. Of these peoples there survive only river, valley or place-names – Pinzgau itself, said to have been developed out of Bisontio, or Rauris, a village near Zell am See, which recalls a tribe that was known as the Raurici. There are also gold-mines, one of which was worked until 1944, and countless sagas, whose historical kernel can no longer be separated from the web of fantasy.

After the Ambisontes and their neighbours had been defeated they probably adapted to Roman ways as rapidly as their Gallic cousins. The occupiers drove a road over the Radstatt Tauer to Italy, made mule-tracks over most of the Alpine passes, built towers and strong-points and organized the ore industry with their usual thoroughness. Over modern Austria, southern and western Germany and France was imposed a new layer of Latin culture which to this day characterizes these regions. What had been Celtic rumbled, like a distant earthquake, beneath a cloak of rationality. But this did not mean that it had disappeared.

In the area between the Bohemian Forest, the Alps and the Main one comes across the *Perchtenläufe*, the most original masque in western Europe, during which young lads can work themselves up into a veritable rage. Anyone who has seen it will find it hard to resist detecting a remnant of something that must once have been practised in the name of Lug or even more ancient gods, an echo from the Nemeta. Not all the participants can be aware of this, although local intellectuals have for some time regarded it as chic to promote an artificial Celtic consciousness and even to speak of a 'league' which has subterranean links with the Scots and the Irish. This may just be fashion, but it does have tradition behind it, for it may be the oldest recorded resistance movement that our continent can show.

From the moment of Viriatus's rebellion the Celts fought only with their backs to the wall. Their withdrawal to a stance of resistance went further in France and southern Germany and was to be continued in the only area in which Celtic tribes still lived independently after the campaigns of Caesar, Drusus and Tiberius – in Britain. Indeed Welsh nationalists whom I know feel that what was then begun is still going on. The struggle, they believe, is not yet over.

TWELVE

Campaigns at the World's Edge

All conquerors have swallowed up their faithful subjects well enough. But conquests are more easily made than kept. There are only three ways to keep them: to kill all the conquered and turn their country into pasture-land; to occupy it with immensely superior force; or to bring to it the blessings of civilization (the Romans' way).

Karl Julius Weber, *Der lachende Demokritos*

The British Isles were probably the first to be settled by Gallic colonists.

Napoleon Bonaparte, in a private note of 1786

Caesar's expedition to Britain, however celebrated in Rome, in truth resulted only in some meagre pieces of information. This island, he noted, was quite densely populated and had tin, iron, timber, game and cattle in large quantities. Its winters were not as cold as Gallic ones. Strabo, who later augmented this from his own sources, notes that there were hilly regions; but the land was generally flat and wooded. This cannot have been anything new even for his contemporaries, but there was interest in what both the general and the geographer had to say of the inhabitants of England. Strabo calls them 'Pritani' or 'Priteni', and says that he knew some of them in Rome: 'They were only young lads, but they were taller by half a foot and more than the tallest of the citizens, though they were somewhat crooked-legged and otherwise not particularly well-favoured.' That the island Celts were related to the continental ones he, like Caesar, simply takes for granted. But both seem to have found them wilder and less developed.

'Their cities,' Strabo says, 'are the woods. They enclose a large area with felled trees and set up huts to house themselves and their animals, never with the intention of staying very long in these places.' Caesar alleges that some of them lived off meat and milk, and that they dressed in animal-skins; 'and all of them paint their faces with woad (the juice of the *isatis*, a hybrid species) which gives them a blue colouring and makes them seem all the more terrifying in battle. They wear their hair long but otherwise shave, except for the head and upper lip.' This almost takes us back to the days of the first Celtic wars south of the Alps; further details confirm this. The moustachioed, blue-painted and long-haired warriors of Britain were not only externally similar to the hordes who had once besieged Clusium, they also seem to have used weaponry from the same arsenal: battle-chariots. Caesar took them no less seriously on this account – on the contrary.

In these vehicles, he noted, 'they swarm round enemy lines, hurl their missiles and, with the terror aroused by their horses and the clatter of the wheels, cause confusion in the ranks; they push forward between their own cavalry squadrons and jump down from the chariot to carry on fighting on foot'. This recalls Brennus's warriors, except that the virtuosity of these Celts is even greater. 'With daily practice they can even manage to stop horses going at full speed down sloping and even precipitous ground, slow them to a canter and make them turn, climbing along the shaft to hold the top of the yoke and then rapidly returning to the chariot.' Roman soldiers were understandably impressed by such artistry.

They must soon have appreciated that this display was part of the Celts' ritualized way of fighting and that the terror thus intended could be frustrated by discipline. In the first expedition of 55 BC Caesar's landing-forces had had to deal with only a disorderly crowd. The second time it was a strong army, led by King Cassivellaunus; but it turned out that the British Celts were as divided among themselves as their continental cousins. After the legionaries had successfully waged three battles, British petty princes came to the Roman camp to surrender and to accuse their sovereign of usurpation. One of them, Mandubracius, king of the Trinovantes, had even arrived with this in view before Caesar left

France, saying that Cassivellaunus had violently subjugated his people and was threatening them with death.

It was by now mere routine for Caesar to restore him to his rights and make him his ally and food-supplier. But he did not spend time playing him off, like Divitiacus, against the other tribes. Instead he fixed taxes to be paid by the defeated tribes, forbade Cassivellaunus, who had also capitulated, to take revenge on Mandubracius, and returned to France without stopping to ask himself whether he had achieved his purpose. It seemed sufficient for him to have added to the list of his glorious deeds and to have shown the islanders what Roman might could achieve. We do not know if Mandubracius long survived the departure of his protector. For the next hundred years the history of the island was dictated by men who passed on their knowledge and experience by word of mouth, as had been the custom for over a millennium.

The question as to when Britain was settled by Celtic-speaking tribes has proved too difficult for archaeologists to answer clearly. Philologists, too, are cautious. The most they will say is that some time between 2000 and 1200 BC Indo-European peoples invaded the island and settled there. The basis of this assumption is a complicated linguistic calculation, resting essentially on two factors. The first is that, of all languages that developed out of the idiom of the central Asian wandering peoples, Celtic was most closely related to Italic, the early form of Latin. Among the differences is that Celtic did without a *p*, where the ancestors of the Romans had one, and used an *a* in place of their *o*. Thus *super* (above) became something like *ver*, as in Vercingetorix; and *gnotus* (knowing) became *gnatus*, as in the Gallic prince's name, Eposognatus (knower of horses). The other factor is that Celtic divides into two great sub-groups, Goidelic and Brythonic. Goidelic, also known as Q-Celtic, survives in Irish, Scottish and Manx languages; while Brythonic or P-Celtic gave rise to Welsh, Cornish and Breton. These letters are used as the distinguishing mark because Goidelic turned the Indo-European *ekvos* into that *equos* the Romans also knew; while in Brythonic the original *k* turned into a *p* not a *q*, thus giving *epos*. There was a similar change, to take a further instance, in the Latin *qui* (who). In Cymric (Welsh) it became *pwy*; while in Q-Celtic it remained *cia* with a hard *k*, closer to the original.

From these factors we can deduce that, roughly simultaneously, there developed two related languages out of the old proto-Indo-European: Italic and an early form of Celtic, possibly identical with Gaelic. Only with the substitution of *p* for *q* did there emerge a younger idiom, called Brythonic by the experts, though it was also spoken by the Gauls and other continental Celts. As Goidelic (Gaelic) can still be detected in several British and Irish dialects, there must have been a time when, at least on some islands off the west European coast, peoples lived who used the elder form of Celtic and then a second era when tribes emerged speaking Brythonic. It can also be supposed that the Goidelic-speakers were driven back by the Brythonic-speakers, forced on to the Isle of Man and to Ireland; or, and this is more probable, that these islands were not touched by the invaders, who themselves must have left the continent under pressure. Their inhabitants retained the older tongue and later gave it renewed currency in the north of Scotland. One thing remains clear: Britain and the neighbouring islands were settled by Celts in two great waves. It is somewhat futile to speculate as to when the first occurred as there is a series of linguistic theories, none of which can be proved; but it seems that the Goidelic wave, perhaps from Spain, affected Ireland above all. The second great wave can be more precisely dated. The Brythonians must have arrived in Britain at the earliest around the beginning of the La Tène era, when Celtic language and culture were already shaped. This expansion was still not over by Caesar's day, as we can see from the *De Bello Gallico*.

In his reports on the Belgae, Caesar says that the Suessiones, who lived north of the Marnex, 'ruled a great part not only of this region, but also Britain'. In another place he adds that in the interior of the island lived 'original inhabitants, while on the coast lived those peoples who had come from Belgium with bellicose intentions, to plunder, and who had then stayed on to practise agriculture. Almost all of them bear the names of the tribes they came from.' Archaeologists confirm the first part of this statement.

In England two types of hill-fort were found: an older one that grew out of places of refuge and later developed into an oppidum, and a second one that has been ascribed to the Belgae. In the former refuge-points, it seems, lived those peoples that had contrived to establish relatively large states, some of which the Alexandrian geographer Claudius Ptolemaius mentions in a map of the second century AD – the states of the Cornovii (whose name survives in Cornwall), the Dumnonii and the Novantae. The Brigantes and Parisii belonged to these groups that arrived later.

The people of Caesar's victim Cassivellaunus, the Catuvellauni, were among the builders of the most recent hill-forts of Belgic type (though of course they also took over older oppida that they had conquered). They seem to have been the last people who attempted to set up great states out of the earlier, long fragmented kingdoms; but they too, as the case of Mandubracius makes clear, must ultimately have failed against the Celts' unwillingness to submit to the rule of others. When the Romans invaded Britain the Catuvellauni were at the height of their newly acquired power; then, and for years after the Romans had left, there were continual arrivals from the continent who joined and reinforced those that had gone in advance. The most powerful body in Britain developed, however, not in the south and centre of the island but in the extreme north. There lived the Picts, a people probably speaking Brythonic, the older Gaelic not being established there until much later. We do not know whether these were Celts, or merely Celticized. Some interpreters have seen in them the descendants of an original population that had quietly survived all invasions and indeed resisted the Romans, who returned for a third time in AD 43.

Tiberius Claudius, son of the Drusus who had defeated the Celts, was by nature far from being a conqueror. Neglected by his parents and avoided by his imperial relatives, he grew up an ugly, stammering and insecure young man, living in some corner or other of the palace. Probably he would have remained there, never becoming anything more than a member of the Julio-Claudian dynasty, had not Praetorians seized him in AD 41 from behind a curtain and proclaimed him successor to his recently murdered nephew, the megalomaniac Caligula.

In the thirteen years of his reign as emperor the poor man never quite comprehended the brilliant maelstrom into which he had been hurled. Everything associated with his name – including constitutional reform – was suggested, planned and carried out by capable Greek freedmen and accomplished generals; and this also applies to the conquest of Britain. Two reasons prompted this step: the conquest seemed desirable to give his weak personality some glory; while the islands, since Caesar's expedition, had developed into a thorn in Rome's flesh. British pirates were doing their best to interfere with French coastal traffic and were also supporting the continental resistance. Moreover, Rome saw increasing numbers of emigrants from the lesser tribes of Britain which the Belgae were subjecting; their hatred and agitation were particularly aimed at Cunobelinus, a successor of Cassivellaunus who, in defiance of Caesar's decree, had completely absorbed the Trinovantes into his own tribe. To bring him down with the help of Roman troops was the chief object of these exiles. Caligula had almost been persuaded to do it. His flag-ship had gone out to sea from Boulogne, but only to fetch some mussels from the water: with which symbolic 'booty' he returned to Rome. Why he went no further has never been clarified. According to rumour, his troops refused to go through with such a risky operation.

When Claudius announced his plans for conquest, there was again not much enthusiasm. Some of the legions stationed in Gaul even refused to move, for some weeks, to embark for Britain; to them, Britain was a refuge of savage, extremely dangerous pirates; they did not believe it was possible for a Roman fleet to get over the Channel in the teeth of such ships. Their fear was by no means unfounded. Caesar himself had had to learn the hard way that Celts could be difficult to defeat not only on land but on the sea. He says of the Breton Veneti that they had ships particularly suited to Atlantic conditions, because the extremely high fore- and after-deck protected them from high waves. These ships were also – 'so as to contain any attempt at attack or boarding' – made of oak and given anchors that did not, like Roman ones, hang on tow-ropes but on chains. Moreover, Caesar said, they did not use linen sails but leather ones, 'whether for lack of cloth . . . or, more probably, because with hoisted cloth sails it was impossible to cope with the strong tides of the ocean or the hurricane-winds, or to steer such heavy ships properly'. The Celtic ships must, then, have been rather heavy and squat; less like the elegant and streamlined Viking dragon-ships than – as Caesar's description suggests – the high-decked cogs of the fourteenth and fifteenth centuries, and thus some way ahead of their time.

The builders had done their work so well that the ships could withstand ramming from a five-oar pentere; as they reached so high out of the water it was difficult to strike the crews with arrows or stones; and 'for the same reason it was still less easy to seize them with grappling-hooks. Moreover, they travelled before the wind and could thus the more easily defy a storm, could stand the open seas and avoid rocks and cliffs at ebb tide. All these dangers were greatly feared by our ships', which were built according to Mediterranean principles.

Caligula probably turned home out of the same fear, before a single British leather-sail had appeared on the horizon. Claudius, however, or more probably his commander, Aulus Plautius, was able to overcome the mutinous troops' fear of the islanders and to mobilize them for the enterprise. Everything then went much more easily than the soldiers had supposed. The British Celts had long disbelieved in any possibility of a Roman attack and they had taken no steps to defend themselves. The invasion force landed without interference, west of Dover, and easily defeated the armies that Cunobelinus had hastily scraped together. They occupied Kent, secured the Thames valley after a two-day battle and finally conquered Camulodunum, modern Colchester, capital of the Trinovantes. There some months later Plautius welcomed his emperor, who received the homage of no less than eleven native rulers. Against all expectation, Britain seemed to have fallen into the Romans' laps like a ripe fruit. Celts had once again capitulated – at least for the time being – to a force led with energy and precision.

Plautius advanced from Colchester into the region of modern Lincoln (the Roman Lindum) and returned in AD 47 to Rome and high honours. What he had begun was continued a little later by his successor, Ostorius Scapula. He secured the whole area west of the Fosse Way, a line from Lincoln to the north-east coast as far as Seaton in the south, and then crossed it into the north-west. He owed his great success, however, not to military capacity but to a woman. She bore the resonant name of Cartimandua and was a princess of the Brigantes. The stormy romance with which she entered the history of her people had at its root that most common of matrimonial problems – the eternal triangle.

Patriotic British historians have sometimes tried to impose on Cartimandua the role of political heroine: a ruler who perceived earlier than many other Celtic leaders that resistance against Rome was senseless and should be stopped. But Tacitus, the most reliable Roman narrator of the British scene, did not believe this; to describe her motives he could use only the word 'scandal'. This is understandable. Cartimandua was married to Venutius, a chief to whom Tacitus ascribes a defiant, warlike spirit and a wild hatred of the invader. Whether his wife was superior, inferior or equal to him in rank, Tacitus did not know. He could say only that 'the British make no sexual distinction among those that enjoy sovereignty', though the point is of little importance in what was to occur.

It must have begun on the day Cartimandua's gaze first fell on Vellocatus, her husband's weapons-bearer. The young man had so much in his favour that from then on she regarded Venutius as an obstacle to her happiness and thought up a scheme to be rid of him. Without asking his advice – perhaps, indeed, when he was not even there – she offered Scapula the tribal area of the Brigantes as a protectorate. He of course at once accepted: the scheme spared him a lengthy war. Cartimandua was now free to present 'her hand and her crown' to Vellocatus, as Tacitus delicately put it, since the way to her throne and her bed was now barred to Venutius, the enemy of Rome. On the surface the tale reads like the plot of a melodrama, but there is more to it. Whatever motivated Cartimandua – whether passion, lust for power, or merely a distaste for senseless bloodshed – she became a factor in history. She thus becomes of interest both for her own sake and for what she reveals about the place of women in Celtic society.

It is clear, from the scheme she instigated, that she must have been able to impose her will on the whole tribe, warriors and Druids alike. She must have had not only a particularly strong will but real power. This in turn implies that the Celts' respect for women, so rightly praised by the classical authors, did not display itself in knightly courtesy alone. In extreme cases, Tacitus himself asserts that female rulers enjoyed the same loyalty as their male counterparts once they had risen to power. We may imagine a breed of strong women able to assert themselves forcefully in a male environment. Cartimandua seems to have been such a Celtic lioness. Her cub was Vellocatus; to protect him she ruthlessly followed her chosen path, committing herself to the Roman cause that she had been compelled to take up.

When in AD 51 King Caratacus summoned the Silures, a people of highly warlike reputation, from South Wales to do battle against the occupiers and hastened east together with the Ordovices from the north-west in order to mobilize the Brigantes as well, their princess cold-bloodedly allowed his forces to fall into a trap set by Scapula. When Caratacus then fled to her capital – we must assume that he was completely unaware of the alliance that had been concluded – he was at once put in chains and sent to Colchester, the headquarters of the Roman commander.

By behaving in this treacherous way Cartimandua, says Tacitus, 'helped Emperor Claudius almost attain the splendour of a triumph'; but his 'almost' shows that, in the end, it was not to be to her benefit. She had strained the tolerance of the Brigantes too far and she was frivolously abusing her good fortune. The scandal of her marriage with Vellocatus was shaking the prestige of her family. Her former husband, Venutius, regained the people's favour and the adulterer was left with only the passion and cruelty of the queen, for Venutius drove the unequal pair from the land. Tacitus goes on: 'Thereupon they sought the Romans' protection, and our cohorts and cavalry squadrons rescued them despite changing fortunes in the fighting. Venutius retained the kingdom, and we had war' – for the Brigantes now returned to the anti-Roman front.

The end of the affair must have been as banal as its beginning. In Colchester Cartimandua languished – an 'older woman' who had lost all her royal splendour – with her young lover, who now had only his dreams of lost majesty. The pair probably became burdensome to the Romans, in the way exiles generally do with their hosts, once they can find no further variations in their tale of woe. At least we do have here a brief insight into the private life of the Celts, which makes it somewhat easier to see them as human beings. There will be mention in our story of another British queen who also ended unhappily, but she was of such stuff as monuments are made of. Cartimandua remains the only one with whom anything like a trace of scent lingers.

AD 59: poor Claudius, poisoned by his wife, had been dead five years and Nero reigned in his stead. Suetonius Paulinus arrived on the island as the fourth Roman governor. Tacitus describes him as 'a conscientious and modest legate' and stressed that these qualities were much needed. The Celts who, in the meantime, had recovered from the shock of their initial defeat, were in full revolt: 'Veterans were massacred, towns were burned down. We were fighting first for our lives, and only later for victory.'

By this time Roman troops had long crossed the Fosse Way and secured considerable areas to the west of it with castles and armed camps; but bloody guerrilla warfare developed around these fortified islands in the frontier areas. The ex-servicemen who had been settled in these outposts had many years' experience but were long past the stamina required to repulse the Celtic hordes. To resolve this situation Paulinus decided to advance against North Wales, which he presumed to be the centre of the rebel movement. Modern Celtic scholars would be happy if they knew something of the factors underlying this plan. They conclude, from the few details supplied by Tacitus, that those fomenting resistance from this area included not only political chiefs but also spiritual ones: in other words, Druids.

What makes the matter still more mysterious is that Mona, the island of Anglesey on the north-western coast of Wales, is supposed – to judge from resilient survivals – to have been a central point of the Celts' religious life. If scholars knew more about what happened there at the time of Paulinus, they might be able to give a more exact idea of the role the priests took in Celtic resistance-movements, both in Britain and in Gaul. But as ever when scholars seek to examine them in detail, the Druids escape from their grasp.

We therefore have to make do with what Anglesey offers to the imagination. It is not much: a few stones set up in the ground, like those in Brittany, Ireland or southern England; little woods, rumoured to have once been sacred groves; a whiff of poetry amid the landmarks of Wales. There is for instance on this island a village that proudly bears, with fifty-eight letters, the second longest place-name in the world – the longest being that of a Maori settlement with eighty-three. The name of this place on the coast of the Irish Sea is: Llanfairpwllgwyngyllgogerychwyrndrobwll-llantysiliogogogoch. Translated, it means: 'Church of Mary near the white-hazelnut spring near the wild maelstrom by the Sysitis-chapel in the red cave.' This jumble of words itself seems to mirror a fairy-tale and deeply religious world, making the rumours surrounding Anglesey understandable. Is it an after-glow of the aura that once lay over an ancient shrine?

Tacitus portrays the Druid situation of AD 61 in a more sinister light. When Suetonius's troops reached the Menai Strait that separated Anglesey from the mainland (today spanned by two bridges), they saw on the opposite shore 'the British, tightly packed together, ready to fight. Women ran wildly through their ranks. They were clad in mourning, letting their hair fly loose in the wind, holding burning torches in their hands and looking altogether like raging furies. The Druids stood in groups, their hands raised up to the sky, and they prayed to the gods, uttering fearful curses.' He goes on:

The strangeness of this sight put fear and terror into the Romans. They stood gaping as if stunned, as if their limbs had frozen and were rooted to the spot – a good target for the enemy. Then their ranks were filled with new strength because their generals reprimanded them; each encouraged his fellow, and the men got into an exalted, warlike state, for they were ashamed that a crowd of women and a band of fanatical priests had made such a deep impression on them. They set up their standards and went over to the attack with a desperate rage.

Tacitus provides a scenario wholly suitable for opera, but whether it fits reality is another matter. The Menai Strait that the legionaries are supposed to have crossed in one wild bound is four hundred yards wide, and besides there are steep banks on either side. Tacitus also describes a second conquest of Anglesey that took place much later and which we shall discuss below. His report should thus be read as an impressionistic amalgam of several sources, unless we assume that the scene actually occurred somewhere else.

It is more regrettable that the Druids he snatches so abruptly from obscurity disappear just as swiftly. The most difficult part of Tacitus's passage to interpret is his last line, where he states that all the sacred places were razed to the ground. As in Gaul, the Romans here applied the principle of tolerating – even promoting – foreign religions. This renews the suspicion that Druidical teachings were too mysterious even for them, though no one says why this was so. Paulinus can hardly have had much time in Anglesey to deal with the riddles of the Druids' world. Immediately after his victory – if indeed it was one – he had to retreat, for in the east the Iceni had risen in rebellion. Their queen was to be the second heroine of the British drama.

No one had really noted how Cartimandua looked and what she wore. But we do have something like a literary snapshot of the Icenian princess Boudicca, showing her life-size. This we owe to the Roman historian Dio Cassius. He lived, it is true, a century after her death; but he was sure of his facts when he stated that 'Boudicca was tall, terrible to look on and gifted with a powerful voice. A flood of bright red hair ran down to her knees; she wore a golden necklet made up of ornate pieces, a multi-coloured robe and over it a thick cloak held together by a brooch. She took up a long spear to cause dread in all who set eyes on her.' It is in this pose the portraitist has fixed her. To complete the picture we might add, to left and right of her, two statuesque daughters, for the Celts in East Anglia had rebelled on account of a feminine triad; though it was not for this reason alone.

As usual when they occupied a country, the Romans had initially left the native princes in their places and treated them as vassal-kings. But they began to infringe their rights as soon as they felt strong enough. With the Iceni, this seemed easy enough. Prasutagus, Boudicca's husband, must have been the man with whom they concluded their first treaty, ostensibly between equal partners. When he died without male issue, the procurator, the civil counterpart of the governor, refused to bestow on his widow and the two girls the rights enjoyed by the dead man, as would have suited Celtic custom. Instead he tried to subject the Iceni to Roman administration. It was one of many similar decisions taken at the time, but on this occasion the occupiers had gone too far.

According to Tacitus the British now said to themselves: 'We can gain nothing by patient submission except that, to those who let things happen to them, worse will come. Earlier they had had one ruler and now they had two, of whom one, the governor, was threatening their lives and the other their property.' In other words the native nobles now realized that the day was not far off when they would lose their relatively unrestricted privileges, while the people appreciated that Rome intended to alienate their old order. Boudicca became the symbol of the fate which seemed to threaten the whole tribe. When this red-haired giantess took up her spear, the men hastened to arms.

Their revolt must have broken out with explosive force. The rebellious Iceni were joined by the Trinovantes, originally the most Romanophile tribe in Britain. The hosts took Colchester, the seat of the governor, occupied Verulamium (St Albans), an oppidum built by the Belgae that the Romans had taken over, and destroyed Londinium (London), the centre of the Roman communications network. These initial successes gave them fantastic hopes of victory. As Tacitus puts it:

What a tiny force was landed in comparison with the numbers of the British. In similar circumstances the Germans [in the battle of the Teutoburg Forest, in AD 9] would have shaken off the Roman yoke, though they were protected by a river [the Rhine] and not by an ocean [from the main Roman forces]. They themselves were fighting for fatherland, wives and parents; the Romans only for greed and lust. Thus the Romans would have to give way, as once their 'divine' Caesar had done, so long as they themselves could proudly imitate the courage of their fathers.

This is certainly good evidence, viewed through Roman eyes, of the Celts' talent for convincing themselves of something; but no more than that.

As with Vercingetorix and Arminius, these rebels had only fanatical rage to pit against the cohorts of Paulinus which had hurried back from Wales. This was however enough to deal the Romans some of the heaviest losses they ever sustained in Britain: the death list is said to have contained seventy thousand names. But it was not enough to decide the campaign in their favour. The governor had prisoners ruthlessly executed, made one bloody example after another and managed, in the end, to break his enemies' morale. It is unfortunately not recorded how Boudicca reacted in this bloody strife. When her situation became hopeless she took poison; her death marked the end of resistance in the south of the island. But in Rome, too, there was not much pleasure at the severity with which Paulinus stamped out the rebellion. The 'conscientious and prudent legate' was removed and replaced by Petronius Turpilianus, in Tacitus's words 'a peaceable man who did not so well know the crimes of the enemy and was therefore more open to their repentance'.

That they had forced a whole people back on to its last line of defence, to the point where women took up arms, seems to have touched even the Romans. In their own myths mothers were the ultimate taboo. No one could harm them without bringing harm upon himself too. They had been provoked by Boudicca. Her self-sacrifice did have the effect of making Paulinus's successors almost completely abandon violent measures for the next eight years and turn instead to the peaceable Romanization of Britain – though not without sinister after-thoughts, as Tacitus, who loved primitive virtue, says: 'Gradually the inhabitants of the island succumbed to pleasure and discovered a taste for colonnades, public baths, splendid banquets. In their want of experience, they mistook all of this for civilization, while in reality it only contributed to their greater subjection.' Not until the governors Petilius Cerialis and Frontinus, who ruled Britain from AD 71 to 78, was a large-scale expedition to the north again undertaken. They subjugated the former subjects of Cartimandua, the Brigantes, annexed the Silures' lands and founded Eboracum, modern York. South of Scotland only the Ordovices, Novantae and Selgovae enjoyed any autonomy. They were to be attacked, after the routine recall of Frontinus, by the general who was to play the most substantial role by a Roman veteran in the British campaign – not least because his daughter married the historian, Tacitus.

THIRTEEN

The Barbarian Conspiracy

Where is the wave that can set my people free? Where is the lonely isle where do not languish the dead of the Celts?

Jean Pierre Callog'h (Breton poet)

According to his son-in-law Tacitus, Julius Agricola was a faultless and immaculate civil servant, a model of honesty and modesty who hated the tyrants with whom he had to deal in his fifty-three years of life. These praiseworthy qualities naturally did not stop him from making a considerable career in politics under six of the seven emperors whom he served. Tacitus, who dedicated to him his first work, the *De Vita Julii Agricolae*, cannot escape the suspicion that, affectionately and deliberately, he credited many of his own ideals to his father-in-law. However we have to take him at his word and accept his biography, which covers the period between the principate of the sinister Caligula (37–41) and that of Domitian whom Tacitus loathed no less (87–96). Agricola died – rumour had it that he was poisoned – three years before the murder of Domitian.

He had been born on 13 June 40, the son of a senator, in Forum Iulii (modern Fréjus). In nearby Marseilles, he spent his adolescence. Then, as he later told, he 'undertook philosophical studies with more passion than befitted a young man of good family'; however his obviously energetic mother prevented worse from happening. No doubt it was bad enough with one intellectual in the family – the father was addicted to similar pursuits, unfitting to his class – and 'she restrained his all too fiery enthusiasm'. She saw to it that Nero had him attached to the British staff of Suetonius Paulinus. As qualification for this post it presumably helped that Agricola had grown up in Gaul and thus may have known Celtic customs and the Celtic tongue. His next great step up the ladder was also indirectly owing to the land of his birth.

In 68 a Gaul cleared the obstacle to the progress of the then Praetor Agricola – the obstacle in question being Nero. Still a young man, the latter had been responsible for so many outrages in his last six years in office – from fratricide and matricide to the murder of his wife – that Agricola and other members of the Roman establishment now felt it incumbent on themselves to withdraw to a position in which, as Tacitus says, 'inactivity was cleverness'. But however necessary this seemed for moral and tactical reasons, it did not foster immediate advancement.

Agricola must have been considerably relieved when news came in from Gallia Lugdunensis – a stretch of land from the Breton and Norman coasts to the Rhône – that the governor, a Celtic nobleman named Julius Vindex, had risen in revolt against Nero. The only disturbing thing was that no one knew who was the real head of the revolt and, hence, the coming man. Vindex himself was too clever to set himself up as the new princeps; he therefore pushed forward as straw-men the two governors of Spain, Galba and Otho, though neither of them managed to stay the course.

After Vindex had been slain in battle against forces from the Roman Rhineland that had remained faithful to Nero, and after the emperor had committed suicide out of pure cowardice, Galba was the first to seize the rudder but lost it shortly after. Otho in turn was defeated and killed by a third competitor, Vitellius, who in his turn was overthrown by a fourth, Titus Flavius Vespasianus. Agricola, observing the drama and confusion of the first Year of the Four Emperors (AD 68–69) from a box in the capital itself, had first backed Galba and then, just in time, the finally victorious pretender. His reward was a second mission in Britain and then his own province, Aquitania, which stretched roughly from the Loire to the Pyrenees. He seems as before to have been considered a Celtic expert.

Having returned from this post as governor he finally attained the social plateau from which a man might become consul and marry his daughter to a rising young patrician politician – Tacitus, his later biographer. Tacitus did not then suspect that six years later the younger son of Vespasian, Domitian, who disfavoured him, would come to power and terminate his career – pushing Tacitus into a stance of opposition that thus acquired literary expression.

The first labour of this young man now ousted from his career was, as has been mentioned, to write a short description of the life of his father-in-law and his deeds in Britain. Agricola was sent there for a third time in 78 by Vespasian; as governor, he was expected to complete what Cerialis and Frontinus had begun: the conquest of the north. However the first armed expedition, undertaken just a few weeks after arriving, led him not to the Scottish moors but to the region where seventeen years before Suetonius Plautinus had encountered the Druids. This might again lend weight to Theodor Mommsen's criticism that Tacitus was not always excessively scrupulous about facts, indeed sometimes contradicted himself.

Tacitus seems not to have known, when writing his *De Vita Julii Agricolae*, that Anglesey had already been taken in 61, though he himself said so in his later work, the so-called *Annales*. There he recorded that Paulinus, in his time, had turned back when he reached the Menai Strait and thus permitted the Ordovices to continue assembling in the island and to plan the attacks that now brought Agricola, the new governor, on his expedition to North Wales. When his troops reached the coast of the Irish Sea, he says, there appeared on the other side of the Straits a final levy, to offer resistance to the legionaries – though at this point Tacitus omits the Druids and the raging women. The contradiction is, however, only apparent, for the earlier work, which in any case also mentions a subsequent attack, gives the more realistic account.

Since Agricola's men – according to this account – did not have at their disposal the ships they needed to cross over to the island,

the commander had native auxiliaries – who knew the shallow places, swam strongly like their ancestors and could therefore cross over with their weapons and horses – lay aside all their baggage and swim across to the bank so suddenly that the surprised enemy, having reckoned with a fleet of warships and transports and with the tides, supposed they were dealing with men for whom nothing was impossible and therefore at once sued for peace and surrendered their island.

Their dread is understandable to anyone who has ever looked down from the bridge over the Menai Strait and on to the foaming currents below. I myself should never have been able to cross these steel-grey depths at ebb or flood-tide. Presumably Agricola also would not undertake the task himself; but even without displaying such prowess, he became a legend for the British.

His next action was prompted less by the need for new spectacular tactics than by administrative requirements. He secured the southern and central English hinterland, reformed the taxation system and did all he could to acquaint the island's inhabitants with Roman ways – that is, as Tacitus sees it, he tried to corrupt them with civilization. The region he then governed ran from the Channel coast to the Solway Firth in the west and modern Newcastle-upon-Tyne in the east. Beyond this line lay the area of the still untamed Novantae and Selgovae; further north still, in the area beyond Glasgow and Edinburgh, began the regions that the Romans called Caledonia. They represented a mountainous, generally barren tract of moorland over which hung eternal rain-clouds. Since its clear streams had not as yet been used for production of a beverage called in Gaelic *uisge beatha* ('water of life') and known to us as whisky, the area can have offered little to attract Roman troops in an armed expedition. But their army was no longer made up of soldiers from the Mediterranean south; already large elements of the army of occupation were composed of Gallic cavalrymen and infantrymen who would find the rain, the fog, the sticky mud and the snow less unbearable than would sons of sun-dried Apulia.

But, Tacitus says, they presented Roman drill-sergeants with the same problem that their ancestors had once given Carthaginian officers. In the summer of 83, for instance, a cohort containing Usipetes took over three fast sailing-boats and made a wild tour of the British coasts. Their unsanctioned leave ended in Holland, where the exhausted deserters were captured by Frisians and offered back as slaves to their earlier masters. The size of the Celtic units serving under Roman standards can be gauged from finds made on the former battlefields. So few items of Roman equipment have been found that we can assume that in Britain it was mainly Celt who met Celt in battle.

We must thus visualize Agricola's armed expeditions in the summer of 80 less as disciplined cohorts than as wild hordes of natives, held together by their officers only with difficulty. No doubt small and reliable elite corps formed the nucleus; but the

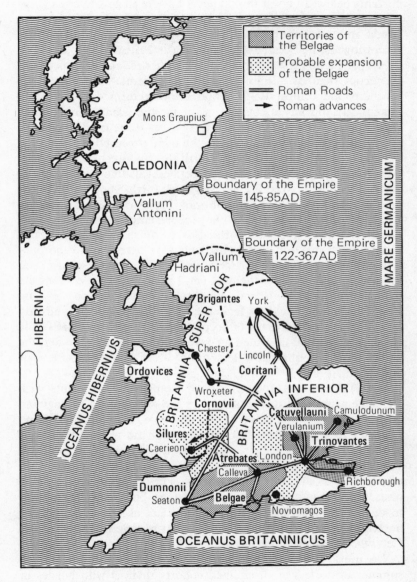

Map 10   Roman Britain

men who strayed on the wings, scouted ahead, attacked villages by surprise, laid ambushes and boasted of their deeds in the evenings round the campfire or became heated in difficult situations – these would be descendants of the people that had driven Vercingetorix to despair. The governor nevertheless succeeded in conquering the whole area between the Solway Firth and the Firth of Clyde and finally in advancing as far as the region of Aberdeen. However he was not to reach the northern edge of the islands. The Pictish 'Caledonii' who lived there would, as if by a miracle, retain their stubbornly defended liberty.

Agricola's final great undertaking, the conquest of this last free part of Britain, is related by Tacitus in the style of the age: with great drama. There are no less than two prologues. As speaker of the first we have Calgacus, the Caledonian prince; though it is not clear how Tacitus came by the text of the address, which runs: 'We, who live on the edge of the earth and who are the last bulwark of freedom, have to this day been protected by our remoteness and by the mystery of our name. But now the frontiers of Britain are open and beyond us there is no people, nothing other than the seas, the rock and the still more dangerous Roman, whose usurpation is not to be escaped by self-abasement or moderation.' These are words that, if authentic, convey something of the Celts' eloquence; however, since their authenticity is open to doubt, it seems that they merely display their real author in that Rousseauesque pose he liked to adopt and which later led him to glorify the Germans as noble savages. But there was a critical element in the words as well. Tacitus meant to hold up a mirror to his own countrymen, whom he thought degenerate; he could thus present a primitive people to them as a model – as has frequently happened in later times. The next section of Calgacus's speech betrays his intentions rather more clearly.

'These plunderers of the earth,' he proceeds, 'are now invading the seas because, having devastated everything, they now have no more land. If their enemy is wealthy, they are greedy; if he is poor, they will be after glory – they whom neither east nor west have satiated. Alone among peoples, they have looked with equal greed upon rich and poor alike. Stealing, murdering and plundering they call government; and where they create a desert they call it peace.' This was powerful artillery; if Calgacus really fired it, he would have to be admired as a statesman capable of surveying the world with

some accuracy, though perched on the extreme edge of Europe.
He might be compared with Brennus, Viriatus and Vercingetorix.

Perhaps he does deserve this comparison. A few sentences later
is a passage that reads as if Tacitus had culled it from authentic
sources – possibly the statements of prisoners – for it displays that
sovereign contempt of which Celts were capable. It reads:

Be not fearful of mere appearance, of glittering gold and silver [on the
insignia of the Roman army] for it neither protects nor wounds: in the
midst of the enemy hordes we shall find our own battle-hosts [country-
men, whom he hoped would desert]. The British will recognize their
own just cause; the Gauls will remember their lost independence; the
Germans will abandon Rome. Then nothing remains to be feared. The
forts are empty, there are only old men in the colonies, there is hatred in
the towns between those who obey unwillingly and those who rule
unjustly.

'Long live the world barbarian conspiracy,' he seems to be saying. From Scotland, the Roman empire was to be rolled up, with a
general revolt of the subject Transalpine peoples. Large as the
element of wishful-thinking must have been, this could have had a
real basis. The lands of the far north must have been, throughout
the years of occupation, a refuge for all who would not submit to
their new masters: that is, for the proud, the resilient, the hard-
core British resistance. Calgacus may have counted on them, which
also explains why Agricola prepared his Caledonian enterprise with
such immense care.

He had not only departed with a large force, he had also established a chain of fortresses and winter-quarters on which he would
be able to rely along the whole coast between the Firth of Forth
and Aberdeen. When Calgacus made his oration Agricola was probably at Raedykes near Stonehaven, where the remains of a tower
were identified. The Caledonians held, opposite him, the hills that
are still unidentified but that are called by Tacitus 'Mons Graupius'.
With the Caledonian hosts in sight, Agricola now spoke the second
prologue of the forthcoming bloody spectacle. His son-in-law con-
veys it much less impressively than he does the words of Calgacus,
but this only serves to make the whole battle tableau more vivid.
He concludes:

As only the bravest wild animal will face the intruder in forests or
ravines, while the fearful and the weak ones will have been frightened off
by the noise of the hunt, so the bravest Britons are already slain and only

the weak remain. Now you have finally stumbled into them and they have halted, not because they wish to fight but because you have pinned them down. The latest happenings, and their crippling fear of death, have nailed them to this spot, where you are to win a magnificent and glorious victory.

This is empty boasting, the product of a mind which sees human beings as merely animals to be hunted down. The speech gives justification to Calgacus. He had right on his side; and it seems as if Tacitus wished to stress this at the governor's expense. In any case Agricola was certainly in error, for the Celts were not cowardly; this he was to learn.

The battle, which took place in 84, began with the usual skirmishing. Calgacus had drawn up his thirty thousand men so that their foremost ranks stood on the plain while the rear stood up on the hillside. Between them, the charioteers went through their virtuoso routines, now known to all of the legionaries. The Romans fired their ballistae and catapults but the British 'with their huge swords and short shields, cunningly avoided them or parried them'. Agricola, who feared the enemy might take him from the flank, pulled his troops as close together as possible. The two armies thus formed two parallel lines. Gauls and Germans opened the attack, as they were the men who knew best how to deal with their own kind. Agricola's calculation seemed to be correct: according to centuries-old practice the barbarian mercenaries so cleverly exploited their sharp-pointed swords and large shields against the long slashing-swords and small targes of the Caledonians that the latter began to crumble. They struck with their shield-buckles, aimed at unprotected faces and were in such a fury that once the Caledonian ranks in the plains had been broken through they were in danger of being surrounded. Agricola then launched a cavalry-force, but this only worsened the position 'since the riders could not hold on in the sloping terrain and were thrown by their horses'. It was now Calgacus's turn to spot an opening.

His hosts posted on the highest part of the hill now rushed forward and tried to encircle all the legionaries already engaged in the battle. Had not Agricola, foreseeing this, kept four further cavalry squadrons in reserve, the manoeuvre might well have worked and the battle of Mons Graupius might have ended in a Pictish victory. But the cavalry succeeded in taking the flank of the Caledonians, all of whom were now fighting in the plain, and put them to flight:

The wounded were pursued, prisoners were taken and struck down whenever others came. On the enemy side, whole armed detachments instinctively fled before small Roman groups; others made off in the opposite direction and ran into the arms of death. Everywhere there was a litter of weaponry, corpses, mutilated limbs; blood reddened the soil. Here and there the defeated put up bitter resistance. . . . Almost ten thousand of the enemy and three hundred and sixty Romans [not including Gauls and Germans] had fallen. . . . Far and wide reigned deathly silence, empty houses and, in the distance, smoking ruins; our troops' spies met not a soul. We learnt through such spies, sent out in all directions, that there was no clear trace of flight and that nowhere were groups of the enemy to be found.

It seemed as if a ghost had been laid: Caledonia open and unprotected before the Roman army; for the legions, a path to the furthest corner of Europe. But they did not take it. On the grounds that the summer was now coming to an end, Agricola moved back south and allowed only the fleet to make a raid up to the Orkneys. Why he did so is artfully concealed by Tacitus: in his hatred of the reigning prince, he maintained that Domitian, who had taken the throne in 81, wanted to stop a lesser general from obtaining greater success and more splendid triumphs than his own, for he had had only a few modest victories over the Germans, the Chatti and the Dacians of Transylvania to his credit. He is accordingly said to have ordered Agricola to break off the Caledonian enterprise.

But there is a much more obvious solution than this malicious suspicion. Vespasian's son, like his father an extremely economical and cautious man, probably could not see why Rome should annex a barren piece of land, the administration of which would cost more than the income it would provide. He was tired of conquest and had severe problems on the Dalmatian border. All of this Tacitus seemingly did not know or preferred to ignore, and for obvious enough reasons. Domitian reigned as an absolute monarch, but he was also a man of the people. His hatred and disfavour were reserved for the senatorial nobility, the class to which Agricola and his son-in-law belonged.

Directly after the victory at Mons Graupius Agricola was recalled and was given no other command. Nine years later he died – as already mentioned, in somewhat strange circumstances. Caledonia, the land he had invaded, was never again attacked by Roman forces; its barrenness was its saviour. In the bleak valleys

of the Highlands the dream of a barbarian conspiracy was kept
alive and would almost be realized some three centuries later. In
the meantime there was a considerable decline in Roman power.

The men who took power in Rome after the murder of Domitian,
who was slain as the result of a palace plot, saw increasingly that it
was senseless to defend territorial possessions to the last square
mile simply because Roman blood had once been shed in their
acquisition. When, therefore, in Hadrian's reign (117–38) the
Caledonian mountain tribes again attacked the garrison and this
time dragged in the Brigantes, the then British governor was
ordered to withdraw his troops to the line that Agricola had occupied when he took up office. There, as earlier under Vespasian,
Hadrian's Wall was to be set up. It ran from the Solway Firth to the
mouth of the Tyne, right across the island. It was a massive structure. At first its western third was of earth, like the earlier wall; the
rest was of solid stone. Behind the wall was a road, itself protected
by a wall and a ditch. In front of the wall were observation-towers
and fortified extensions; it was manned by the garrisons of several
forts, with legionary camps to the rear and smaller outposts every
mile. A graduated defensive system almost sixty miles long was
thus developed. Why Hadrian's Wall was erected was explained in
an inscription at its eastern end – *necessitas*.

Antoninus Pius, successor of that most important and most mysterious of the so-called 'adoptive' emperors, clearly no longer
believed in such necessity. He once more had the troops advance to
the Firth of Clyde and there set up the *vallum Antonini*, which fulfilled its purpose for about forty years. Then the north again
became ungovernable. After an attempt by the governor Clodius
Albinus to seize the then empty throne in Rome, Celtic tribes
advanced to the southern borders of Scotland which were now
without troops. In the summer of 196 they even overrun a large
part of England and twelve years later the reigning emperor had to
come in person to beat back the Caledonii. This was Septimius
Severus, an experienced general who spent three summers on this
campaign. He died soon after in York.

After his death, the tide of Roman power in Britain ebbed further and further. Caracalla (211–17) even emptied Hadrian's Wall
of all permanent garrisons and replaced them with the so-called
exploratores, irregular troops made up of natives who fought a

defensive guerrilla war against their countrymen. It must have been something like Red Indian wars: half-bandit against half-savage, sometimes joining up, then ambushing one another, doing business, plundering and killing. There were desertions on both sides, but rules on neither.

Behind these fluctuating frontiers, however, two Roman provinces developed in brilliant style: in the west, Britannia Superior; in the east, Britannia Inferior. Cloth and pottery works were established, gold, lead, copper and iron were mined and exported. Five towns had the rank of *municipia* or *coloniae*, with full Roman citizenship and rights: Eboracum (York), Verulamium (St Albans), Glevum (Gloucester), Lindum (Lincoln), and Camulodunum (Colchester), with Londinium (London) progressively becoming the leading trading centre of the country. At its height in this early period London had a population of twenty-five thousand, served as centre for corn, ore and the slave trade, and had the largest town-hall in Britain – some one hundred and thirty yards long – which was the hub of finance and the seat of the state mint. A man who had acquired wealth and a villa here could enjoy magnificent baths and efficient drainage, could undertake business trips by regular shipping lines to Gaul or to York – the headquarters of the military, who also wanted their share of the profits. For his health, however, he would travel to beautiful Somerset, to Aquae Sulis (Bath). There, around Britain's only thermal source, elegant baths were built, of which there survives today the Great Bath decorated with statues and surrounded by colonnades.

However, away from the towns, in the countryside, life seems to have gone on in the old Celtic fashion. At South Cadbury in Somerset, where archaeologists have dug intensively in the hope of finding an oppidum – the castle of the legendary King Arthur – they came up with only a few Roman finds: some fine tableware, some coins, a few fashionable ornaments. But there are signs that the inhabitants of an old fortified post were violently taken from their hill and settled, as elsewhere, in an open village at its foot. The occupying power clearly would tolerate no walled places in the hinterland. Their suspicion was justified.

Admittedly, if during the three centuries of the *pax Romana* there were troubles in the southern part of the island, these occurred less for national than for social reasons. As in Gaul most of the native peasants can have been little better than serfs, ex-

ploited to the marrow by Roman or Romanized British lords. If
they were *colones*, a sort of share-cropper, they would have to give
up half of their produce; if their possessions were rather larger,
they would be victims of the usurers. This pressure from above
grew proportionately with the increase of taxes by the rapid succession of second-century emperors, who had to contend with rivals
within or with intruding Germans, Parthians and Sarmatians
without.

Whether the British rebelled against the social conditions of the
time we do not know, but the Gauls certainly did. When by 286
conditions in northern France became insupportable, the rural
proletariat formed *bacaudae* (bands) and started a proper revolution. The leaders, the two 'peasant emperors' Aelianus and
Amandus, set up residence on the banks of the Marne near
Vincennes, a 'court' that, as Jacob Burckhardt says, must have
been 'colourful' and 'individual'.

They were able to hold out for only a few years. Diocletian's
lieutenant in Gaul, Maximianus Herculius, defeated the movement, with the help of the plague. This had indirect consequences
in Britain. Maximianus was given higher honours and more important duties in gratitude for his eradication of the *bacaudae* rebellion.
His subordinate Carausius, the Celtic admiral of the Channel fleet,
set himself up on his own, proclaiming sovereignty over the island
and himself emperor in London. This too had a short and bloody
sequel. Diocletian, who had ruled the empire since 293 as one of
a total of two *Augusti* and two *Caesares*, first recognized the
usurper as fellow-emperor but later declared him to be an enemy
of the state. Carausius was assassinated in 293 by his chief minister,
Allectus. He ruled for a mere three years until an Illyrian praetorian
prefect, Constantius Chlorus Caesar, reconquered the island for
Rome in 296 and was established as governor in York. From there
he managed once more to assert Roman hegemony over the most
westerly provinces and to repel the aggressive northern tribes. But
on his death what he had built up rapidly crumbled again. The *pax
Romana* was losing its strength. Constantius's son, the Emperor
Constantine the Great, transferred the capital of the empire to the
Bosphorus, to Constantinople; and from there Britain was only a
shadowy outline on the horizon of the western sky. The Romanized
part of the island now seemed so exposed to the barbarian threat
that it is conceivable that some of the islanders must have reflected

that it might after all have been more sensible to have let Agricola complete what he had planned.

Tacitus's father-in-law had felt that to secure a lasting peace on the westerly borders it was necessary not only to subdue the Caledonians but also to occupy Ireland. As neither Domitian nor his successors could be convinced of this, the emerald isle remained completely free of Roman troops. This was not to go unpunished. In the next decades the Saxon pirates, who since the mid-third century had been returning again and again from the North Sea coasts of Germany and Denmark to raid British shipping and coastal towns, were increasingly associated with the Picts from the Caledonian north and the Scots from Ireland. In craft called 'curuci' by England's earliest historian, Gildas Bandonicus, they crossed the stormy waters between the two islands and gave endless trouble to sailors of the imperial navy.

Since these 'curraghs', as they were called in Gaelic, were only light wooden frames covered with animal skins, men on high-decked galleys could not easily tackle them. They could avoid the rams and gave no opportunity for grapnels to be used. They could be effectively contained only by equally small boats which, hidden behind cliffs and camouflaged, could themselves take these pirates by surprise. This tactic was adopted by the Romans. But it was an odd kind of naval warfare: deer-stalking through the waves, duels in the surf. A fishing-trip along the Irish coast gives an inkling of what such fighting must have been like – these ancient curraghs are still in use, though the skins have been replaced by hulls of tarred cloth. Their ancestors had, by the summer of 367, become particularly active; what they started was called by Ammianus Marcellinus a *conspiratio barbarica* – a term which suggests that Calgacus's hopes had finally been fulfilled. Picts, Scots, Angles, Saxons and Jutes jointly, and from all sides, fell upon the Roman island provinces. The occupiers were threatened with the loss of booty that had been theirs for centuries.

Whether this sudden attack really was concerted, we do not know; nor what damage it did. Only one thing became clear: Agricola's opponent on Mons Graupius may have prophesied correctly, but he was not right in the end. The Romanized Britons whom he hoped would join the barbarian conspiracy were no longer barbarian. Now their free cousins seemed to them to be enemies, menacing everything to which they had become accustomed: prosperity, the benefits of civilization and – even exploited *colones* appreciated this – stability and the rule of law. As they fought not only out of compulsion but also out of conviction, the *conspiratio barbarica* called forth a new Vercingetorix-type figure of legend, though this time he did not wear a torc. It was not some Pictish or Scottish chieftain whom they worshipped as their liberator but, somewhat grotesquely, a Roman officer, Magnus Maximus, whom the Welsh call Maxen Wledig. He had beaten the invaders back and thus passed into Celtic tradition as a Celticized hero. Those who composed his legend endowed him with a native bride and said he would tolerate around him only men from Segontium (Caernarvon). Most of them must have been slain at Aquileia, in northern Italy, where in 388 Maximus failed in his attempt to set himself up as second Augustus to Theodosius I.

For the Britons he had abandoned, marauding pirates and attacks from the north became the order of the day. The barbarians were becoming increasingly impudent and the legionaries saw increasingly less reason why they should be ground down in the furthest and most forgotten province of the empire. When therefore another governor was sent from Ravenna, the new administrative centre of the western provinces of the Roman empire, these legionaries forced him to attempt to repeat his predecessor's usurpation.

Flavius Claudius Constantinus, as this man was called, went at the Gauls' behest to France, fought successfully against the joint hosts of the Vandals, Sarmatians, Alani, Suevi and Alemanni who had crossed the frozen Rhine in January 407, and set himself up as Emperor Constantine III – to be defeated and beheaded four years later by another Roman general. The post he had once held in Britain was no longer filled, which greatly diminished the islanders' anxiety to continue paying their taxes. Native nobles took the place of Roman officers and civil servants, set up private armies, established new principalities in place of the old provinces and seem to have perceived that they themselves belonged to the barbarian world – or at least that they lived in it and had to come to terms with it. It might be said that these Celts found themselves, briefly, back at the roots of their old culture; in Gaul it seems to have been much the same.

At Mackwiller in the French department of the Moselle a sacred spring was discovered in 1953 which was originally consecrated to native gods and then, about the mid-second century, became a sanctuary of the Iranian god of light, Mithra, so beloved of Roman legionaries; finally, one hundred and thirty years later, the grove once more reverted to its original deities. Their power, never entirely forgotten, must have revived in proportion to the decline of Rome's; and with these miniature Celtic renaissances, which can also be shown to have taken place elsewhere, the Druids too made a come-back. That they still existed they had already shown, as in the Year of the Four Emperors (68–69) which brought on the first of Rome's great internal crises. On such occasions the Druids always seemed to sense an advantage, not always without reason.

It was a Gaul, Julius Vindex, who launched the struggle for Nero's throne; and it was Vitellius, commander of the army of the Rhine, who fed the flames. Both men are used by historians as evidence of the new grip of a Celtic-German nationalism on France and the eastern neighbouring provinces which Caesar had conquered – a nationalism that also infected the legionaries stationed there. They argue that Vitellius's attempt to seize power in Rome from the north ought to be regarded as a reflection of this new spirit.

Right or wrong, after Vitellius's death the Batavian Julius Civilis certainly did try to channel his predecessor's attempt at usurpation into the paths of rebellion, with the help of north Gallic and Germanic tribes. Tacitus says that when this occurred a Druid, 'on the basis of empty nightmares, foretold that world hegemony would henceforth pass into the hands of the Transalpine peoples'. He was referring to the terrible eruption of Vesuvius which, on 24 August 79, destroyed Pompeii, Herculaneum and Stabiae, and also to the fire that, a year later, destroyed the field of Mars, the Capitol and the Pantheon. Both disasters were, for him, 'portents that the end of the empire was at hand. The Gauls themselves had once taken the city, but the sacred seat of Jove and with it the Imperium had remained intact; now this fire showed the anger of the gods.' It did indeed look as if, since the fall of Alesia, the whole Gallic people had been waiting for the day when it could throw off the Roman yoke in a *conspiratio barbarica* with the Germans.

That Civilis's rebellion failed does not rule out the possibility that this might have happened. The Druids seem to have been keeping alive the spark of resistance in the whole of Gaul and to have been waiting for their chance. We must of course ask ourselves where they hid, survived and worked at a time when most of their compatriots were collaborating with the garrison, creating the Gallo-Latin culture that is considered to be at the root of the French one. The answer is less surprising than might be thought. Some of the 'wise men of the oak' had simply accepted the *interpretatio romana*, the Romans' way of fusing the Gallic gods with their own. They served as priests in the official temples, as such also practising some of their own traditional rites, particularly the medical practices. Others had retired to remote areas such as the Vosges, the Palatinate and the Black Forest, the Rhineland, the Massif Central or Normandy and lived hardly differently than in the days before Caesar's conquests. As there were no large estates or *colones* far from the great economic centres and communication arteries, the old village social structure and the traditional customs were preserved. The dead were still buried beneath hut-like gravestones, much as in the Bronze Age tumuli; temples retained their rectangular shape; the gods were worshipped in the traditional fashion.

This reveals that in some corners of France remnants of old Gaul survived and that, as in the temples of the larger towns, there were centres of resistance that could be rapidly activated. If gaps were ever torn in the proud façade of the Imperium, the guardians of the Celtic inheritance would certainly try to widen them: partly by force, perhaps through the vain prophesie mentioned by Tacitus, but more likely by a clever attempt to win round influential Romans to their teachings. It is said of Caracalla, for instance, that he worshipped a native god in Baden-Baden; Diocletian and Maximinian bent the knee before Belenus of Aquileia; and Constantine the Great himself nearly became the Druids' greatest prize. It was in a Gallic temple that he had the vision from which he later took the sign that adorned his standard: a large 'x'. French scholars see in it the spokes of the Celtic wheel of rebirth and assume that he, the last ruler to undertake complete reorganization of the empire, at least toyed with the idea of taking the religion of 'the wise men of the oak', though of course in the end he preferred to make Christ, and not Lug, his ally and to give to the X the significance of the Greek *chi*, the initial letter of 'Christ'. With the addition of a *rho* this switch was finally confirmed, and both letters were incorporated in the words a celestial voice had called out to him on the Milvian bridge: *In hoc signo victor eris* ('In this sign, you will be the victor'), the sign being 'XP'. Lug and his supporters had finally lost the battle, as this little story so picturesquely showed. Against Christianity, which now spread over Gaul as well, they could achieve nothing – even with their own comforting doctrines of reincarnation. But they did not disappear in the Roman empire, which the Druids survived quite well; they did not finally collapse until the confusion of the great migrations that reached France in 407.

This event thrust the British back into independence. In 410 Honorius, emperor of the west, informed the *poleis* of the island – literally, its city-states – that he could no longer concern himself with them and that they must look to their own defence. As he wrote this the Goths under Alaric were already before the gates of Rome, which they took shortly afterwards. While in the coming years Gaul was traversed, plundered and split into several states until the Franks managed to unite the bulk of the country under their rule, in England an era opened that was shaped by Latin-speaking and predominantly Christian Celts. To investigate this we can no longer turn to Roman historians and have to make do with more dubious sources – the sagas. However, according to some scholars, this is not necessarily a bad thing; for in these old stories, with their fairy-tale embellishments, we hear not the voice of some outside observer but – for the first time – that of the Celts themselves. This applies particularly to the Irish, whom Agricola never conquered.

FOURTEEN

Ireland: the Fly in the Amber

Disdaining fortune, with his brandished steel,
Which smoked with bloody execution,
Like valour's minion carved out his passage
Till he faced the slave;
Which ne'er shook hands, nor bade farewell to him,
Till he unseamed him from the nave to the chaps,
And fixed his head upon our battlements.

Macbeth, Act I, Scene II

Men were killed, women raped, cattle driven off.

Irish Anonymous, *The Cattle Raid of Cooley* (twelfth century)

When the roast arrived at the table, the heroes became cheerful.

Cet said, 'Unless we fight over it, I'll take a slice of that pig.'
'But,' said a large, flaxen-haired warrior from the ranks of the men of Ulster, 'you're not the right man to start.'
'Who is it, then?' asked Cet.
'Eogan MacDurtacht,' they all replied, 'who is king of Farney.'
'I know him already,' said Cet.
'Where did you see me?' asked Eogan.
'At the entrance to your house. I was just driving cattle from your meadows. When there was an alarm, you came out and threw your spear at me, but it was my shield that it hit. I threw it back and hit your eye; I can still put out the other one.' Then Eogan sat down.
Cet said, 'Let's go on fighting, men of Ulster.'

'You shall not be the first to cut that pig,' said Muinremor Mac-Gerginn.

'Is that not Muinremor?' said Cet. 'Not three days ago I cut off the heads of three of your warriors and your eldest son.' Then he too sat down.

But when Cet now took up the knife in his hand and approached the pig, Conall Cernach entered and made a salmon-leap in the centre of the house. The men of Ulster gave him an enthusiastic greeting.

'I'm happy the food's ready,' said Conall. 'Who's cutting first for you?'

'He who's already at it, Cet Mac Magach,' said Conor Mac Nessa.

'Is it true that you're cutting the pig first?' asked Conall.

'Leave it alone.'

'Why should that be your affair?' asked Cet.

'I have the right to challenge you,' answered Conall, 'and by the gods of my people, I swear that since the time I first took a spear in my hand, no day has gone by where I've not killed a man of Connaught, no night where I've not got one, and I have never slept without having the head of a man of Connaught under my knee.'

'Truly,' said Cet, 'you're a better man than I, but if my brother Auluan were here, he would be your match. It's too bad for us he's not here.'

'But he is,' said Conall, who took Auluan's head from his belt and hurled it at Cet's chest. Then Cet turned away from the pig, and Conall took his place.

This was the climax of the story, which had begun because of a dog.

This animal, Ailbe, was so strong and savage that it could replace a whole army. Three kings fought for possession of it: Mac Da Thó of Leinster, Ailill of Connaught and Conor Mac Nessa of Ulster. Mac Da Thó, to whom it belonged, had invited both his rivals in the hope that they would fight over Ailbe, kill each other and leave him on the field as *tertius gaudens*. The plan seemed to work but, as we have seen, by verbal fighting alone. Cet Mac Magach, a warrior from Munster, Connaught's ally, asserted himself until the Ulsterman Conall Cernach came in and proved that he had killed more men than Cet, which settled the contest. Conall could now relax and divide the pig up as he thought fit. The whole rear part of it, 'a portion fit for nine men', he allotted to himself, the men of Connaught getting only the head and the foreparts, which was too little.

Their protest began the battle on which Mac Da Thó had

been counting. When it was in full swing, the cunning king of Leinster unleashed Ailbe and the giant animal chased the whole crew out of the hall. It was a triumph for Mac Da Thó; but the price was a bitter one. Fer Loga, a charioteer from Connaught, raced unluckily (or perhaps cunningly) straight into the dog, whose head was speared on the vehicle's shaft. The place where this happened (in the Darrow valley) is still called Mag nAilbe, or 'Ailbe's plain'.

This Irish popular epic, with the innocuous title *The Story of Mac Da Thó's Pig*, may strike confusingly familiar chords among continental readers. These chords can be arranged, however, according to a well-known pattern. Fighters, whose reputation for having 'rubbed out' a number of enemies has won them a privileged place at table or at the bar, appear in countless Westerns. Heated debates, where everyone boasts of his own adventures, occur whenever men sit together. 'Salmon leaps' of the sort that Conall Cernach is supposed to have executed can be seen at most football matches, for almost every goal-scorer celebrates a success by running and hurling himself into the air like a fish in a stream.

In this way we can perhaps sympathize with Diodorus Siculus when he read in Posidonius that it was Celtic custom to save the best part of a roast animal for the best warrior. It reminded him of customs described by Homer. It reminds us, in fact, of Diodorus. The Irish sagas seem to describe a world where things happened much as in old Gaul. Among the first modern scholars to be struck by this were the British archaeologist Ridgeway and the German philologist Windisch, early in this century. Neither would go further than a suspicion that stories such as that of Mac Da Thó's pig described old Celtic ways; and they had good reason to be cautious. The *Book of Leinster*, which contains the earliest extant version of the battle for Ailbe, dates roughly from 1160, so that it seemed very bold to assume that its authors, medieval monks, could possibly have described what Posidonius had noted twelve hundred years before in Gaul. No tradition, it was felt, could possibly have remained alive for that length of time, even if it were suggested, as it was by Ridgeway, that Mac Da Thó's business took place two hundred years after Posidonius's journey to Gaul.

On the other hand, the alternatives seemed hardly more credible. Was it conceivable that the monks were describing occurrences that were contemporary, or at most a few centuries old? That would imply that the Irish nobility were still going in for head-hunting and racing across the land in battle-chariots when, on the continent, Christian civilization had long been flourishing, not least because it had received some vital impulses from Irish scholars. These sagas thus posed a considerable dilemma for their interpreters. To solve it, the suppositions made by Ridgeway and Windisch were combined with new ones, though there was no

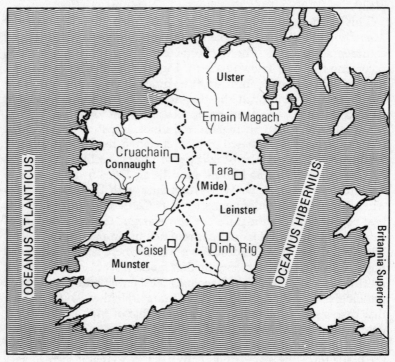

Map 11   The 'five-fifths' of Ireland

evidence that the version thus obtained was correct. Scholars looked with some fascination at a world of which it could legitimately be said – the more contours the picture developed – that it was astonishingly similar to that described by Diodorus, Strabo, Athenaeus, Caesar and others. Ireland's popular epics – this could, after a time, simply no longer be denied – in fact give us the most detailed picture that we have of the Celts.

As in old Gaul, the heroes of the sagas of Ireland liked to wear woollen cloaks, pinned together at the neck by a brooch. Trousers were worn only by the poor, noblemen preferring *léine*, knee-length linen tunics. The weaponry of a warrior consisted of two or three javelins or of the long lance and sword which, as in the La Tène era, was suitable for cutting but not for thrusting. Bows and arrows seem as unknown to the early Irish as to the Gauls before Caesar's day. Many of their hand-weapons corresponded to the descriptions of Diodorus: their spears had blades that were indented at the side, even three- to five-pronged forks. Another characteristic was that, in general, less work went into their shields, which were of alder-wood, circular in shape, with a metal boss in the middle.

A further point already noted by the Greeks and Romans was that spear and shield marked only the ordinary foot-soldier or, as he was called in Gaelic, *gaiscedach*. The *eior* – roughly translatable as 'lord' or 'knight' – had an additional weapon, a two-wheeled battle-chariot pulled by a team of two horses. It was on this, and not on horseback, that the knights rode into battle, with a special driver for the chariot. We thus have to imagine all the great heroes sung by the poets as a team: two men between whom, in the course of their adventures, all kinds of relationship could exist – comradeship, friendship, even love. Such feelings were even imprinted on the weapons. The Irish equivalent of Achilles's shield or Siegfried's Balmung was the Caladbolg, a legendary sword later to be found in the hands of King Arthur, where it was called Caliburnus or Excalibur. It must have been a masterpiece of the Celtic smith's art, glinting with the precious metals with which heroes used to adorn their persons.

In the story *Bricriu's Feast* a chariot-team is described with these words:

At [the rider's] side hung a sword with a golden handle; on the copper frame of the wheel, a blood-red spear was fixed. . . . Over his shoulder he hung a carmine shield, the silver edge of which was decked with golden animal-figures. . . . The driver was a slight, freckled lad with a shock of loose red hair; his forehead was shielded from the flowing locks by a bronze visor, and golden ear-plates contained the mane. . . . In his hand he held a whip of reddish gold.

But men did not, of course, automatically become part of the exclusive caste represented by this *eior* and his jockey-like driver;

they had to be elected. Young men of reasonably good birth would
be given all the equipment needed for a hero's life as soon as they
reached the age of maturity – probably sixteen or seventeen. They
were dubbed, as it were, knights. But they then had to show that
they could, with their companions, take part in a raid on the nearest
enemy territory. Its success would be judged by the booty with
which they returned; this had to include cattle and the inevitable
severed heads.

This special method of documenting a victory was not quite as
common as on the Celtic mainland; in Ireland it was 'refined' in a
way the classical authors did not know. The men of Ulster, it is
reported, kept on their trophy-shelves at home not the skulls of
their victims but only their brains, formed into a little ball with
gypsum. But the banquets were more humane.

From all the reports we have of the Celts it emerges that they
liked to sit together and to eat a great deal, enjoyed getting drunk
and, in general, tasted the joys of life in great, noisy festivities. The
Irish epics confirm this. According to these the banquets took place
in great halls, each prince having one such in his own residence.
Mighty carved and painted wooden pillars supported a wooden
shingle-roof, while between the pillars were placed enclosures like
boxes in a theatre; in these sat and perhaps even lived the noblest
warriors, together with their staffs. Above their heads ran a bal-
cony, reserved for the women. The seating-plan followed strict
protocol. From a book of customs of the eighth century we can
judge that the king's seat was always opposite the entrance-doors
opening to the east, while 'to the west of him sat the ambassadors,
and after them the foreign guests, then the poets and finally the
harpists'. The whole scene was foggy with smoke from the hearth
in the middle of the hall; and it was here, too, that the kitchen
probably was.

We can guess what form these festivities took, the favourite dish
of all Celts being boiled or roast pork. It was served, from the left,
with wine, beer or mead. The dessert would consist of pastry
sweetened with honey. This was hardly a slimming diet, though of
course the calories would be burned up again in debates, 'salmon-
leaps' and all kinds of contest and rough-and-tumble. The banquets must have been noisy and turbulent: a motley throng in the
boxes, the crack of breaking pork-bones, witty sallies, laughter,
yelling. Then from time to time it would go quiet, whereupon the

singers would rise. This, too, was part of the ritual of a warrior-society.

Men who would gladly undergo the most dangerous adventures for the sake of getting an especially large piece of meat – the hero's portion, comparable to a military decoration – can ultimately have had only one criterion of value: the honour which is manifested in glory. These warriors wanted to be talked about. This was particularly evident in the address of Cú Chulainn, the most celebrated of all the heroes of Irish sagas. A Druid who prophesied to him in his youth that he would not live long was given the answer: 'If it makes me famous, a single day of life would be enough.' But men could not acquire fame through deeds alone: there had to be people who would report the deeds.

Such a need for propaganda would give even young noblemen with no warlike inclinations the chance of succeeding in life. They could join that profession of which Posidonius's successors had already noted that its members were called in Celtic *bardi*, roughly translatable as 'singers'. In reality the word denotes those who not only performed stories and songs but also composed them: in other words, poets. Nowhere did they enjoy such prestige as in Ireland. There were whole groups: on the one hand the 'bairds' who sang and lectured; on the other the 'filids' (*filid* originally meant 'seer') who also counted as priests and scholars and gradually came to outrank the Druids. Both were trained in schools similar to those of the 'wise men of the oak' in old Gaul. In courses lasting from seven to twelve years, they would be crammed with everything their masters knew. The method of teaching must have been that of question and response – the master singing out, the pupils answering in chorus – for there were no written lessons. One was taken through the favourable and unfavourable days of the calendar, the rules according to which a poem should be composed, genealogical data and of course all of the old stories circulating that the public invariably wished to hear again and again, in the same traditional form. The whole corpus of knowledge, the whole 'literature' of a people, were thus stored not in dead archives but in living brain-cells.

Not much was changed in these practices even when the Irish – presumably in the fourth century AD – invented the Ogam alphabet (it is not known what 'Ogam' means). This was a primitive script which contained, on a vertical line, represented by means of dashes

and dots, nineteen of the letters that we use. But it was not suitable
for anything other than the inscription of simple grave-stones or
mnemonics, and both the filids and the bairds had to rely on their
memory. They correspondingly acquired respect. When they rose
to tell the old stories, to report on heroes still living, the warriors
would hang on their every word, like actors waiting to learn
whether they had performed well or not. Adverse or favourable
criticism from such a source could alone set the seal on, or ruin, a
reputation; woe betide the prince who failed to reward a singer
properly. One who did prove to be tight-fisted had a poisonous
quatrain directed at him: 'I know him/He'll give no horse for a
poem;/He'll give you what his kind allows,/Cows.' This kind of
thing struck home, and noblemen tried to be generous, to reward
good singers, with at least a horse. The old Irish intellectuals were,
moreover, more than just court-poets and chroniclers.

The knowledge that the filids stored served many ends, not just
conversation, teaching or enlightenment. The sagas were also
regarded as collections of legal precedents. If there was any doubt
as to how one of the complex Irish laws, transmitted in verse-form,
should be applied in a difficult case, the legal men – who had to
know the whole corpus of unwritten material – would look for what
British or American lawyers call a 'leading case': a (mythical)
situation similar to that in which their client was placed. What
would then happen is well demonstrated in an example from the
Christian epoch, which began in Ireland during the fifth century.

The question arose whether a contract had to be kept even if one
of the parties would thereby have to face unforeseen and harmful
consequences. In this case the opposition lawyer felt that it had to
be kept, and the argument he used was an episode not from a saga
but from a work that his countrymen had already worked into their
own traditions: the Book of Genesis.

Adam, it was argued, had made a contract with the Serpent in
Paradise, expecting nothing more than enjoyment of the apple. But
in God's eyes this contract was still binding even when it became
clear that a great deal more was involved; namely Adam's expulsion from the Garden of Eden, the Fall of Man, the entry of death
into man's existence – in short, as the biblical text has it, the ruin of
the world. This goes to show that a deal is a deal, whatever the unforeseen consequences, and has to be adhered to. How the judge –
a prince – decided this case, we do not know: it is not clear whether

he accepted or rejected this unorthodox interpretation of the Bible. One possible objection – that it had really been Eve who had made the contact – he would not have accepted, for in old Irish law a woman could not enter upon a contract on her own, and her husband was thereby required to honour any agreement she might make.

Whether the filids could argue as pettifoggingly as their Christian successors, we do not know. Probably they could, and did. Mythological situations could seldom be taken over directly to apply to ordinary ones. But if the traditional corpus of precedents did fulfil its purposes, this was to some extent because it was designed for lords who could, if need be – and quite legitimately – assert their rights by force of arms. Ordinary people are seldom mentioned in the sagas, which deal mainly with kings and well-born heroes. Old Irish law was feudal law; probably it was applied only when a man had infringed really vital principles – for instance, if he murdered hostages. The noblemen's daily behaviour, their relationships with one another, were governed by a sort of informal code: there were certain things that a gentleman simply did not do to a gentleman. He could kill his enemy only in open battle, and had to pay all the required respect to the better man; he had to be generous and, above all, fair. There were precedents for this, too: the most popular being the case of the famous Cú Chulainn, a Celtic Heracles.

Like the son of Zeus and Alcmene, Ulster's greatest hero had shown at a very tender age that he was not to be measured by ordinary standards. Heracles strangled two snakes that slithered into his cradle; Cú killed, with his bare hands, a dog of Ailbe's breed. Later, having already been informed that he had not long to live, Cú fought with such fury against the battle hordes of Connaught that, as we have seen, he had to be cooled off in a tub of cold water, as his glowing body would otherwise have singed his clothing. This shows that, according to Celtic custom, he went naked into battle. But he was not hard-hearted or unfair.

When his best friend, Fer Diad, drunkenly challenged him to a duel and was of course slain, the hero complained: 'All the fighting I have ever been involved in has been only a game or a sport in comparison with my fight with Fer Diad.' When Étarmacol, a much inferior man, similarly pitted himself against Cú, he gave him endless chances to break off the hopeless encounter: 'He smote with his sword at Étarmacol's armpits so that his clothes fell away from the body without the skin being touched, and said: "Now go." Étarmacol would not. Then Cú Chulainn swept his sword over his head and shaved off Étarmacol's hair; but when the churl went on whining, he lifted his sword above the skull and split him to the navel.'

Both of these episodes come from the *Táin Bó Cúailnge*, the Irish *Iliad*. (Its title may be roughly translated as 'The Cattle-Raid of Cooley', or 'How the Bull of Cooley was driven off.') The event that it deals with has been conveyed to us in several different versions, the best known being that in the *Book of Leinster*.

Maeve, wife of King Ailill of Connaught, desperately wished to replace a white bull that had run away, but the only animal of similar value for miles around was the Bull of Cooley, which belonged to the men of Ulster. It was black and so large 'that a hundred warriors could find shade from the heat in its shadow'; and it was uncommonly potent: 'Every day it would bestride fifty cows, which calved the very next day.' Understandably, the ruler of the north did not wish to part with it voluntarily. The animal would have to be stolen, which gave Cú the chance to use his superhuman strength in battle with the cattle-thieves from the west. But the story does not end as one might imagine. Almost all the warriors from both camps are indeed slain, but the last word belongs to the bulls. With elemental force beside which all human endeavour pales, the bulls storm on to the battlefield and fight. The black bull of Ulster wins, though it dies from its wounds. Cú Chulainn, however, survives to undergo further adventures in other sagas.

We encounter him again in the traditional quarrelling over the hero's portion, or in battle with demons and giants; but there is always an aura of tragedy about him. He seems – and it is this that makes him the true mythical hero – always to have lived under the shadow of an early death; and sometimes he even defied it with an almost exaggerated sense of fair play.

When at the court of the king of Ulster at Emain Macha, a ghost one day appears in human guise and offers to let three outstanding champions strike its head off provided it can do the same to them the next day, the three agree to make the attempt. They indeed cut through the monster's throat, but without killing it; whereupon they flee, refusing to accept the role of victim.

Cú is different. Since the ghost's head grows again on its

shoulders even after Cú's terrible blow, the next day he lays his head on the block. He is as good as dead. Yet the ghost strikes, to universal surprise, with the blunt and not the sharp edge of his weapon, declaring there to be in all Ireland no greater warrior than Cú Chulainn, to whom is to be given, from now on and wherever he goes, the hero's portion. The whole affair was only a test. The ghost had expressly required fair play from the people of Ulster but only one met his demand. This shows that it was not just a record number of severed heads that entitled a man to the highest honour; he also had to be prepared to keep his word, even at the cost of his life.

But, noble as Cú Chulainn was, he could not escape the envy of the gods: the metaphor in this case is an obvious one. On another day he was walking with his sweetheart Emer over the fields, when he came across an uncommonly impertinent lad who had already challenged two of his friends and had defeated the strong Conall Cernach.

'Stay away from him,' said Emer, 'for he is one of your sons.' But Cú would not let a child call in question the honour of the men of Ulster. To his surprise, he was then thrown three times on to his back; when the fight continued into a nearby lake, he did no better at striking the lad down and seemed likely to be drowned. He was forced to use a foul trick with his javelin, which no one else knew: he threw it through the water towards the lad, whose vitals it pierced.

'Scáthach never taught me that one,' cried the boy, 'and it is dreadful that you have wounded me so.'

'It is,' replied Cú Chulainn.

He took the boy in his arms and carried him over to where the men of Ulster were.

'Men of Ulster,' he declared, 'this is my son.'

The narrator asks,

Why did Cú Chulainn kill his son? The reason was simple: Cú Chulainn had learned the art of weaponry from Scáthach, the daughter of Airdgeimm, in Letha, and he soon had a mastery of it. Aife, Airdgeimm's other daughter, went to him, and he left her pregnant, telling her that one day she would bear him a son.

'Keep this thumb-ring,' he told her, 'until it fits the boy. Then let him go and look for me all over Ireland, and charge him that he must be stopped by no man on the way, must not refuse a fight with anyone, and must give his name to no one.'

The boy, who had also been taught by Scáthach, kept to this, and met death at his own father's hand. One of the many authors of the story *Bricriu's Feast* describes Cú Chulainn later as 'a melancholy man, the bravest in the land'. It is possible that a warrior somewhat similar to him really did at one time exist in Ireland.

All the sagas in which Cú Chulainn appears belong to the Ulster Cycle. These describe the wars of the north Irish king Conor Mac Nessa against his enemies Maeve and Ailill of Connaught. These kingdoms probably existed, and their rulers no doubt contended for the mastery of the northern half of Ireland. There is nothing unlikely in their using men who were, thought and acted just as Cú Chulainn. But this is speculation, bordering on the mythological.

The cycle of Ulster sagas is relatively late, being superimposed on a much older sequence, the mythological cycle. These tales all relate to the occupation of Ireland by the Celts, and to the overcoming of the original population by the invaders. Pre-Celtic gods are fused with Celtic ones, and motifs of earlier poems were taken over. All creators of myths have applied similar techniques. The authors of the Ulster sagas did so as well, with the result that a figure such as Cú Chulainn would assume more and more features as time went by. He was probably not much more than a particularly energetic warrior to begin with; but soon, with the help of some motif in the saga, he was ascribed more of the miraculous strength that had already enabled him as a child to tear apart the giant dog. To explain this, he was described as son of the god Lug.

The suspicion that gods are really created in this way by their human worshippers was expressed as early as the third century BC by the Greek writer Enhemeros, and even he was by no means the first. Nowadays we regard his interpretation with scepticism, though we cannot deny it a certain plausibility. Barbarossa in the Kyffhäuserberg has Odin's ravens flying about him; Charlemagne, in French and German sagas, is considered a superhuman hero. If Christian and rational thought had not stopped them from developing into myths, they would have become European demi-gods. There were no such obstacles to block Cú Chulainn's path to the heavens.

As Lug had a firm reputation for sometimes procreating sons on earth – just like Zeus or Poseidon – his countrymen would see no

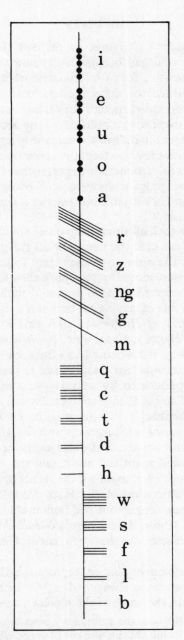

The Ogam alphabet

reason not to consider Cú as one, or perhaps to lend his name to some demi-god who had become well known from elsewhere. Of course it is impossible for us to tell quite what happened here. The monks who edited the sagas tried to extinguish all heathen features in Cú's biography, though they made rather a mess of it. They failed to see that the two bulls on whose account the men of Ulster and Connaught fought had a suspiciously large part to play in the Cooley story, and they also forgot to strike out the reference to Scáthach. Consequently, modern interpreters have seen in the bulls old Indo-European gods, who were still being worshipped in animal guise, and in Cú's mysterious teacher a kind of Irish Pallas Athene.

Druids and filids took all three from older sources; and because this was how they worked, the heroes of all the great myths have certain similarities, the more so as they stem from common traditions. One comparison serves to exemplify this. Cú Chulainn had premonitions of an early death, in common with Achilles; similarly, he shared the fate of slaying his own son with the chief figure of the Germanic *Lay of Hildebrand* and with Rustem, a central personage in the Persian national epic, *Shah-nameh* (Book of the King) of Firdawsi – all three being Indo-European. The boy who is so tragically slain has a distant resemblance to the young Parsifal: he too, after being educated by women, went out into the wide world and accepted any challenge to fight. As will be shown below, Wolfram von Eschenbach's Parsifal was, in his original form, a British Celt. If he really was taken up into the Ulster cycle, then the motif that he embodied could quite easily be passed on elsewhere, to be reworked again and again into the myth of Parsifal. All in all the boy and, even more so, the father appear to be blueprints for the chivalric ideal of the High Middle Ages: both of them nobles who were courageous and honourable. This may make us wonder – with *Minne*, *Minnesang* and *Minnedienst* in mind – what relationship there was between these Ulster heroes and women.

In the Irish sagas women play an important and sometimes predominant part. They were always ladies: for instance Maeve, of whom it is related in the story of the Cooley bulls:

Although King Ailill was the ruler, his queen always had the final word in the land of Connacht, for she could order whatever she liked, take as lover whomsoever she desired, and could get rid of them as she felt inclined. She was strong and restless, like a goddess of war, and she knew no law other than her strong will. She was, it was said, tall with a long, pallid countenance and she had hair the colour of ripe corn. When [the adventurer] Fergan came to see her in her palace at Roscommon, she gave him her love as to many others before.

– and also worked out with him the plan of depriving the men of Ulster of their black bull.

Maeve was indeed a suitable object for enthusiastic veneration, but this is to be explained by her mythological origin. She was – and this is evidence of the dual origin of the old sagas – identical with a fertility goddess called Medb. Everything happening in connection with her was both real and unreal; it had an added dimension. This was even more true of the fairy-story, *The Competition for Étain*. It belongs to the mythological cycle and takes place mainly among divine beings. The heroine of the title was kidnapped by the god Midir, just as the Greek Persephone was kidnapped by Pluto. There was already a woman in his house, the sorceress Fuamnach, and this gave a fantastical twist to her fate. Fuamnach turned her rival into a blue-bottle and chased her out to sea. Blown around by the winds, the insect survived for seven years and then took refuge on the roof of a house; it fell down the chimney into the kitchen, and then into the second-best cup. The wife of the king of Ulster swallowed it without noticing; but that did not mean death for the bewitched insect: the princess bears a daughter who is none other than Étain; and that is the end of the first part of the story.

The second part begins with a very human tale. Étain married Eochaid Airem, king of all Ireland. When one day he left his house to go round his vassals courts, one of his brothers told his sister-in-law that he was sick with love for her. Étain then fixed with him upon a hide-out in the hills above the castle, 'there to assuage his pangs with tenderness'; but in her brother-in-law's stead there appeared a man whom she did not know and to whom she refused her favours. The stranger then told her: 'It would be better for you if you came with me, for you are still Étain, daughter of the god Ailill, and I am your husband, Midir.' But she refused to follow him and Midir tried another tack. He appeared before Eochaid and challenged him to a game of chequers; three times the king won large sums of gold and silver, and the fourth time they played for a stake that the winner was to name. Now, Midir won; and he demanded a kiss from Étain. For better or worse, the loser had to have his wife brought forward, but as soon as she embraced the god, he disappeared with her through the roof of the hall.

Eochaid, not to be cheated in this way, went with his men to the old burial-mound in which the Irish believed supernatural beings lived and extracted from Midir a promise to give back Étain. He kept this promise, literally, fifty times over – because he sent not one Étain to the royal residence but fifty, each identical with the rest in looks, manner and voice. Eochaid, understandably at a loss, chose one of them, but she was not the original: she was indeed Étain, but at the same time his own and her daughter. This leads him to commit a serious crime for the daughter she later bore him was conceived in incest and had to be left out to die. But this, as often happens in myths, was prevented by a shepherd, who found the child, brought it up and finally took it – the girl's fame having meanwhile spread far and wide – to the court of another Irish king.

Thus the ending of the saga makes it self-explanatory. It is a description of the tortuous process by which gods and goddesses can become ordinary mortals; that is, by repeated rebirth. The belief that death was only a pause in a long life seems also to have governed the Irish Celts. At all events it legitimized the devices of their poets. If a hero appeared in one story as an Irish warrior and in another as a god, there would be a plausible explanation to hand: here was a man, here a rebirth; and the converse was also true.

Étain, who had first appeared as a supernatural being, could, after her threefold transformation, be taken into the more earthly Ulster Cycle. Here she was described in the following terms:

Her hair was the colour of the summery iris, of pure, beaten gold. . . . Her hands were white as the snow of the night, and her lovely cheeks were soft and even, red as the mountain foxglove. Her eyebrows were black as a beetle's back, her teeth were as rows of pearls, her eyes were blue as hyacinths. . . . Her hips were white as foam, long, slender, soft as wool: her thighs were warm and soft, her knees were small and firm. . . . It was said of her that all who might before have been thought beautiful are as nothing beside Étain; all blondes cannot match her.

This is reminiscent of *Minnesang*: worship and glorification of women accompanied by unmistakable erotic overtones.

The miniature novel, *The Exile of the Sons of Uisneach*, also deals with a romantic theme, but in tragic fashion. Deirdre is misfortune incarnate. Even before she was born, a Druid prophesied that she would one day bring great misfortune upon the men of Ulster. Conor Mac Nessa therefore has the child brought up far from human contact and forbids his followers to have anything to do with her. But the course of fate cannot be stopped. Deirdre, who has taken on masculine qualities, takes as lover Noísi, the handsome son of Usneach, whom she persuades to flee to Scotland with her. Her two brothers accompany the pair, so that they too become outlaws; pursued by the curse of Mac Nessa the four lead a shifting, homeless life in the northern part of Britain. They have to conceal Deirdre. But the king of the country discovers the beautiful girl and seeks to win her; Deirdre does not reject him, but neither does she give way, keeping him waiting and informing Noísi in advance of all the traps that the Scotsman sets for him. But the exiles' situation gradually becomes so intolerable that, in the end, they return to Ireland in the hope of gaining Mac Nessa's pardon. They wish to seal peace with him with a banquet.

But the king of Ulster will not let them enter his hall, where the laws of hospitality have to be observed. Instead he tells one of his allies to intercept the exiles on the border and to render them harmless: 'Eogan received them with a blow at Noísi's head, and his neck was broken.' Deirdre is captured and taken to Emain Macha. For a whole year she refuses to 'laugh, to eat enough, or to sleep, nor would she lift her head from her knees'. When Mac Nessa finally realizes that nothing can be done with her, he asks her whom among men she hates the most. For obvious reasons, she says that it is the one who slew her lover. 'Good,' says the king; 'then you can spend a year with Eogan.' Whereupon she smashes her head against a stone and dies. It is this fearful end that is the most touching side of the story of Deirdre. A creature whom fate had given no chance from the beginning escapes the final humiliation by suicide. This shows, too, that the myth-makers were no simple-minded tellers of fables. They also saw men as prisoners of their own existence and showed how they must always hurt themselves against the bars of this prison.

Beyond that, Deirdre rounds off their picture of the female sex. Together with that highly earthbound virago Maeve, and the transfigured dream-creature Étain, she is a woman fated to make the man who loves her unhappy. Her story also records how

Irishwomen never let themselves be deprived of their basic rights, despite the laws that made them powerless. But the question remains open whether what the sagas relate can be generally applied to the Celts as Windisch and Ridgeway supposed.

Up to a few years ago, nationalistically inclined lovers of Irish folklore – which means most Irish intellectuals – would react with some vehemence whenever the stories of the Ulster and other cycles were used as illustration of what Posidonius's successors had, somewhat more austerely, described. As the writer M. A. O'Brien said in a radio-talk, it might have been the case that Posidonius had come across some early version of, say, *Bricriu's Feast* and interpreted it after his own fashion. His mocking objection was still valid in 1953; but nowadays – to be more exact, since 14 May 1964 – it would not be admissible. On that day Kenneth Hurlstone Jackson, Professor of Celtic Philology in the University of Edinburgh, gave a lecture in which he unequivocally demonstrated that Ridgeway and Windisch had been on the right lines.

Professor Jackson had hitherto believed that the sagas of the Ulster Cycle could only have referred to the La Tène era. This must have ended in Ireland around 150 because on the continent it lasted only up to the time, roughly, of Christ's birth or, in Britain, a century longer. He came to this conclusion through data afforded by the *Book of Leinster*, the *Book of the Dun Cow* and the *Yellow Book of Lecan* – the three most important sources of Irish mythology, according to which Conor Mac Nessa must have lived shortly after the death of Christ and may even have been baptized.

By 1964 Jackson had come to regard this as quite impossible; the twelfth-century monks, he said, were in no position to establish an accurate chronology going back to the beginnings of Christianity. To create some continuity, they merely linked the family tree of the historical kings with those of the saga-kings and sought subsequently to clear their heroes of the condemnation of going to Hell.

But this was to fly in the face of the fact that Ireland had been christianized only in the fifth century. Ridgeway, too, failed to take sufficient account of this. Moreover, Jackson went on, there is no satisfactory reason to suppose that the La Tène era finished in Ireland in 150. Why should it have done so? In Gaul, Germany and Britain the Romans put an abrupt end to it; but they never took

Ireland. It is thus not only possible but even altogether probable that the La Tène culture flourished in Ireland until the third, and even the fourth, century AD.

By this time the sagas must have been so clearly formulated that they could be passed on orally for another few generations. Rudolf Thurneysen of Basle, probably the most respected of Celtologists, believes that it can be proved that the story of the Cooley cattle-raid was first written down around 700; the manuscript has long been lost, but the twelfth-century monks must have known and used it. In other words, Ridgeway did not have to be nearly so cautious in formulating his views as he was.

The authors of the *Book of Leinster* and of the other magnificent medieval manuscripts of Ireland were in fact able to rely on a virtually uninterrupted literary tradition, and could thus describe an epoch seven or eight centuries before their own day. However, Ridgeway and Windisch were wrong in supposing that the sagas must have taken place in Posidonius's life-time or a mere one hundred and fifty years later: they could equally well have taken place at a later date. It was simply that, in Ireland, the clock of history had moved in a different way from on the continent. Thus a living model of the Celtic world survived into the fourth or fifth centuries, as it were frozen by the myth-makers and passed on to us as intact and complete as a fly in amber. Its value is inestimable.

It is only Cú Chulainn, Cet Mac Magach, Conor Mac Nessa and the others who can give shape and colour to the rather meagre descriptions of the ancient authors. Maeve and Deirdre allow us to imagine the Celtic contemporaries of Cartimandua and Boudicca: we can see, and say, how they lived, what they were. They took pleasure in murderous slapstick, pithy speech which, leaving no space for reflection, would drive a plot on to cruel climaxes; but they also loved ornate descriptions of beautiful women, sad love-stories, fairy-tale speculations about complicated cycles of rebirth: a warlike race with an inclination to poetry. Had Rome not simply broken off the history of the continental Celts, the Germans might also have had narratives such as Étain's story. We may presume that traces of the Celtic imagination have survived in fairy-tales, as an inheritance buried under Latin culture and Germanic tradition. It is clear that the old Irish were a part of the people that built Manching and almost defeated Caesar.

As mentioned, the first Celtic-speaking tribes came to Ireland as far back as the Hallstatt period. After the beginning of the La Tène era these were followed, via Britain, by other wandering hordes, who spoke a Brythonic, that is a P-Celtic, dialect. Once they had settled in Ireland, however, they took on the old Goidelic language, although it was their art that established itself. Their swords, torcs and vessels were almost identical with those of the continent; as in Germany and France, the wheels of their chariots had iron tyres which were laid glowing on to the wooden rims – a Celtic invention.

But such technological developments hardly affected the archaic life-style of the islanders. Oppidum-like hill settlements, of which there were in England almost innumerable instances, were hardly set up at all in Ireland. Instead the migrants made do with the original population's refuges: circular walls of stone, put together without mortar, and with a diameter of 25–30 yards. Around them, widely separated, were the individual farms. Only when danger threatened did men take refuge behind the walls and close the low gates.

Somewhat larger, though still not towns, were princely seats like that of the legendary Conor Mac Nessa in Navan near Armagh. The earth wall of his Emain Macha enclosed a surface of some seventy-three thousand square yards, giving space for extensive living-quarters, sanctuaries, stables, barracks for the retinue and a large banqueting-hall. Probably this 'palace', in which Cú Chulainn also lived, should really be visualized as a kind of extended farm. Its owner can have been nothing less than an absolute monarch. Irish society was ordered in countless – it is assumed, more than two hundred – túatha (from túath, 'people'), of which each had its own king, the rí, like Eogan Mac Durtacht of Farney, mentioned earlier. None of these peasant communities can have had more than two or three thousand members, for the island's population in the La Tène period was at most half a million.

Within this tiniest of political units there existed clan-like social groupings. These were extended families to whom all male descendants of the founder and their wives and children, down to the fifth generation, might belong. They were called fine, and it was to these, and not to individuals, that the land controlled by the clan belonged. They alone were empowered to make agreements. Individuals had only limited rights. But there was no organic link between the clan and the túath or between the túatha and the larger units. When opportunity arose the *rí* might make himself subject to a high king, who in turn could make his group part of a larger federation. In the era of the Ulster sagas there were five such federal states in Ireland: in the north Ulaid (modern Ulster); in the centre Mide (Meath); to the east Laigin (Leinster); to the south-east Mumhain (Munster); and in the west Connachta (Connaught). Their chiefs must have sometimes been wholly engaged in keeping all the lesser chieftains in order – not the best situation for dictatorial aspirations.

They were elected, according to myth, in a strange ceremony. Bulls would be slaughtered; a man would eat some of their flesh and be put to sleep with the help of Druids; he would then be asked who had appeared to him in his sleep as ruler of all. For prudence's sake he had to name the most powerful, for the highest office of state could naturally be given only to members of great families. Nobles of lesser rank would attain at most the position of leader of the retinue; beneath them were the classes of landed peasantry and *fine* members, who were free, and the workers and entertainers – such as flute-players – who were unfree. But the bairds counted among the upper class and the filids were aristo-crats. This confirms data that Posidonius gave us; what he did not know was that, at least in Ireland, mastery of an art or craft enabled a man to climb the social ladder. Harpists, doctors and smiths were released from the slave-class if they were sufficiently qualified; as an old Irish proverb runs: 'Every man is better than his birth.' This is almost redolent of an achievement-oriented society, but it also corresponded to the competitive principles by which the warriors lived. It must have been a continual struggle to remain on top in the battle for recognition and the hero's portion.

The islanders' financial arrangements have a considerably less modern ring. They still calculated, as their nomadic forefathers had done, in natural goods and not in their metal equivalents. The smallest unit was a cow not yet capable of calving; the next was a female slave – equivalent to six heifers, but also convertible into a given amount of land. This was also true for each individual: social status was measured in terms of head of cattle. A man who slew another who was worth, say, forty cows had to pay this amount to his heir. On the other hand, a man could undertake business only up to the limit of the value he represented – his credit rating was fixed.

Ireland's federal states, traditionally called 'the five fifths', must have flourished on the basis of this archaic order well into the fourth century. Some time thereafter, Emain Macha was destroyed and Ulster itself was pushed to the edge of insignificance. A powerful new family, the Uí Néill (Sons of Niall), extended their own territory of Meath so far that it included virtually all the northern half of the island, including large parts of Connaught. The Uí Néill even seem to have had something of a grand design. Their original holdings, the old Mide, had grown out of a small district that probably included no more than the surroundings of the hill of Tara, near Dublin. Tara must, however, have been an ancient sacred place, the seat of a sort of priest-prince. On this basis the Uí Néill, who had conquered this Irish Delphi, laid claim to high kingship of the whole country. But they could not found anything more concrete than a new myth, and to this day it is not clear whether the title they claimed was based on recognized tradition or was merely an invention of monks dreaming of having their own Holy Roman Emperor.

Archaeologists can demonstrate only that there was at Tara an old royal castle, of which there remains nothing save a few circular elevations in the surrounding pasture-land. These can scarcely be made out with the naked eye. Underneath, the archaeologists found among other things the remains of a passage-grave of the second millennium BC, Egyptian faience-beads of the first millennium and traces of a banqueting-hall that was two hundred and fifty yards long and twenty wide – which gives some idea of the size of the roofs under which these old heroes feasted.

The neighbours of the Uí Néill, the Eoganachta family, did not recognize the power that such a building must have embodied. From their own residence in Cashel they ruled over a state made up of Munster and parts of Leinster. The island was in their day divided into northern and southern halves, with the successors of the Ulster heroes confined in this new system to a small region on the coast of the Irish Sea, the kingdom of Dál Riata, and even it was dominated by descendants of the Uí Néill. But they were not resigned to their fate and instead extended their power in the only direction still open: by settling in Scotland.

On Pictish territory an offshoot of Dál Riata arose, which was later to be called Argyll. Memory of this incursion survives only in the name of Scotland, for it was Irishmen, and not Caledonians or other British peoples, whom the Romans labelled 'Scotti'. Now they imposed the name, together with the Goidelic language, on the neighbouring island. In exchange for this, as it were, they were given the territory they wanted. In Wales, where smaller Irish kingdoms also grew up, the sons of the Emerald Isle were called *gwyddel*: roughly, 'savages'; hence the term *geidil*, the Goidels. This term gives obvious enough indications as to the behaviour of these Ulster conquerors in Britain. If men who, to Tacitus, were the essence of savagery could themselves call foreigners savage, these foreigners must have appeared in the bloody aura of Cú Chulainn and his comrades, with severed heads at their belts, boastful speech on their tongues. But here there is a surprise, for the founder of the Scottish Dál Riata appears in history not as a savage but as a Christian saint.

FIFTEEN

The Mild and Primitive Celtic Saints

> I am from Ireland
> From the holy land of Ireland
> I ask you, lord
> Come dance with me in Ireland
> For Christ's own sake.
>
> Irish Anonymous, Twelfth Century

The curragh that, some time in 563, approached the island of Iona can hardly have aroused any suspicion that it was the harbinger of momentous changes. Nor was its purpose such that extensive defences were required against a possible onslaught. Iona (in Gaelic, Hy) is a flat, treeless piece of land off the north-west coast of Scotland, hardly three miles in length and one and a half across. Tossed by spray, exposed to all four winds, it is a nautical mile from the larger island of Mull and is more a refuge for sea-birds than for people. It now has a population of 150, though in the tourist season there are three times as many, despite the short duration of the summer there.

The traveller going past the island sees grey houses on top of grey rocks and the reddish nave of a chapel; but there are surprises on landing. In the cemetery are buried all the kings of Scotland up to the eleventh century, including Duncan I and his murderer, Macbeth. In the shadow of the almost eight-hundred-year-old church (it was reconstructed only recently) stands a ninth-century cross, lavishly decorated with stone carving, dedicated to St Martin, the national hero of the Franks. In the ruins of the old Benedictine abbey the visitor is shown a little room which local historians maintain was the cell of St Columba, who brought his curragh from Ireland in 563. His countrymen call him Colum Cille, 'dove of the church'; but to historians he is St Columba the Elder. In his lifetime he was both abbot and statesman.

Columba first saw the light of day at a princely court in the Irish Dál Riata. He belonged to the family of those Uí Néill who, as against the larger branch of the family, sought to preserve the old Ulster inheritance and were thus pushed more and more on to the defensive. When finally they elected to seek their fortune in the Pictish part of Britain, the then forty-two-year-old prince and abbot was among those sent out as pioneers. He did not however travel with an armed band but rather as a pilgrim accompanied, like Christ, by twelve companions. We can therefore assume that he had stronger weapons than swords and spears. One of these was his own origins and another the reputation he must have enjoyed as healer of souls. Descent from the Uí Néills would make him the legitimate successor of the priest-princes of Tara, which must have impressed the Picts as well. His spiritual eminence buttressed all the claims that might derive from it and also helped him acquire the status of missionary. He must have chosen Iona as landing-place because from there he could make contact with the British princes and simultaneously maintain his links with Ireland.

His first labour was to establish a monastery. The thirteen seafarers took pieces of stone lying around to build little primitive shelters and probably an equally simple church. Then began the missionary work. They pushed on into Scotland proper, whose princes came to meet them. Iona developed into a spiritual centre for all the tribes of coastal Scotland; other Irishmen followed and set up the British Dál Riata. It must have come about quite peacefully. In the course of lengthy negotiation, Brude mac Maelchon, the most powerful of the Pictish kings, was won over to the new state as its ally; and later Columba made Aidan, one of his relatives, its head.

All this sounds strange, even incredible. Members of one of Europe's most savage warrior-peoples using spiritual methods to create a new kingdom? Pugnacious, boastful Irishmen landing on a strange coast, cross in hand? But such an estimate would be, to say the least, hasty. Irish monks were not necessarily gentle friars, their hands hidden in their sleeves; they too could fight where need arose. A Welsh clergyman who visited the monastery of Llanbadarn Fawr, founded at the end of the twelfth century by Irishmen in Wales, reported that the abbot was a 'layman distinguished for his sins' who celebrated the Mass assisted by his own sons. Moreover, the brothers attended the service armed. A Breton knight who asked the head of this community whether he had no other badge of office than a spear received the blunt reply: 'No.'

St Columba has to be visualized in similar terms and surroundings. When he died, the headship of the monastery at Iona was handed over not to a successor of special worth or appointed by the church but, in accord with ancient Irish inheritance customs, to a member of his *fine*. Adamnán, the most talented writer to be abbot of Iona (around 650), was the great-grandson of a nephew of Columba and produced a biography of him. It would therefore be correct to compare an Irish monastic community with what, after Benedict of Nursia, came to be known in Europe as a monastery. The early missionaries from Ireland, the founding fathers of the later kingdom of Scotland, built no extensive constructions with cloisters, refectories and monumental churches; they made do with a few cells strewn about the grounds, a modest church, a cemetery and a fence round the whole settlement. Their models were the original founders of the monastic system, the Syrian and Egyptian saints who had starved in the desert.

If, at the time Ireland was converted, it was fashionable to withdraw like St Antony the Great into some wilderness and serve God by asceticism, before long it became a form of resistance to the official church: a spiritual struggle against Rome. The early Popes did not have an easy time with their Celtic flocks, neither Irish nor Gallic.

The gospel of the New Testament reached France along paths already smoothed by the legions. The church fitted in with the Roman administrative structure of the country. Each *vicarius*, the governor of one of the administrative units, 'dioceses', created by Diocletian, was associated with a bishop who was responsible for the baptized citizenry. In 395, four years after the installation of Christianity as state religion, the Gallic church had been almost completely organized and was widely respected. It was socially desirable to take the Cross and, if sometimes without much fervour, to fulfil the duties it required.

Decimus Magnus Ausonius, a high Roman official who had retired to his estates at Bordeaux and from there confirmed his reputation as one of the most gifted writers of the fourth century, relates that every morning 'he would pray in his private chapel and then, God having been sufficiently honoured', would go with some relief to the kitchens to arrange the midday menu. In this, one of the richest provinces of the empire, many other aristocrats must have lived and thought in this way: they were thriving, life was agreeable, there were marbled towns, with large theatres, efficient water-supply and drainage, places full of wit, culture and activity. They had little reason to take the Cross with particular seriousness, let alone to suffer for it.

This was true even of descendants of the old Druidical families. Those of them who no longer saw sense in serving the old gods in secret had long been in the habit of attending the civic schools of rhetoric, drawing profit from the mystery attached to their ancestors and giving themselves prettified names such as Phoebicius or Dephidius. It is entirely conceivable, and even highly probable, that many of them exploited their gifts to undertake a career in the clergy. They were of course soon involved in the first disputes over principle that the young church had to undergo: one of these was started by the theologian Pelagius, who came from Ireland; another by the Gallic monks.

Pelagius had asserted that man could overcome evil by his own strength and his own will: he should simply do good. This contradicted the doctrine of one of his most prominent contemporaries, St Augustine, who postulated that temptation through the mind, possessions, the flesh or power was a force that no one could resist without the help of the church. Now, summoning all his oratorical powers, he turned against the Celt's arguments and with magnificent hyperbole sketched out a picture of a terrible God, against whose vast power of Grace no mortal could prevail even if he was relying on help from the religious community. Yet, exaggerated as were these arguments, they caused Pope Zosimus to declare Pelagius a heretic and the western Emperor Honorius to outlaw the Pelagians.

The monks were a more complex problem. Among the first in France to be gripped by a desire for a life of sanctity, in quiet and isolation, was a man who bore the belligerent-sounding name of Martinus. Martinus, who had indeed served as a soldier in his

homeland, Hungary, before becoming a Christian and follower of
Hilary of Poitiers – after Augustine, the most important Latin
theorist – went from Italy to Gaul. There, probably following the
advice of his spiritual father who well knew the eastern practices,
he went with a few companions into the woods of the Loire and
near Tours set up the first monastic community in the country.

The church, it seems, permitted him to prosper. In 370 he
became bishop of Tours and is today canonized. His *cappa*,
the cloak that he is said to have shared with a frozen beggar at the city-
gate of Amiens, was carried on all campaigns by the French kings
as a national treasure that brought victory; and its keepers were
later collectively called the *capella*. Despite these later honours,
resulting from early missionary activity, the Gallic bishops were
not enthusiastic about Martin. Communities of hermits were hard
to reconcile with the picture they wanted to see of the church; these
often self-appointed or elected abbots were not easy to categorize
in juridical or hierarchical terms. Their attempt to meet sin by
renouncing comfort and concentration on good works seemed to
smack of the Pelagian heresy; and their constitution was too
democratic.

They therefore received all the criticisms that solid citizens
make nowadays when they come across social orders outside their
own system: for these early monasteries were none other than
communes. Their members, Pope Celestine I complained in 428:
'have not grown up in the church, they wear mere cowls with a
string at the loins. . . . Why must they wear this garb and exchange
. . . the habits of so many years' standing for others?' The letter
containing this stiffly correct, conservative objection was sent to the
bishops of Vienne and Arles. Gaul had developed into a centre of
the monastic movement. But its most objectionable flowering
occurred not among the continental Celts but among their Irish
cousins.

In Ireland there were no dioceses, no legionary roads, no ports
from which ships could regularly go to the Continent. But
Christianity also arrived there, indeed considerably earlier than the
annals of the church suggest. According to them, Rome in 431 –
still in Pope Celestine I's pontificate – sent Palladius to the island
to convert its inhabitants. Later the Briton Patricius, called by the
Irish 'Patrick', was sent across. By his own account St Patrick was
a Latinized Celt of a land-owning family. In his early years he had

been carried off to Ireland as a slave but escaped home again after six years. There, his own account runs, a man called Victor (whom legend has turned into an angel) gave him the task of returning to missionary activity 'at the world's edge'. Whether this can be taken literally is doubted by modern scholars. The late Nora Chadwick, one of the greatest experts on early Christian Britain and Ireland, believed that both Palladius and Patrick were less concerned to convert heathens than to get converts back into the ways of the Roman church; the 'Celtic church' flourishing in the island was older than both Irish apostles, and different from what the pope desired.

How it could have started we still cannot tell. Let us give just two of the many suggestions made. First, Ireland may have been linked by the ancient tin-trade route via Spain with the eastern Mediterranean and thus may also have imported spiritual goods, including reports of Christ and the Syrian anachorites. The second, which seems the more probable, is that Ireland was influenced from the Aquitanian coast of Gaul. We can at least assert that the Irish were more strongly affected by the eastern notion of serving God in the wilderness than by the Roman concept of a strictly hierarchical church with bishops, presbyteries and the whole lower clergy. It may have suited the Celtic peasants and warriors better to carry out their religious practices where the old priests had worked: under the sacred ash-trees, in the sanctuaries depicted by Lucan.

In such places they would set up their cells and chapels and would live together less as a fraternal community than as an extended spiritual family. What they possessed belonged to all; the abbot, usually a layman, was their representative in the outside world. Women, who had originally been included, were gradually pushed out as the hermit ideals asserted themselves; but they never totally disappeared from the communities, for how otherwise could the still-prevailing rule of *chom-arba* (co-inheritance) be preserved? The Irish could be brought neither by Patrick nor by Palladius to abandon their own particular way of bearing the Cross. Their Celtic church produced no heresy worth mentioning. They were good Catholics; except they showed it not in cathedrals or elaborate hierarchies but instead, almost exclusively, in monastic communities great or small. Moreover, their church was accepted almost without a struggle.

So far as we can know, Ireland produced no equivalent of the martyrs who elsewhere marked the church's passage into the heathen world. Christianity seems to have advanced by the power of persuasion alone. Charioteers, spear-men, bairds and filids laid down their multi-coloured cloaks, their bronze visors, were baptized and took to the woods: at least, such is the impression given by the facts we know. If it is right, we are here confronting the greatest mystery in Irish history, a metamorphosis that cannot be explained and can hardly be illustrated. We have only fragments of what caused this: a few descriptions of life in the Celtic monastic communities.

> Grant me, sweet Christ, the grace to find –
> Son of the Living God! –
> A small hut in a lonesome spot
> To make it my abode.

Thus wrote, in the ninth century, the adaptor of an Irish poem that was in his day already two hundred years old. He went on:

> A little pool but very clear
> To stand beside the place,
> Where all men's sins are washed away
> By sanctifying grace.
>
> A pleasant woodland all about,
> To shield it from the wind,
> And make a home for singing birds
> Before it and behind.
>
> A southern aspect for the heat,
> A stream along its foot,
> A smooth green lawn with rich top soil
> Propitious to all fruit.
>
> And all I ask of housekeeping
> I get and pay no fees;
> Leeks from the garden, poultry, game,
> Salmon and trout and bees.
>
> My share of clothing and of food,
> From the King of fairest face,
> And I to sit at times alone
> And pray in every place.

This is, in somewhat over-sweet tones, the description of an idyll that many of us today might wish for – a peaceful, carefree, isolated life reduced to the bare essentials for contemplative tranquillity. The pious fathers of the day saw it differently. For them, flight from the world was one of three possible types of martyrdom, each of which had its special colour.

The white one, as it was called in the oldest extant piece of Irish prose, the Cambrai *Homily* (a Biblical exegesis), meant separation from family, friends, home; the green one was the hermit life; the red one involved sacrifice of life for the faith. It has been suggested that, in accordance with mystical terminology, red does not necessarily indicate blood, nor is green necessarily associated with meadows and woods, though it is possible that less esoteric thinkers decoded the catalogue in this way. Green is the Irish national colour; and as the Irish did not have to undergo the red martyrdom, they may early on have adopted the green one the more readily – although, as the Venerable Bede said, it did have its thorny side.

An early medieval monk and historian who was given the title 'Venerabilis' by his contemporaries, Bede knew Irish monasteries very well. We can take him at his word when he writes in his *Ecclesiastical History of the English People* that they were 'poor settlements whose houses were hardly suited to civilized life. Their inhabitants had no money, only cattle; if a rich man gave them money they would at once give it to the poor, as they themselves had no cause to collect money or erect buildings for great lords. They and their like would go into their church to pray and listen to the Word of God.'

Bede's picture of these closed communities becomes even greyer when we consider the description of the monks' disciplinary system. This was strict. A brother who failed in the honest discharge of his duties could be punished with up to a hundred lashes. Besides he periodically had to confess in person to the abbot, in some places even two or three times a day – a practice not yet current among the continentals. He had thus to submit to an unflinching self-examination, though this was still not the harshest of rules, for the anachorites worked on their souls even more devotedly than the ordinary brothers.

These more direct successors of the oriental saints of the desert did not live, as was usual in Egypt or Syria, on trees, cliffs or pillars, but generally within the monasteries. They were there subjected, however, to particularly harsh observance of rules. Even when they wished to leave the monastic world they would head in small groups for tiny Atlantic islands. Among the most famous of these refuges is the island of Shelbig Michel, eight miles west of the Kerry coast. It is like the top of a great mountain-chain sunk into the ocean; steep, jutting almost vertically from the water, with a narrow and frequently broken path leading to within a few yards of the top. There, spread out over rock terraces, are six beehive-like cells and two chapels in the shape of upturned boats. All these buildings are made of flat stones and so skilfully fitted against the gable that the rain washes off them, although there is no mortar to fill in the gaps. The air inside is completely dry, though musty. By virtue of their small size, these primitive but ingenious dwellings even have an air of cosiness; yet they cannot have been centres of relaxed contemplation. Living year in, year out in the middle of the sea, amid storms and bird-cries, must have subjected a man to psychosis, exposed him to lunatic schemes: one would need strength of character, or of faith.

Some hermits did indeed fall victim to a kind of holy madness, *geilt*. They wandered homeless over the country and lived off herbs. Others would climb into a boat and let themselves be swept oarless across the open sea – some are even supposed to have reached Iceland and the Faroes. None the less, Nora Chadwick says, it was not so much these extreme features that characterized the era of the Irish saints but rather what she describes as the 'all-pervading rays' of a lasting beauty. What she means by this can for instance be seen in the remnants of the monastic communities: such as the community of Glendalough.

Glendalough, in the 'valley of the two lakes' some twenty miles south of Dublin, was still a completely inaccessible place when around 619 a man named Kevin settled there. On a reef above the waters, accessible only by boat, he set up a little beehive-like cell, with the intention of living out his life there. News of his saintliness spread so far abroad that pupils came to live nearby. Thus there was at first a tiny church, and later four large ones, with a cemetery in which the better-class people of the area could be buried. Finally one of those slender round towers was added, a characteristic feature of Irish monasteries. In time of war they served as refuges, a kind of castle with an entrance several yards above the ground. At its height, Glendalough was thus a little walled town dominated by monks: a cultural and educational centre, a refuge for the homeless, perhaps even a market-place. It is difficult to imagine a more peaceful spot than Kevin's settlement, with its shady firs, rustling streams and brilliant green meadows – even today, when it is overwhelmed by picnicking tourists.

But it cannot have been from this that its *genius loci* emanated, as Nora Chadwick shows. It must rather have come from the illumination radiating from the *sancti*, men whom the Middle Ages called holy without equating them with martyrs or patron saints. *Sanctus* applied to any learned and pious ecclesiastic, and there were, contemporaries said, more of these in Ireland than elsewhere in Europe during the fifth, sixth and seventh centuries. This naturally raises the question as to why they were so numerous: were they perhaps the pupils of the baird and filid schools, those walking libraries, who had gained a secure place in a society of seekers after God and of hermits? They were, after all, best suited to storing, digesting and passing on knowledge. Their understanding of complicated cycles of rebirth may have enabled them to give explanations of Christ's death and resurrection and, perhaps, unknowingly, to link this with their own traditions.

Archangel Michael – to whom the Irish, like the Germans later, were particularly attached – was early on reshaped after the model of their old heroes. There were even hymns to his horse, Brian, who was 'swift as the swallow in spring, swift as the March wind, swift as lightning and almost as swift as death itself'. Brigit, too, the goddess of priests, doctors and smiths, was admitted to the Christian heaven. As 'Maria of the Gauls' she became native to the Celticized regions of north-western Spain and Portugal, while Brendan, one of their seafaring holy men, became confused with Maelduin, the legendary discoverer of the Islands Beyond, somewhere to the north of Scotland. Tempting as it is to believe that it was filids who sublimated their heritage as *sancti* and thus were the source of that poetic brilliance so characteristic of the Celtic church, we cannot prove it. We know only that the monks and the singers were not enemies but, on the contrary, that they worked closely together.

The death of St Columba, for instance, was mourned by a *fili* who had been a close friend. His elegy is the oldest extant poem in the Irish language. Neither do we know whether Myrddin of Wales, the possible prototype of the wizard Merlin, was a heathen bard or one of the *geilt*-ridden hermits from the depths of the

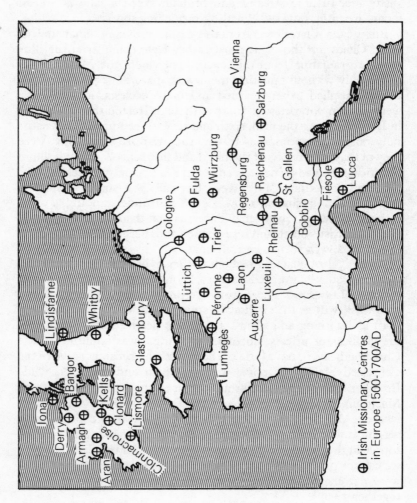

Map 12   Irish missionary centres in Europe

wilderness. Such sparse evidence does however suggest that the border between the old saga-heroes and the new saints' world was at least penetrable, and that the men and women who adopted the green martyrdom did not break with their people's traditions but sought to continue them. The world in which they lived was a copy of that known to us from the sagas; monasteries resembled large ring forts and became associated with others in centrally directed federations. Spear-carrying abbots preferred the 'Johannes tonsure' as well: they did not cut out a circular patch at the back of the head but shaved from ear to ear, leaving the hair long at the back – in the Druid style, as many interpreters have suggested.

All this – their eccentricities, their poems, their way of life, their individual conception and practice of Christianity – makes them valuable guides in any search for the Celts. If Irish sagas relate how the Goidels lived, at least in their heroic age, then the monks show how the same people absorbed the doctrines of Christ. On the continent a Latin cultural layer separated the new faith from the old; in Ireland the two met directly and fused much more completely than elsewhere. That in itself was astonishing enough, as we might have expected that the island barbarians would have resisted Christianity at least as stubbornly as did later peoples such as the Frisians and Saxons. This clearly did not occur, however, and we have to ask whether Celtic fantasy provided better soil for Christianity than German myth, whether Christianity would have been accepted as easily on a Celtic continent as in Ireland.

Both problems stem from a great enigma rooted in the strange phenomenon that Ireland has no martyrs. Not only can the question not be answered; it is beyond speculation, for we are apparently forced to the absurd conclusion that even in the Cú Chulainns and Cet Mac Magachs there is something of the substance, however unrecognizable, that produced the Irish *sancti*. We can hardly assume that Ireland in the fifth century suddenly produced a wholly different kind of individual from those that had been living there for centuries. In St Columba's personality alone we can see how the archaic material was fused with the new; warlike tradition with Christian humility. The next, considerably later model in the same style is the knight, also a warrior bearing the Cross. The ideal he embodied seems to be a distant reflection of that beauty to which Nora Chadwick was referring. It also surrounds the Anglo-Saxon classical scholar, the gentleman of the intellect who, humble, dreamy and courageous at the same time, was both scholar and poet at once.

What strikes the later observer as so agreeable about the Celtic church – its pastoral way of life, its uncomplicated fervour, the dislike of its representatives for all manner of officialdom and organization – was precisely what the men of Rome so disliked. The bishops had reluctantly had to accept that Scotland had been converted from Iona and not from Canterbury, the Catholic centre of Britain; but they fought hard to make sure that this was not repeated in Northumbria, the most northerly of the Anglo-Saxon kingdoms which had meanwhile been established. They sent the priest Paulinus to King Edwin's court and won him round to their side. But the official church was to have only a short-lived success. Oswald, the next occupant of the Northumbrian throne, felt more strongly attracted to Irish piety and brought the abbot Aidan from Iona to England. He set up a new monastic community on Lindisfarne, now Holy Island, off the north-east coast. Its members converted the whole Germanic community settled south of Hadrian's Wall, with the result that there were now two ecclesiastical orders, Roman and Irish. Canterbury was not prepared to let this reverse continue.

Oswald's successor was again won round to the Pope's cause. Simultaneously episcopal scribes in Armagh in Ulster set about appropriating for their cause the kings of Tara – as whose heir Columba himself had emerged – and thus remodelling the senior branch of the Uí Néills into a kind of Irish imperial dynasty. These kings were also associated with the new long-dead and almost forgotten St Patrick, as apostle of Ireland. It was the classic medieval combination of temporal and spiritual arms; and, as we know, this version held up for centuries to come for Patrick won, though only posthumously. The champions of Rome sought the real decision of this battle in another area: they reproached the Irish abbots because their followers did not, like Celtic Christians in France and north-west Spain, celebrate Easter on the Sunday following the first full moon of spring but, in accordance with Greek custom, only on the third day after this phase. This ran counter to an ecclesiastical ruling established after much debate and was regarded as heresy. The Irish defended it stubbornly.

There was a first encounter between representatives of the two sides somewhere in the English Midlands. The British bishop

Augustine had received seven delegates from the monastery of Bangor, founded by Irishmen, and these had been enjoined by an anachorite to give way to Augustine if he rose to greet them; if he did not, they were to keep to their standpoint. Augustine would not get up. The debate thus had to be decided at a council. Oswiu, successor of Oswald of Northumbria, summoned it in 663 at Whitby, a coastal town in Yorkshire. The Irish representative was Colmán, then abbot of Lindisfarne; the Roman, a bishop called Wilfred.

Colmán opened the debate and declared, according to Bede, that Easter had been celebrated by his fathers and forefathers on the day he himself celebrated it: 'It is the Easter of John the Baptist, the favourite disciple of Our Lord, and is adhered to in all churches over which he presided.' Wilfred countered with a corresponding argument. The new Easter, he said, followed the tradition of Rome, 'the place where the apostles Peter and Paul lived, suffered and were buried'. Then he added that the decisive point was that the Celtic custom was accepted only by a minority, while the Roman one was that of the greater part of Christendom. This finally convinced Colmán and his companions. The monasteries of the southern part of Ireland were the first to give way and thereafter celebrated Easter according to the Pope's rules. Adamnán, abbot of Iona – Columba's relative – was among the last. Rome had triumphed; but this was not, by a long way, the end of the Celtic church, whose representatives now began to swarm all over Europe, converting men to their way of life and thought.

One of the earliest Irish *peregrini* was Columban the Younger who, born in Leinster in 530, went sixty years later to France, like Columba with twelve companions. He swept through the country like a whirlwind: he hurled the crockery at the feet of the Merovingian king because his court was so un-Christian in its ways; peasants said to each other that he even terrified bears in the forest. The Erlangen historian Arno Borst calls him 'a sturdy berserker of Christianity', though he was also a highly educated man.

On the south-western slopes of the Vosges, Columban founded the monastic communities of Luxeuil and Fontaine, mother-foundations of the Benedictine movement; then he continued towards Switzerland. At Lake Constance his companion Gallus fell ill, stayed behind and laid the foundation of the monastery named after him, St Gallen, which even in 801 still had a pronouncedly

Irish character: it was then a village of huts dominated by two slender round towers. Columban himself crossed the Alps and set up his next and final monastery in Lombardy, at Bobbio near Pavia. There he lived as a strict father to his monks, never sparing them blows, and he died there on 23 November 615.

The road he had taken became that of dozens of his fellow-countrymen: Irishmen covered all of France and the greater part of Germany in accomplishing what is one of the great missionary feats of the church's history. Cilian (or Kilian), Colmán and Totnan, to name only the more important, converted the East Franks. Fergal (Vergilius) from Aghaboe in Leinster became bishop of Salzburg: 'All four of them,' says the Franconian local historian Baron von und zu Aufsess, 'preached to men of their own people, their own language and their own ways.' To this day, pious south Germans sing hymns to St Kilian.

The 'Exulantes Christi', as these Irish wandering monks described themselves, were more than witnesses of the faith in a land that, since the great migration of tribes, had once more become virtually pagan. They also represented the entire corpus of contemporary knowledge and culture and carried it about with them – more in their heads than in manuscript, though they were also capable of writing it down. 'Pugilatores Scotorum' – Irish writing-tablets – was the name given in seventh and eighth-century Germany to their most important piece of equipment; and the name 'Scottus', borne by many of these voluntary exiles, almost acquired the significance of a high academic title. Thus in Liège there worked the rather worldly poet, writer and theologian Sedulius Scottus; similarly, in the Paris court school of Charles the Bald, Johannes Scottus Eriugena. Like most of their emigrant countrymen, they were also rebels, who resented the constraints of the Roman order. Fergal, archbishop of Salzburg, suggested that there might be another world, with different human beings, under the earth's surface. He was threatened with excommunication for this. Sedulius Scottus and Eriugena tried to combine late Greek philosophy with Celtic belief in re-birth.

Such futile speculations did not deter the Carolingian kings and emperors from inviting Irish and Anglo-Saxon scholars to their courts. Alcuin, Charlemagne's confidential adviser and friend, came from Northumbria; Jonas, Raefgot, Dungal and Cadac, four of his colleagues, came from Ireland. A contemporary, Heiric of

Auxerre, wrote that Greek civilization had, thanks to the Irish scholars, been extended over the Carolingian empire. Indeed these scholars did, in the ninth century, still have stronger links with the eastern Mediterranean and its doctrines than with Rome. This can be explained by the sudden turn to scholarly writings with which Irish monks responded to the Easter debate and other acts of provocation made by the established church.

Early in the seventh century the Venerable Bede, who had grown up in an Irish monastery, noted: 'Besides observance of the rule and the daily duties of praying together in church, it was always my good fortune to study, to teach and to write.' This, at the time, was a wholly new feature of life in the Celtic monastic communities.

Until far into the sixth century, men who adopted the green martyrdom relied far less on the written word than, following tradition, on memory. Not only sagas and folk-songs but also hymns and articles of faith were passed on almost exclusively by word of mouth. As such practices could only with great difficulty help defend the Celtic church against a church apparatus that was accustomed to making a careful record of its views, opinions and instructions, the companions of the Irish founding abbots now took up the pen and established a new rule by which there were to be 'three daily obligations of prayer, work and reading'. Instead of the ears, the eyes were to be used; and books were now produced.

At first the still uncertain *scriptores* wrote mainly what the Fathers had taught. But soon they discovered Jerome, Augustine, Cicero, Horace, Virgil and the Classical Greek writers themselves. To be able to read them, they had to learn their language and alphabet. Somehow, even on their isolated island, they managed this so well that a product of an Irish monastery, the Sedulius Scottus mentioned above, could become the leading Greek scholar of western Europe. Young Britons came to Ireland to absorb what otherwise could be learned only in Alexandria, Antioch or Byzantium.

The next step on the way to literature was necessarily the discovery of Ireland's own folklore and language. Monks extracted from members of the old filid-families sagas like that of Cú Chulainn, of Maeve or of Deirdre, wrote them down and even composed sagas themselves. Altogether this provided them with a rich store of motifs: Latin *sententiae*, Greek theories, Celtic legends. How the monks set about composition can be seen in the decoration with which they lovingly endowed many of their books, rather than in the texts themselves. For instance in the *Book of Kells* – the *pièce de résistance* of Irish illustrative art: a New Testament that was probably made in the monastery of the same name, near Kilkenny in Leinster – Nora Chadwick discovered, among other things, human figures that are otherwise found in the same form only in certain early Greek vases along with a whole series of typical La Tène motifs. In another work of equal splendour, the *Book of Durrow*, Coptic and Syriac elements can be detected in the decoration. Both thus represent a remarkable synthesis of almost all the elements in early European culture. We may thus conclude that Ireland was not at all 'the edge of the world' but rather had links, in ways we cannot know, with all the important centres of spiritual life.

No such effort of scholarly comparison and speculation is required, however, when we come to consider the products of the monastic metal-smiths and sculptors who also flourished between the ninth and eleventh centuries. Their output clearly recalls overwhelmingly that which was produced in Gaul after 450 BC. The solid silver chalice of Ardagh, near Limerick, is ornamented with a strip of subtly interwoven gold foil, studded with plaques of red enamel; its base is covered by a thick mesh of spiral patterns and serpent-headed mythical figures, similar to those on the Gundestrup Cauldron but much more elegant, slender and delicately worked. The most famous of the stone crosses characteristic of the island bear sun-wheels (or as some believe, wheels of rebirth) around the crucifix, and they are covered to the last square inch with decoration, sometimes abstract, sometimes representational: there are saints at prayer, doves in flight, bulbous plants intertwined with tendrils, or soldiers piercing the Lord's side with their spears. The Celtic artist's fear of an empty space seems to have still been alive in the Middle Ages.

It was also clear that foreign (usually Germanic) motifs were not only appropriated but also elaborated, particularly those that were odd, fantastic, abstruse; the same was true of the monks who painted or wrote. In the many books produced in Ireland one sometimes finds tiny foreign elements, which on closer examination turn out to be the root-strands of new myths. One instance is the *Codices Celtici*: additions inserted into the Vulgate, St Jerome's Latin translation of the Bible. These were produced in Irish and

Scottish cells and were probably written in the eighth century; they are famous because, for no apparent reason, a sentence was inserted from the Gospel according to St John into St Matthew's account of the death of Christ.

It has been suggested that this was a scribal error; but the philologists reject the suggestion and prefer to see in the additions an early manifestation of the spirit that would later produce the most beautiful of Celtic sagas, the story of the Holy Grail and King Arthur's knights. To trace its origin we must return to the days when Honorius informed the British that he could no longer provide for their defence.

SIXTEEN

The Celtic Court of King Arthur

The historian describes what happened; the poet shows what might have happened, and so poetry is a more philosophical and serious activity than historical writing.

Aristotle, *Poetica*

'So tell me who is the purest knight?' 'That is King Arthur.'

Wolfram von Eschenbach, *Parsifal*

Rome's former Celtic subjects had, after 403, to deal not only with attacks from without; they also had to fend off barbarians who were native to the island. There were Irish on the Welsh coast and to the north of Hadrian's Wall; and there were Germans on the Channel coast. Roman commanders had allowed these blond savages to settle in Kent and Wessex as a reward for military service. The natives appear to have accepted this without resistance, for achaeologists have been unable to discover any traces from the second or third centuries that might suggest there were battles between worshippers of Odin and those of Lug. These were to break out later.

The Venerable Bede reports in this context that a Celtic nobleman called Vurtigernus – to later writers, Vortigern – followed the Romans' example after their departure and recruited a large number of Saxon warriors to defend himself against Picts and Scots. This must have been the origin of the first conflict. The Germans, led by the legendary chiefs Hengist and Horsa, now claimed not only the right to settle near the existing settlements: they also tried to set up their own state on the island. They were strong enough to assert this claim by force, and fighting broke out between them and the natives. Vortigern appears to have supported the former, though we do not know why.

Constantinople viewed this with such seriousness that an army was sent – probably in around 417 – once more to Britain. Clearly it was feared that its former, long since Christianized subjects might be exterminated by the heathen Saxons. Legend thus attached a bishop to the troops, the saintly Germanus of Auxerre, who is alleged to have inflicted a bloody defeat on the savage heathen in the 'Hallelujah Battle'. But the hero of this war of liberation was made out to be a Roman cavalry commander named Ambrosius Aurelianus. Who he was is again so uncertain that we cannot even be sure that he ever existed. Tradition has it however that he defeated Vortigern, drove out Hengist and Horsa and later, after the renewed withdrawal of the legions, became *Vicarius Britanniae*. In this capacity he is said to have ruled southern England once more on behalf of the emperor at Constantinople, and some historians have even regarded him as the factual kernel in the myth that later became the Arthurian cycle.

The real literary starting-point was to come in the eighth century, with the unrestrainedly inventive historian Nennius. In his history of the British he said that 'Arthur fought together with the other British kings against the Saxons, and was their commander-in-chief'. Further we read that the Celts fought in all twelve battles with the Germanic invaders, the last of them on Mount Badon, in which 'there fell in one day nine hundred and forty men. Arthur killed them at the first attempt. No one other than Arthur was capable of defeating these enemies. He was victor in all the action.'

This information could easily be put into the class of incredible tales heaped up by Nennius, except for two things. Firstly, the tale occurs in the *Annales Cambriae* (Annals of Wales) a century later; secondly modern research has found that Nennius based his remarks on authentic, though no longer extant, reports from the fifth century. Moreover, rumours of an 'Arthur' have survived much more stubbornly than many of the stories that chroniclers regularly examined and handed over intact to later generations. The victor of the battle of Mount Badon was the object of such

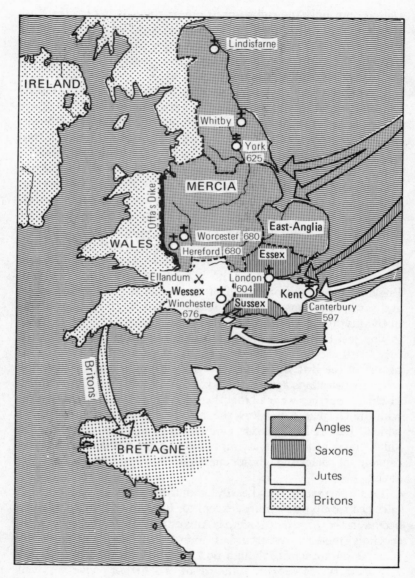

Map 13 Britain after the Anglo-Saxon conquest

insistent imaginative curiosity on the part of a whole people that, given any familiarity with the laws governing the development of myths, it becomes absurd to describe him as purely the product of fantasy. Just as there was presumably a historical prototype for Homer's Agamemnon, just as Dietrich of Bern may be traced back to Theodoric the Great, so also there must, in the fifth century, have been a commander who inspired contemporaries and posterity alike to erect an indestructible monument. Latterly, this is the view scholars have taken.

They cannot yet say where Mount Badon was, but they suppose that the battle took place between 490 and 499 and that the victor must have been a successor of Ambrosius Aurelianus. The name sounds Latin enough to support such an assumption, though it may go back to the Celtic god, Artaios. In any event Arthur must have been a Romanized inhabitant of Britain, possibly a Christian and – to summarize further conjectures – the leader of an alliance of petty native kings who together tried to fend off the Saxons. He was killed by a Celtic, not a Germanic, sword; his final battle, that of Camlann (probably in Somerset), was part of a civil war between previously allied princes. We may take it that they had been unable to agree on which of them was to rule the reconquered lands – a situation by no means uncommon in Celtic history.

It is unlikely that we shall ever be able to know what manner of man Arthur was; nor does it much matter. It would indeed have been remarkable if in 1967 the English archaeologist Leslie Alcock had been able to prove beyond all doubt that a ring-fort discovered near Cadbury in Somerset really was the Celtic leader's head-quarters in his wars against the Saxons – and it is by no means out of the question. But this would have added nothing essential to what we know of the legendary Arthur. It is really the way in which he was transfigured that is interesting in the overall context of the last days of Roman rule in Britain. Much more vividly than the reality could have done, it documents how an epoch of history came to an end, how a dream was dispelled, how a culture died – and how it went on living just the same.

After their final resistance in the fifth century, the successors of Cassivelaunus and Cartimandua were pushed back further and further out of their southern British settlements by Germanic tribes from the mainland. Many took refuge in Wales, where strong native principalities were set up, with Irish help; others fled to

Cornwall or – as Gildas Bandonicus says, singing psalms – to France. It was through them that the province then called Armorica acquired its modern name; from the Latin Britannia Minor to Bretagne. The various reverses, defeats and expulsions were remembered not only in lugubrious ballads of hopeless struggle and tragic downfall, but also in the fairy-tales that preserved the essence of the Celtic world from earthbound influences. This happened because of grief and despair; yet it suited the Celts' style, for they were people who never came to terms with reality, which was why they suffered defeat. If conditions became unbearable – and this was both their strength and their weak point – they always had a refuge: their imagination. This being so, their most successful political creation was the community ruled by King Arthur.

The founder of this state of Never Never was the probably historical Vortigern. He already had attached to his court the second chief figure of Arthurian legend, the magician Merlin; from him, he learnt that his fate had long since been determined in the battle of two mythical dragons. One of these, the red one, symbolizing the Celts, had already been driven off by the other, white one, which stood for the Saxons; and this, said Merlin, would happen in reality. The tragedy of the expulsion of the Celts is outlined in this account, which is abbreviated to pure symbolism: outlined, and almost overcome. What follows is a mingling of fact, probability, dreams and vague hopes.

Vortigern, who sought to have Merlin slain, is defeated and killed in the story by two Celtic chieftains who return from Brittany. One of them has the name of the presumed last Roman commander in Britain, Ambrosius Aurelianus; the other, his brother, is called Uther Pendragon (Dragon's Head). Ambrosius, in many of the versions, is Merlin's father, which makes Uther his uncle. Both princes rule, in succession, over the lands they took from Vortigern and retain the young magician as their closest adviser. Arthur has not yet been born. He was born through the unwilling adultery of the beautiful Igerna, wife of Duke Gorlois of Cornwall. Uther, wildly in love with her, pushes his way into Gorlois's castle of Tyntigaill (now Tintagel) and, transformed by Merlin into the form of her husband, embraces her. The boy resulting from this union later appears at a meeting of Celtic noblemen in London. The lords were just then dealing with a

difficult problem: they had come across a stone into which a sword
had been stuck, bearing the inscription that he who would extract it
should become true king of England. Hitherto no one had managed
the feat; and now it was Arthur's turn. He withdrew the sword
effortlessly and thus succeeded the now dead Uther. At the same
time he also had the weapon destined for him, Excalibur.

The island now enters on a great chivalric epoch. Arthur selects
Camelot – a place no one has identified – as his residence and
marries Guinevra (in Cymric, Guanhumara, or 'the White One'),
daughter of the dwarf-king Leodegrance. The king takes one
hundred and fifty knights to follow him because he receives, as part
of her dowry, a huge round table that can accommodate that number of guests (it must have been at least forty metres in diameter).
It is supposed to have been a brilliant assembly. The knights'
swords were to prove vastly superior to all mortal foes. With them,
Arthur defeated the Picts, Saxons and Scots. When Lucius
Hibernus, a Roman emperor not noted in any of the historical
works, summons Arthur to pay tribute, he even goes to the
continent and drives the Roman armies step by step back to the
Tiber. Returning from this campaign, he fights against rebellious
British chiefs; thereafter he is content to preside at the Round
Table and to send out his followers on stranger and stranger
adventures.

Tristram of Lyonesse, one of Arthur's knights, falls in love with
Isalt, fiancée of his uncle, Mark, and elopes with her to France;
there he falls in battle, and she dies of a broken heart. Launcelot
seduces Arthur's own wife. Gawain, son of the king of the
Orkneys, fights against the Green Knight, a magical being whom
no one can defeat – not even Gawain – but who salutes Gawain,
who fought valiantly against him, as the most noble of living
swordsmen. Launcelot's son Galahad and the quiet Welshman
Percival take up the search for the Holy Grail as the great task of
their lives. They leave Camelot for ever.

Finally, Merlin, the magician who also advised Arthur, goes to
Rome to visit Julius Caesar, makes a pilgrimage to Jerusalem and
converses with Virgil – the author of the *Aeneid* being allegedly
conversant with magic. Later, Merlin retires with a lady of the
court, Viviane, to the Breton wood of Broceliande, where he merges
with the trees, the stones, the ferns and the owls to become the
spirit of that melancholy landscape. Arthur is gravely wounded

while fighting his relative, Modred: this may have happened to his historical counterpart. Before he dies, mysterious women take him off to the island of Avalon, from where one day he is supposed to return.

Thus ends this brief account of a fairy-tale biography, filling a whole century of British history in such a way that to this day, we cannot be sure where it overlaps with reality, where it veils facts and where it underlines them. The Celts shrouded a whole epoch of their island's past in mystery, their final refuge. It has always inspired writers, the story of Arthur being told in almost all European languages: latterly by the German Karl Immermann (1831) in his verse-drama, *Merlin*; somewhat later by Tennyson, in the poem-cycle *Idylls of the King* (1885); and, in our own times, by Mary Stewart, whose novels about Merlin have reached the top of the American bestseller list. The topic fascinates to this day, and it is perhaps worth asking why.

The Arthurian legend can satisfy tastes both simple and subtle. Into its ornamental refinements we can read as much as is already there, though we can never be certain that all such details were consciously woven into the text. As its originators never gave it literary shape, the material itself was constantly reworked, in the modes of succeeding centuries.

Its lasting fascination is to be explained, if at all, only in that it was the quintessence of the history of a whole culture. The Celts, who entered the European landscape as head-hunters, now leave it as Christian knights, though without – as the legend of Arthur shows – ever being untrue to themselves. At its centre is a classical Celtic couple, the lord of a retinue and his Druid, stylized into a magician. Merlin lived in the forest like the priests of Gaul or Irish hermits; he had brought up his prince, advised and tutored him, perhaps as Columba did for the kings of Dál Riata. Moreover the knights of the Round Table, for all their chivalric refinement, resemble both the heroes of Ulster and the men of Ambiorix.

This is particularly obvious in the case of Gawain's ghostly adversary, the Greek Knight, who is *mutatis mutandis* none other than the monster whose head Cú Chulainn severed without killing it. Like this monster, the Green Knight declares that Gawain is a model nobleman; and we may assume that at the Round Table of Camelot, too, the hero's portions were served up, if only on the golden plates of fable. Finally, Launcelot and Tristram suffer fates much like those of the lovers of Étain and Deirdre. Rank is conferred not on the field but in the king's banqueting-hall. The Round Table itself is a perfect symbol of the companionship that had such great, even ritual meaning for Celtic warriors.

On closer examination, Arthur's Italian campaign may be taken as an echo of the day when the islanders or their continental neighbours fought the Romans. The island to which the dead king was spirited away must have been one of those refuges in the ocean or in rivers, topped with gloomy castles, which had long since come to replace those undefined realms where the dead Celts would spend 'the pause in a long life'. Men always returned from them to the world. It was thus out of the timber of an ancient and still living tradition that Arthur's knights were hewn; their deeds and their way of life could still, therefore, inspire the whole High Middle Ages in Europe. The Norman kings of England, above all, consciously tried to promote this: to justify themselves in Anglo-Saxon eyes, they simply claimed Merlin, Gawain, Tristram, Percival and their lord as their own ancestors.

In 1066 William the Conqueror defeated, at the battle of Hastings, the last ruler of the people which, five centuries before, had subjugated the Celts; afterwards he had a round table made for himself at which, if they sat close to each other, twenty-four guests could be accommodated. Its surface was of thick oak-trunks; it had a diameter of eighteen feet and it today hangs, painted green and white and with the names of Arthur's knights engraved on it, in a hall of the castle at Winchester. Beneath it, the Winchester jury usually meets.

The next monarch to have a similar piece of furniture made was Philip II Augustus of France (1180–1223). His reason was similar to William's. In his wars with John Lackland, brother of Richard the Lionheart, he had won the continental British duchies of Brittany and Normandy. But since the successors of the Norman kings had also revived Celtic traditions on French soil, he too was obliged to step into Arthur's shoes and thereby gave the poets of the country a welcome opportunity to write about its knights. Their 'Chansons de Geste', epic glorifications of native heroes such as Charlemagne and his paladin Roland, had so satiated their audience's imagination that it was becoming difficult to arouse much enthusiasm for them. The public wanted new heroes in new circumstances, and there was an obvious alternative in the adventures of a Gawain or a Merlin and, as the literary historian Paul Wiegler puts it, in 'the mysterious and cloudy poetry of a primitive people, with its tales of sorcery, mysterious encounters of hunters in the deep forests, isolated refuges, appeals from fairy-land'.

The continent now fell under the spell of the British-Celtic imagination. The ecclesiastic Wace of Jersey turned Geoffrey's book into the *Roman de Brut*, a history of the Bretons; other Frenchmen introduced their countrymen to the story of Tristram and to the adventures of the Irish island-seeker, Maelduin. Finally, Chrétien de Troyes, the greatest troubadour of France, took up the tales of Camelot. Living at the court of Countess Marie of Champagne, he reworked the love-story of the knight of Cornwall which would much later fascinate Wagner. Then, in succession, he took up the other members of the Round Table: first Erec, a surly tyrannical husband, then 'Gauvain' (Gawain), Launcelot and finally 'the quiet Welshman', whom he called Perceval. However he was unable to complete this last poem, for he died before he had sifted through all the material on the Holy Grail. This permitted a German, Wolfram von Eschenbach, to give the material the shape in which it is best known to us.

Wolfram was a poor follower of the Franconian Count of Wertheim, born in 1170 and dying fifty years later. With his *Parsifal* he created one of the most profound, moving and finely drawn epics of Middle High German literature. He expressly referred in it to 'Master Christian of Troyes', his great colleague, though he wondered whether Chrétien had not incorrectly dealt with 'the tale of the Grail'. He himself saw this mysterious Grail in quite different terms from his French colleague, for whom it had been merely a bowl and 'something sacred'. For the Englishman Robert de Borron it had already become the bowl into which Christ's blood had dripped; but Wolfram regarded it as a magical healing-stone that could also provide exquisite food and drink. He claimed that this information had been passed on to him by a Provençal called Kyôt. Who he was is not at all clear; but mention of him indicates that there were in Wolfram's day several schools of mysticism which considered they had exclusive knowledge of the Grail. The phenomenon was the product not of one but of several cultures, though Celtic and oriental influences were strongest. This can be detected even in such minor indications as the insertion of the verses from St John's gospel into the Vulgate to be found in the *Codices Celtici*.

The Irish exegetes clearly imagined that Matthew had withheld something important when he described Christ's death (Matthew 27, 50) with a simple sentence to the effect that Christ had cried out loud and died. They therefore added what St John had transmitted; namely the blow from the spear which caused blood and water to flow from Christ's body. Why should this have mattered? Konrad Burdach, that great scholar of Germanic philology, feels that the answer lies in the first Epistle of John, for there (John 5, 6) it is said that the Son of God will come with blood and water. The intention behind this was symbolic: the blood representing Christ's human form, the water his divinity. It was thus almost purely on symbolism that the legend reworked by Chrétien and Wolfram was based.

A mind accustomed to thinking in images will be open to quite different interpretations than a mind accustomed to sober reasoning; it moves by association, not deduction. To simplify: water also baptizes, the Spirit of God was above the waters before Genesis, which then becomes the Word, transmitted to us in Jesus. All this was worked into the idea of the Grail. As the receptacle described by Chrétien de Troyes it contained blood and water: the double nature of Christ. It also contains his spirit, the third of John's elements. With Wolfram there is a further idea that such power could, as with the loaves and fishes, easily manage miracles such as the production of food and drink; and among the magic healing forces there was also the spear which could relieve pain that plays such an important part in Wagner's *Parsifal*. In its original form it is of course the weapon with which Jesus was wounded. According to an apocryphal source, it was carried by the Roman captain, Longinus. A symbolically minded interpreter would not leave this out.

Under the dome of Hagia Sophia in Constantinople, for many years the largest church in Christendom, Byzantine priests divided up the host with the Longinus lance. Later on, it was said to have come into Charlemagne's possession and to have accompanied all the Holy Roman Emperors in their wars; Hitler was the last statesman to take an interest in it. He had an imitation of it – reputed to be the original – taken from the Hofburg in Vienna to Nuremberg. Today it hangs in its old place, where it can still be seen.

It was Irishmen who wove the first legends around this sacred weapon. They turned Longinus into a blind man who had been made to see again by blood from Christ's wound, a tale as profound as it was poetical. Adamnán, abbot of Iona, brought the cup that Jesus passed round at the Last Supper into the story and for the first time identified the Grail with a distinct object. The name, Burdach believes, probably stemmed from *garalis*, the word for the cup from which English monks drank their fish-soup during fasts. Thus, everything was brought together: the bowl, the spear, the doctrine of blood, water, spirit. Only one link remained to be made between the mystery incorporating these elements and the court of King Arthur; and it was made by Norman kings and British abbots.

The Roman church, for understandable reasons, disapproved of the Grail just as much as it had earlier done of Irish monasteries. The Grail seemed to be institutionalizing a super-sacrament that was parallel to Rome's own orthodox Grace and which could dispense blessings by virtue of its fairy-tale perfection. It was thus interpreted as a manifestation of reservations towards the Roman order; the Grail in eleventh-century England was indeed just that.

Unlike their predecessors, the Anglo-Saxon kings of Kent, Sussex, Wessex, Essex, East Anglia, Mercia and Northumbria after 700, the Norman kings had no desire to be subject to Rome's jurisdiction. For the Normans, the bishops and priests installed by Canterbury were representatives of a people they had conquered and whose identity was to be stamped out if the Normans were to remain in power; hence their efforts to exploit the older Celtic tradition for their own purposes; hence too the effort to interpret Christian doctrine in ways other than the traditional Latin ones. An opening seemed to be afforded by the monastery of Glastonbury in Somerset, probably the oldest on British soil; it could not have been better placed for the purpose.

This island in a river where the monastery stood was, according to an old saga, Avalon, the place to which the dead Arthur was taken; besides, another legend had it, its founder was the very man who had taken Christ's body from the Cross and buried Him – Joseph of Arimathaea, who had been entrusted by the Apostle Philip with journeying to Britain to preach the Word. In the course of this mission, he was supposed to have taken all his relics with him and to have set up an altar to them on this island, surrounded by cliffs; these relics included the vessel that had once held Christ's blood. Later, the monastery was said to have been stormed by Arthur; but Gildas Bandonicus reconciled him with the abbot, and both men agreed to make Glastonbury the central sacred place of the land, a place that was never to be subjected to 'the chief town' – that is, to Rome. This sounds like a mixture of legend and history – Gildas did live in the sixth century, around Arthur's time – and also a late reminiscence of the British Celts' attempt to assert their independence from Roman ways and to start a Christian tradition directly going back to Jerusalem. The Norman kings and their monastic collaborators intended this mixture to serve a rather similar purpose: to secure themselves from Rome and Canterbury, to set up a national church that they – and not the bishops – would dominate.

In 1191 the abbots of Glastonbury set the seal on all this with the news that Arthur's bones had been found in the monastery's grounds, dug up and reburied with due ceremony. Today we know that this was not all pure invention, for the brothers had indeed dug up a particularly large skeleton, but they had failed to draw the obvious conclusion that it might be the remains of some other, later contemporary of a particularly large build. Still, it is now possible to visit Arthur: there is a large rectangle on the grassy ground of the ruin that once was Glastonbury. The monastery was destroyed during the Reformation. Its nave walls, with their Gothic windows towering up above the green turf like a set for a romantic opera, are all that remains.

The knights of the Round Table have for many years been familiar from the stage; they even figured in Frederick Loewe's musical, *Camelot*, and they gallop around film and television screens. But these knights are not an integral part of the Grail myth, to which Wagner felt he could do justice only in his 'Bühnenweihfestspiel', or festival play to consecrate a stage: *Parsifal*. The Arthur figure was associated with it thanks to the manipulations of the monks of Glastonbury and their patrons, as well as to Robert de Burron, a nobleman who had set himself the task of assembling figures from the Celtic saga and the Bible in a monumental tableau and creating relationships between them. He lived in the house of the Count of Montbéliard and wrote not in his English mother-tongue but in French.

All these attempts at fusion succeed only in one case, that of the seeker after the Holy Grail. He is called Bron by Robert; in the most popular English version of the saga, Galahad. But these are in fact outsiders at the Round Table of Camelot; they do not fit in with the joyous Gawain, Launcelot, Tristram or Kay. They are a thin strand connecting the warrior-ethos with the ideal incorporated in the guardians of the Grail, Wolfram's *Templeisen*, Knights of the Order. This in turn shows that Celtic material alone would not have sufficed to create the legend of Arthur; and that it became thinner and had to be stretched with all kinds of symbolical speculations, partly of oriental origin. The Middle Ages themselves were illuminated by it, though with a distinctly unreal, moonlit glow.

Nor was there anything surprising in this. By the twelfth century the nucleus, the people that had started it all, lived hardly anywhere in the old way, save in the far north of Scotland, the edge of Wales or those areas of Ireland that had escaped control by Vikings or Normans. Its sagas became, more and more, a kind of underground, in which it now had to live and which it sought to conserve rather than to extend. The heroes became petrified in the images familiar to us.

Bron, Galahad, Percival were the last to escape the prison and to be taken up into more recent myth. If we bear in mind the origin of at least one of these – the shores on which his prototype had fought the heathen demi-god Cú Chulainn – this was an astonishingly long way to go. No poet could have invented a more beautiful ending than in the castle of the Grail, one of the most brilliant products of the European imagination. It is as if history had thereby tried to erect a final monument to the Celts.

Chronology

264–241 First Punic War, Celtic mercenaries taking part.

226 Rome concludes the Treaty of the Ebro with Hasdrubal, to forestall alliance of the Celts and Carthage.

225 The Celts again advance on Rome: Battle of Cape Telamon.

223 The Roman legions begin to advance along the Po valley, conquer Mediolanum, capital of the Insubres, and found colonization.

218 Outbreak of Second Punic War. Hannibal with allied Celtic tribes marches across southern France and over the Alps. After battle on the Ticinus, the Insubres join the alliance. In the battle on the Trebia the Celts forfeit some of the fruits of Carthage's victory; their power is broken, and guerrilla warfare between Rome and the Celts of northern Italy continues until about 175 BC.

CHAPTER 3   *The Heirs of Alexander and the Celts*

335 BC Alexander advances to the Danube and there encounters Celts.

323 Alexander dies in Babylon; his generals, the *Diadochi*, begin to quarrel over the inheritance.

301 Asia Minor and parts of Macedonia fall to Lysimachus, the rest of Macedonia to Cassander; Egypt stays with Ptolemy, Persia and Syria with Seleucus.

283 Lysimachus is abandoned by his chancellor Philetairos, who invests the embezzled money in property round Pergamon.

281 Seleucus defeats Lysimachus and takes over his lands. Ptolemaios Ceraunos murders Seleucus. Antiochus I succeeds to the Seleucid throne.

279 Celtic invasions of Greece under Bolgios and Brennus. Antigonus Gonatas drives Ceraunos from the Macedonian throne, Ceraunos falls in battle with the Celts.

277 Antigonus Gonatas defeats the Tectosages, Trocmians and Tolistoagii in a night action at Lysimacheia and is then recognized king of Macedonia. Nicomedes, disputing the Bithynian region of Asia Minor with Antiochus I, recruits the three Celtic tribes as auxiliaries.

275 Antiochus I defeats the Celts in Asia Minor; Nicomedes gives them an area of settlement near Ankara. The community of Galatia emerges. Byzantium suffers attacks by Tylic Celts.

263 Eumenes I becomes ruler of Pergamon.

230 Eumenes's nephew Attalos I defeats the Galatians in the Caicos valley and has the so-called great Gallic consecration-gift put up in the shrine to Athena in Pergamon.

189 A Roman punitive expedition advances into Galatia.

165 Eumenes II severely defeats the Galatians.

133 Attalus III bequeaths Pergamon to Rome.

47 Caesar conquers Pontus. The whole of Asia Minor including Galatia now in Roman hands.

CHAPTER 4   *Four Greeks discover Gaul*

POLYBIUS, son of Lykortas of Megalopolis:

c. 200 BC Born.

170 Hipparch of the Achaean League.

167 Invited to Rome, becomes friendly with Scipio Aemilianus.

146 Takes part in the capture of Carthage, returns to Achaea, begins work on his *History*, travels, researches, and is also politically active.

c. 118 Dies.

POSIDONIUS:

c. 135 BC Born in Apameia, goes as a young man to Rhodes and becomes a pupil of the Stoic Panaitos. After the latter's departure from the island, forms his own academy.

c. 105 Begins extensive journeying through Spain, southern Gaul, Italy, Sicily. Also concerned with the Celts, whom he describes.

After 101 After the wars against the Cimbri and Teutoni, undertakes a final journey to find out to which people these tribes belong.

70 His *History* begins to appear.

51 Dies, on a last journey to Rome.

STRABO:

64/3 BC Born in Amaseia (Anatolia) in an upper-class family.

29 Begins extensive travel for study and pleasure through Asia Minor, Greece and Ethiopia.

27 Starts work on his historical *Commentaries*.

18 He complements these with *Geographical Commentaries*.

after 26 Dies.

DIODORUS SICULUS:

Date of birth unknown; lived in the first century BC; worked for thirty years on a universal history that he called 'Historical Library', assembled from several sources.

CHAPTER 5   *It Began on the Volga*

c. 3000 BC Asiatic nomadic steppe peoples, among them the Kurgan people, tame the horse.

2400–2300 Kurgan people break into the Caucasus and advance to the Black Sea, where a mixed culture with Indo-European features emerges.

c. 2200 The Indo-European Hittites occupy Anatolia. Indo-Europeans also appear for the first time in Greece.

c. 1800 Rise of the Únětice civilization, from which emerge the later Italic, Venetian, Illyrian and Celtic peoples.

CHAPTER 6 *When Atlantis Sank*

5000 BC Beginning of long summers and mild winters, probably throughout the world.

c. 4000 Establishment of the first large stone graves in the lands on the Atlantic seaboard.

c. 1500 Apogee of the Bronze Age cultures on the western coasts of the Continent and the southern coasts of England and Ireland.

1470 Eruption of the volcano on Santorin (Thera).

c. 1300 Climatic conditions reach catastrophic heights with a worldwide period of heat.

c. 1250 Volcanic upheavals in Sinai, Iceland and Sicily; earthquakes, seismic storms, tidal-waves; part of modern Schleswig-Holstein sinks into the sea; the Egyptians pursuing the Israelites drown in the Red Sea; start of central European migration.

1200 End of the period of drought.

after 1197 'Sea Peoples' attack Egypt.

c. 1150 Dorians arrive on the Peloponnese.

CHAPTER 7 *The Birth of Celtic Europe*

900 BC Etruscans settle in Italy.

800 Scythians advance into western Europe.

700 The Hallstatt era opens.

600 Between the upper Danube and the French Mediterranean coast a well-developed trade-route opens.

520 New troubles on the upper Danube: in consequence, the whole of the Rhône valley is devastated. One can now speak of Celts, and the first of their tribes advances into Italy.

450 End of the Hallstatt era.

CHAPTER 8   *Head-hunters, Artists and Entrepreneurs*

450 BC Beginning of the La Tène era.

460–430 In Greece, Phidias sculpts the Zeus of Olympia and the Athena Parthenos.

443–429 Periclean Age in Greece.

400 Celtic invasion of Italy.

399 Socrates condemned to death.

333 Alexander the Great defeats the Persians at Issus.

304 In Egypt, Alexander's general Ptolemy sets up his kingdom.

c. 300 In Rhodes the Colossus, one of the Seven Wonders of the World, is erected.

175 End of the Romans' struggle against the north Italian Celts.

113 War of the Celtiberians against Rome.

61 Caesar breaks the last Celtic resistance in Spain.

58–51 Caesar conquers Gaul.

after 50 End of the La Tène era on the Continent.

CHAPTER 10   *The Coming of Caesar*

209 BC Publius Cornelius Scipio, called Africanus Major, drives the Carthaginians out of Spain, and presents himself to the Celtiberians as liberator.

197 The Celtiberians stage their first revolt against Rome.

133 Publius Cornelius Scipio Aemilianus, called Africanus Minor, conquers the Celtiberian redoubt of Numantia and receives the honorific name of Numantinus.

77–71 Gnaius Pompeius Magnus defeats the Lusitanians, who had once more risen against Rome, under the leadership of Sulla's enemy, Sertorius.

61 Gaius Julius Caesar conquers Brigantium, one of the Celtiberians' last refuges.

60 Pompey, Crassus and Caesar form the first Triumvirate.

59 Caesar becomes Consul. He is assigned the provinces of Gallia Cisalpina, Illyricum and Gallia Narbonensis for five years.

58 Caesar arrives in Gaul. He defeats the Helvetians at Bibracte, the Suebi at Mulhouse.

57 Defeat of the Belgae.

56 Renewal of the Triumvirate; occupation of Brittany and Normandy; victory over the Aquitani.

55 Caesar repulses the Usipetes and Tencteri, crosses the Rhine and the Channel for the first time.

54 Caesar's second crossing to Britain, victory over King Casivellaunus.

CHAPTER 11   *The Vain Struggle of Vercingetorix*

54 BC Death of Dumnorix. Caesar travels to Britain for the second time. The Eburones under Ambiorix and the Treveri under Indutiomarus rebel and the latter is killed.

53 The Eburones are also defeated.

52 Vercingetorix begins all-out guerrilla war and is defeated.

51–50 Caesar pacifies Gaul.

49 A final resolution of the Senate declares Caesar to be a public enemy. He crosses the Rubicon and defeats Pompey in a three-year civil war.

46 Vercingetorix is executed.

44 Caesar is assassinated.

15–14 Tiberius and Drusus advance to the upper Danube, destroy Manching and other towns and set up the Roman provinces of Rhaetia and Norisum between the Danube and the southern reaches of the Alps.

CHAPTER 12   *Campaigns at the World's Edge*

c. 900 BC Goidelic-speaking peoples advance into England and Ireland.

after 500 Brythonic-speaking Celts reach the island.

c. 75 Belgic Gauls begin to cross the Channel.

55, 54 Caesar travels to England and fights the Belgae who have settled there, though they continue to spread over the country.

AD 40 Caligula attempts to conquer Britain.

43–47 On the order of Emperor Claudius, Aulus Plautius occupies the southern part of England.

47–52 Ostorius Scapula advances on Wales.

51 Queen Cartimandua allies with Rome.

61 Suetonius Paulinus fights at Anglesey and in this campaign defeats the rebellion of the Iceni under Queen Boudicca.

62–69 The governors Petronius Turpilianus and Trebellius Maximus successfully strive to Romanize southern Britain.

71–78 Ordered by Vespasian, Frontinus and Petilius Cerialis overthrow the Brigantes and the Silures.

CHAPTER 13 *The Barbarian Conspiracy*

AD 40 Birth of Julius Agricola.

60 Agricola takes his first command in Britain.

68 The Gaul Julius Vindex rebels, causes Nero to fall and thus assists, within one year, four generals to become emperor. Agricola supports first Galba and then Vespasian.

71–3 Agricola holds office for the second time as legionary legate in Britain.

74–6 He administers the province of Aquitania.

77 Tacitus marries Agricola's daughter.

78–84 Vespasian confers on Agricola the governorship of Britain. He conquers the island of Anglesey, reforms the administration in Britain, undertakes some campaigns, advancing over the Forth–Clyde line and founding several forts in eastern Scotland. In his last year of office he defeats Calgacus, leader of the Picts, on Mons Graupius. Then he is recalled by Vespasian.

93 Agricola dies, without again having had state office.

98 Tacitus publishes a biography of his father-in-law.

c. 122 Emperor Hadrian has the wall named after him erected between the Solway and the Tyne.

c. 140 Antoninus Pius builds a second line of fortification further north, between the Clyde and the Forth.

166–7 The *vallum Antonini* has to be abandoned.

193 Clodius Albinus tries to become emperor with the help of troops from Britain.

208–11 Emperor Septimius Severus travels to Britain to fight the rebel tribes there. He dies at York.

after 211 Caracalla, like Septimius Severus before him, withdraws all garrisons from Hadrian's wall and replaces them with irregular native troops.

286 Bacaudae rebellion in northern Gaul.

287 Carausius becomes ruler of Britain. 293 He is murdered.

296 Constantius Chlorus regains the island for Rome.

after 300 Saxon pirates begin to raid Britain.

367 Combined attack of Picts, Scots, Angles, Saxons on the Romanized part of Britain. Magnus Maximus repulses it and thus becomes, in tradition, a Celtic hero; in 383 he becomes Augustus.

388 After an attempt to usurp, Maximus is beheaded in Aquileia.

410 Emperor Honorius informs the British that they must henceforth look to their own defence; end of Roman rule on the island.

CHAPTER 14 *Ireland: the Fly in the Amber*

c. 600 BC Goidelic-speaking Celts from Spain arrive in Ireland.

300 Tribes from Gaul speaking P-Celtic reach Ireland via England. Beginning of the Irish La Tène era. Creation of heroic and royal sagas.

c. AD 450 The capital of the legendary kings of Ulster is destroyed. The Uí Néill and Eóganachta form respectively a northern and a southern kingdom. End of the Irish La Tène era. Christianity spreads.

CHAPTER 15 *The Mild and Primitive Celtic Saints*

c. AD 360 St Martin founds the first Gallic monastery near Tours.

391 With Theodosius I, Christianity becomes the Roman state religion.

c. 400 St Jerome produces a Latin edition of the Bible, the Vulgate. The Augustinian doctrine of Grace is contested by the Irishman Pelagius.

412 First condemnation and outlawing of the Pelagians.

431 Pope Celestine I sends Palladius as missionary to Ireland.

486 The land between the Somme and the Loire is occupied by Merovingian Franks.

c. 500 St Patrick goes to Ireland as missionary.

563 St Columba begins conversion of the Picts and lays the foundation of the Scottish Dál Riata, his base being the island of Iona.

590 St Columban the Younger goes from Ireland to France and founds the monasteries of Annegray, Luxeuil and Fontaine. His companion Gallus founds the monastery of St Gallen on Lake Constance. In 614 Columban founds the monastery of Bobbio near Pavia, where he dies in 615. Other Irish missionaries follow.

597 Abbot Augustine travels to England at Pope Gregory the Great's request and is assigned a ruined Roman church at Canterbury by King Ethelbert, ruler of Kent. From there, he tries to set up in England a church on the Roman model.

625 King Edwin of Northumbria is baptized by the Roman bishop Paulinus, from York.

635 King Oswald, Edwin's successor, brings the Irishman Aidan from Iona to take Paulinus's place. Aidan founds an abbey at Lindisfarne, and uses the 'Celtic church' as model for his conversion work in England.

663 At the Council of Whitby, the battle between Roman and Celtic

churches is decided in Rome's favour, the cause having been the 'Easter question'.

after 741 The Frankish kingdom becomes Carolingian. Pippin, son of Charles Martel, makes the Irishman Fergan bishop of Salzburg.

793 Lindisfarne and, two years later, Iona, are destroyed by Vikings. Ireland itself is invaded and partially occupied. More and more Irish monks and scholars emigrate to continental Europe, among them Sedulius Scottus from Leinster and Johannes Scotus Eriugena. The *Codices Celtici* date from this time.

after 1000 The Irish defeat the northern invaders. Their church and culture flourish anew. There are high crosses and artistic metalwork with, among other things, the *Book of Kells* and the *Book of Durrow*.

CHAPTER 16 *The Celtic Court of King Arthur*

AD 417 (according to the saga) Emperor Constantius sends a legion to Britain, which defeats the Saxons in the 'Hallelujah Battle'.

c. 440 (saga) The Roman groups are withdrawn. Ambrosius Aurelianus takes power in Britain.

c. 450 (saga) The Saxons again gain ground, but are again defeated by King Arthur, in a total of twelve battles.

after 491 (saga) Angles, Saxons and Jutes are finally victorious, and gradually grind down the Celts to form seven kingdoms, which are later united and promote the establishment of a church of Roman persuasion.

1066 William of Normandy defeats Harold of England at the Battle of Hastings and conquers the land. His attempt to revive the Celtic tradition promotes the legend of King Arthur and the Holy Grail.

c. 1180 Chrétien de Troyes writes *Perceval*.

c. 1210 Wolfram von Eschenbach writes his *Parsifal*.

1202 John I Lackland loses the greater part of formerly Norman possessions in France to the Capetian Philip II Augustus.

Select Bibliography

Alcock, L., 'By South Cadbury is that Camelot . . .' (London 1972)

Ammianus Marcellinus, History (Res Gestae: trs. J. C. Rolfe) (London 1935–7)

Atkinson, W. C., A History of Spain and Portugal (Harmondsworth 1960)

Beer, Sir Gavin de, Hannibal (London 1969)

Bittel, K., Die Kelten in Württemberg (Berlin, Leipzig 1934)

Brailsford, J., Early Celtic Masterpieces from Britain in the British Museum (London 1975)

Brogan, O., Roman Gaul (London 1953)

Caesar, Julius, The Conquest of Gaul (trs. S. A. Handford) (Harmondsworth 1951)

Carney, J. (ed.), Early Irish Poetry (Cork 1965)

Chadwick, N. K., The Age of Saints in the Early Celtic Church (London 1961)

De Vries, J., La Religion des Celtes (Paris 1963)

Dillon, M. (ed.), Irish Sagas (Cork 1970)

Dillon, M. and Chadwick, N., The Celtic Realms (London 1967, 1972)

Diodorus Siculus, History (ed. C. H. Oldfather) (London 1933)

Duval, P.-M., Les Dieux de la Gaule (Paris 1957)

Fox, R. Lane, Alexander the Great (London 1973)

Gimbutas, M., Bronze Age Cultures in Central and Eastern Europe (The Hague 1965)

Green, R. L., King Arthur (Harmondsworth 1973)

Hawkins, G. S., Stonehenge Decoded (London 1966)

Herodotus, *The Histories* (trs. A. de Sélincourt) (Harmondsworth 1954)

Hubert, H., *Les Celtes et l'éxpansion celtique* (Paris 1974)

— *Les Celtes et la civilisation celtique* (Paris 1974)

Jackson, K. H., *The Oldest Irish Tradition* (Cambridge 1964)

Jacobsthal, P., *Early Celtic Art* (Oxford 1944)

Jakobi, G., *Die Ausgrabungen in Manching* (Wiesbaden 1974)

Joffroy, R., *La Tombe Princière de Vix* (Châtillon s. B. 1968)

Jones, H. L. (ed.), *The Geography of Strabo* (London 1969)

Kendrick, T. D., *The Druids* (London 1927)

Klindt-Jensen, O., *Denmark* (London 1957)

Livy, *The Early History of Rome* (trs. A. de Sélincourt) (Harmondsworth 1960)

— *The War with Hannibal* (trs. A. de Sélincourt) (Harmondsworth 1965)

Luce, J. V., *The End of Atlantis* (London 1969)

Mansuelli, G. A., *Les Civilisations de l'Europe Ancienne* (Paris 1967)

Mauduit, J. A., *L'Epopée des Celtes* (Paris 1973)

Noelle, H., *Die Kelten und ihre Stadt Manching* (Pfaffenhofen 1974)

Piggott, S., *Ancient Europe* (Edinburgh 1965)

— *The Druids* (London 1968)

Plutarch, *The Fall of the Roman Republic* (trs. R. Warner) (Harmondsworth 1958)

Polybius, *History* (trs. W. R. Paton) (London 1922–7)

Powell, T. G. E., *The Celts* (London 1958)

— *Prehistoric Art* (London 1966)

Rolland, H., *Glanum* (Saint Remy-de-Provence 1974)

Ross, A., *Pagan Celtic Britain* (London 1967, 1974)

Stone, J. F. S., *Wessex* (London 1958)

Strabo, *Geography* (trs. H. C. Jones) (London 1917–33)

Suetonius, *The Twelve Caesars* (trs. R. Graves) (Harmondsworth 1957)

Tacitus, *The Histories* (trs. K. Wellesley) (Harmondsworth 1964)

— *On Britain and Germany* (trs. H. Mattingly) (Harmondsworth 1948)

— *On Imperial Rome* (trs. M. Grant) (Harmondsworth 1956)

Tarn, W., *Hellenistic Civilisation* (London 1959)

Taylour, Lord William, *The Mycenaeans* (London 1964)

Wheeler, Sir Mortimer, *India and Pakistan* (London 1959)

Index